TEACHING IN A NONGRADED SCHOOL

ABOUT THE AUTHOR

LEE L. SMITH is now a nationally known consultant in the area of nongrading. While he was principal of the Brunswick Elementary School in Brunswick, Maryland, he led the development of the highly acclaimed nongraded, team teaching program. This led to his authorship of a landmark book in the field, "A Practical Approach to the Nongraded Elementary School." He has since been promoted to a larger school, South Frederick Elementary, where he developed still another successful nongraded program. Probably no other educator in America is more qualified to write on this subject.

0-13-893602-1

TEACHING IN A NONGRADED SCHOOL

LEE L. SMITH

PARKER PUBLISHING COMPANY, INC.
WEST NYACK, N.Y.

PRINTED IN THE UNITED STATES OF AMERICA

0-13-893602-1 B & P

This book is dedicated to
the STAFF
at
SOUTH FREDERICK ELEMENTARY SCHOOL

FOREWORD

Teaching in a Nongraded School is a follow-up to Lee Smith's first book entitled *A Practical Approach to the Nongraded Elementary School.* In that book Mr. Smith achieved the objective of writing a very practical book explaining how to reorganize the curriculum from the traditional to a nongraded plan. In passing this milestone Mr. Smith wrote what is unquestionably the best book yet to be written on the topic of nongrading the elementary school. He accomplished this by explaining in detail the techniques for converting from conventional to continuous learning in education.

In his second book on this topic, Mr. Smith is adding to the field of literature in nongraded education and at the same time contributing something entirely new. Teaching in a nongraded school is different and requires diversified approaches.

To sit and talk with Lee Smith is a rare experience as one finds here a practicing educator who understands theory, philosophy, and methodology. Furthermore, here is an education author who is practicing in his field. This in itself is a rarity.

As Mr. Smith himself says, "Living and teaching in a nongraded school can be a very rewarding experience."

The significance of Mr. Smith's writings in the field of nongraded education lies in the fact that he has pulled together the best practices into a system, and he explains this system in detail so that anyone interested has a blueprint to follow. The big difficulty with the nongraded elementary school in the past has been the fact that there has been a lack of a system and the techniques for operating such a school have been largely amorphous.

Mr. Smith's book on teaching in a nongraded school will help to alleviate this problem and provide guidelines for both teachers and administrators for the climate and environment for this type of school.

Through his very practicality Mr. Smith has made a major contribution to the field of nongradedness.

DR. B. FRANK BROWN
Director, Information & Services Division Institute for Development of Educational Activities, Inc. Melbourne, Florida

A PROGRAM GEARED TO THE INDIVIDUAL CHILD'S DEVELOPMENT

Once an Australian native was given a brand new, shiny, golden boomerang. He was thrilled — really excited about it. A major problem developed: he went crazy trying to throw his old boomerang away. Some teachers who accept the nongraded philosophy are experiencing difficulties in forgetting some of their obsolete teaching techniques.

Teaching in a nongraded school is a twofold job. Not only must one know *how* and *what* to teach, but also he must know the *why* of what he teaches. Too often teachers accept the principles of individual differences, but only give lip service to meeting the needs of each child.

A nongraded school is an organizational plan — a different, flexible way of grouping. The continuous movement of children according to their own rate of maturation is an administrative tool to encourage and promote the philosophy of continuous growth. Instruction must be geared to meet the needs of each child and must be individualized as much as possible.

The primary function of the teacher in a nongraded school should be to provide an environment which would enhance the development of values and attitudes. Emphasis should be placed on the personal development of each individual and on self-understanding.

Although it is important for each child to learn to live with other people, it is imperative that each child learn to live with himself. The teacher in a nongraded school must provide many opportunities for a growing, responsible independence, so that each child will gradually accept more responsibility for his own learning.

The scope of this book suggests that teaching in a nongraded school is different from teaching in a traditional graded school. I'm sure you've heard a teacher say, "I have had 25 years' experience." Does she really mean that she's had one year's experience 25 times over?

The principal focus here is to share ideas, experiences, and activities which have been used successfully by teachers in nongraded schools. The actual experience described should be quite valuable to teams of teachers as they plan for individualized instruction.

Through the activities outlined in the chapters which follow, children should learn to understand personal differences in others and to prize these differences. Children should learn to accept as reality in our society differences in race, socio-economic status, speech patterns, etc. Each child should begin to see himself as a worthwhile human being with a contribution to make to the society in which he lives.

A teacher who witnesses this kind of growth and understanding in children realizes that living and teaching in a nongraded school can be a most rewarding experience.

LEE L. SMITH

CONTENTS

1. **WHAT THE TEACHER SHOULD KNOW ABOUT THE NONGRADED SCHOOL** **21**

   THE NONGRADED PROGRAM 22
   THE NONGRADED CURRICULUM 23
   THE TEACHER IN A NONGRADED SCHOOL 24
   THE PRINCIPAL IN A NONGRADED SCHOOL 26
   THE PUPIL IN A NONGRADED SCHOOL 27
   THE SCHOOL BUILDING FOR A NONGRADED PRO-
   GRAM 31
   GOALS AND OBJECTIVES OF A NONGRADED PRO-
   GRAM 31

2. **TEACHING FOR SELF-DIRECTION AND SELF-DISCIPLINE** . . . **34**

   GENERAL GUIDELINES FOR TEACHERS 34
   PROVIDING A VARIETY OF EXPERIENCES 37
   PROVIDING SECURITY FOR CHILDREN 41
   THE TEACHER IS THE HUMAN RESOURCE 41
   ENCOURAGING CHILDREN TO SOCIALIZE 43
   THE GROUP PROCESS 44
   STUDENT GOVERNMENT AND SELF-DIRECTION 45

3. TEAM TEACHING IN NONGRADED LEARNING CENTERS..... **59**

VARIOUS CONNOTATIONS OF TEAM TEACHING   59
PROS AND CONS OF TEAM TEACHING   59
CHARACTERISTICS OF A TEAM-TEACHING PLAN   61
A PRACTICAL APPROACH TO TEAM TEACHING   62
TEAM ORGANIZATIONS   63
TEAM PLANNING TIME   66
THE LEARNING CENTER APPROACH   70
LEARNING CENTER TEAMS   71
INDIVIDUALIZED SCHEDULES   72
STAFF PLANNING TIME   73
FACILITIES FOR LEARNING CENTERS   74

4. TEACHING IN THE LANGUAGE ARTS NONGRADED LEARNING CENTER.. **76**

GUIDELINES FOR TEACHING LANGUAGE ARTS   76
GOALS AND OBJECTIVES   77
TEACHING TECHNIQUES FOR LANGUAGE ARTS   78
MATERIALS FOR LANGUAGE ARTS   79
ACTIVITIES IN THE LANGUAGE ARTS CENTER   82
LANGUAGE ARTS SKILLS AND EVALUATIONS   83
          LANGUAGE ARTS — LEVEL A   84
          LANGUAGE ARTS — LEVEL B   85
          LANGUAGE ARTS — LEVEL C   88
          LANGUAGE ARTS — LEVEL D   93
          LANGUAGE ARTS — LEVEL E   95
          LANGUAGE ARTS — LEVEL F   100
          LANGUAGE ARTS — LEVEL G   102
          LANGUAGE ARTS — LEVEL H   108
          LANGUAGE ARTS — LEVEL I   110
          LANGUAGE ARTS — LEVEL J   117
          LANGUAGE ARTS — LEVEL K   120
          LANGUAGE ARTS — LEVEL L   131
          LANGUAGE ARTS — LEVEL M   134
          LANGUAGE ARTS — LEVEL N   136
          LANGUAGE ARTS — LEVEL O   144

5. TEACHING IN THE MATHEMATICS NONGRADED LEARNING CENTER. **148**

GUIDELINES FOR TEACHING MATHEMATICS 148
GOALS AND OBJECTIVES 149
TEACHING TECHNIQUES FOR MATHEMATICS 150
MATERIALS FOR MATHEMATICS 151
ACTIVITIES IN THE MATHEMATICS LEARNING CEN-
TER 152
MATHEMATICS SKILLS AND EVALUATIONS 152
    MATHEMATICS — LEVEL A 153
    MATHEMATICS — LEVEL B 156
    MATHEMATICS — LEVEL C 159
    MATHEMATICS — LEVEL D 161
    MATHEMATICS — LEVEL E 165
    MATHEMATICS — LEVEL F 168
    MATHEMATICS — LEVEL G 171
    MATHEMATICS — LEVEL H 177
    MATHEMATICS — LEVEL I 181
    MATHEMATICS — LEVEL J 184
    MATHEMATICS — LEVEL K 187
    MATHEMATICS — LEVEL L 192
    MATHEMATICS — LEVEL M 196
    MATHEMATICS — LEVEL N 200
    MATHEMATICS — LEVEL O 204

6. TEACHING IN THE SOCIAL STUDIES NONGRADED LEARNING CENTER. **209**

PHILOSOPHY OF SOCIAL STUDIES 209
MAJOR OBJECTIVES OF SOCIAL STUDIES 210
DEMOCRATIC VALUES IN SOCIAL STUDIES 211
TEACHING FOR CONCEPT DEVELOPMENT 211
ACTIVITIES IN SOCIAL STUDIES 212
TEACHING TECHNIQUES FOR SOCIAL STUDIES 213
How is an activity selected . How does a teacher build a rich background of experience . How are purposes stated . What are some techniques for initiating an activity . What are the criteria for a good

6. TEACHING IN THE SOCIAL STUDIES NONGRADED LEARNING CENTER *(Continued)*

initiation . What are the criteria for determining major problems and needs . What are the criteria for selecting culminating activities . What are some types of culminating activities . How may an activity be evaluated

MATERIALS FOR THE SOCIAL STUDIES LEARNING CENTER   215
BASIC GUIDELINES IN SELECTING MATERIALS   215
EVALUATING MATERIALS   216
COMMUNITY RESOURCES   217
SAMPLE FIELD TRIP PLAN   217
MAPS AND GLOBES   219
CONSTRUCTION AND PROCESSING MATERIALS   220
CREATIVE EXPERIENCES   220
EVALUATION IN THE SOCIAL STUDIES   221

7. TEACHING IN THE SCIENCE NONGRADED LEARNING CENTER **223**

PHILOSOPHY OF SCIENCE TEACHING   223
GOALS OF SCIENCE TEACHING   224
TEACHING FOR CONCEPT DEVELOPMENT   225
Concepts in the area of living things . Concepts in the area of the earth and the universe . Concepts in the area of materials, energy and change

SUGGESTED PROBLEMS FOR STUDY   227
TEACHING TECHNIQUES FOR SCIENCE   228
LIVING THINGS   229
How can we find out what animals need to live and grow . How are human beings like other living things . How are human being unique

THE EARTH AND THE UNIVERSE   232
What conditions of the atmosphere affect the weather . Why does man want to explore and travel in space

MATERIALS FOR THE SCIENCE LEARNING CENTER   234

7. TEACHING IN THE SCIENCE NONGRADED LEARNING CENTER *(Continued)*

OTHER RESOURCES 238
The earth and space science laboratory . The Frederick County outdoor school . Resource People

EVALUATION IN SCIENCE 240

8. UTILIZING THE INSTRUCTIONAL MATERIALS CENTER **244**

PHILOSOPHY OF THE INSTRUCTIONAL MATERIALS CENTER 244
PERSONNEL FOR THE INSTRUCTIONAL MATERIALS CENTER 245
SELECTION OF MATERIALS 246
SERVICES PROVIDED BY THE IMC PERSONNEL 247
PHYSICAL ARRANGEMENTS 249
MATERIALS AND EQUIPMENT 252
SCHEDULING 252

9. SPECIAL TEACHERS, TEACHER AIDES, VOLUNTEERS, STUDENT AIDES IN THE NONGRADED SCHOOL **254**

UTILIZING AUXILIARY PERSONNEL 254
SCHEDULING AUXILIARY PERSONNEL 261
AUXILIARY PERSONNEL IN LEARNING CENTERS 263
EVALUATION OF AUXILIARY PERSONNEL 264
THE ROLE OF SPECIAL TEACHERS 265
THE ART CENTER 265
THE MUSIC CENTER 267
THE PHYSICAL EDUCATION CENTER 269
UTILIZING PEER TEACHERS 271

10. EXTENSIONS OF THE NONGRADED PHILOSOPHY **274**

THE "LIVING ROOM" APPROACH 274
OBJECTIVES OF THE EXPERIMENT 275

10. EXTENSIONS OF THE NONGRADED PHILOSOPHY *(Continued)*

DESCRIPTION OF THE EXPERIMENT   276
EVALUATION OF THE EXPERIMENT   280
SUMMARY OF "LIVING ROOM" EXPERIMENT   283
COMMUNITY SCHOOL PROJECT   284
PHILOSOPHY OF THE COMMUNITY SCHOOL
PROJECT   284
PLANNING THE ACTIVITIES   285
THE NATURE OF THE ACTIVITIES   288
EVALUATING THE PROJECT   289

**11. TEACHING FOR CONTINUOUS EVALUATION IN THE NON-
GRADED SCHOOL**. **290**

CHARACTERISTICS OF EVALUATION   290
STEPS INVOLVED IN EVALUATION   291
MEETING INDIVIDUAL NEEDS   292
THE LEVELS APPROACH   292
REPORTING TO PARENTS   300

INDEX. **311**

TEACHING IN A
NONGRADED SCHOOL

WHAT THE TEACHER
SHOULD KNOW ABOUT
THE NONGRADED SCHOOL

Nongrading is a way of life — a style of living. The philosophy of nongradedness is known by many names, with the emphasis of the plan and the years covered reflected in the name. Some of the names mentioned in the literature on the subject are nongraded primary, primary unit, continuous progress, primary cycle, levels system, flexible primary unit, primary block, and nongraded school. Although some use the term ungraded, most systems prefer nongraded.

A nongraded school organization is a vertical one which provides for the continuous progression of all students, with recognition of the variability among them in all aspects of their development. This type of school organization provides for differentiated rates and means of progression toward achievement of educational goals.

I define nongradedness as: "A philosphy of education which makes possible the adjusting of teaching and administrative procedures to meet differing social, mental, and physical capacities among children. It uses an organizational plan which eliminates grade labels, promotes flexible grouping and continuous progress, and permits the utilization of meaningful individualized instruction."

Every child has the potential for many types of growth. Some of these potentials lie dormant throughout life. Others are developed in part. The determination of which possibilities are realized, and the degree to which any is fulfilled, are functions of the environment.

If children are to develop their intellectual potential, the school must provide an environment that is intellectually stimulating and in which achievement of an intellectual nature is respected and nurtured.

The emotional climate of a learning situation determines how well the pupil will obtain functional behavioral changes. Unless the emotional content of the situation is conducive to the acceptance of new information, that information will appear irrelevant and will be rejected. In every situation, boys and girls are striving to feel right about themselves, to feel that they have worth, to feel that they are accepted.

Each child is uniquely different. Meeting individual differences is not a technique; it is a way of living — a style of life. It includes accepting others, respecting their contributions, working for the kind of group operation in which each individual knows he has a part, and encouraging each child to give his best in each situation.

The determination of group direction and policy is based upon the individual decisions of group members. If the society is to improve, or even sustain itself, its individual members must be able to make wise decisions. Each must be able to decide for himself what he values, what he wants, and what is the best method of obtaining it. Thus, in our democratic society, the nongraded philosophy must be applied in schools because the nongraded school places a major emphasis on helping the individual become self-directed and self-disciplined.

THE NONGRADED PROGRAM

Although it is quite important to learn to live with other people, it is imperative that each child learn to live with himself. Each must learn to understand his assets and use them constructively. He must discover his shortcomings and, if possible, improve on them. He must develop a sense of self-protection sufficient to keep him functioning at an efficient level.

Complete understanding of oneself is continuous and on-going. Successful living is not a thing but a process, a continuous movement toward ever changing value goals. The primary function of the nongraded school program should be to provide an environment which would enhance the development of values and attitudes.

There should be many opportunities for a growing, responsible independence, with each child gradually accepting more responsibility for his own learning and assuming greater self-direction. Emphasis should be placed on the personal development of the individual and on self-understanding.

The curriculum should not be a formal one which emphasizes mastery of subject matter as an end in itself, but rather it should emphasize the development of the child and take into consideration his interests, abilities, and experiences. The subject matter should be presented in such a way that it helps him grasp its functional value in relation to the problems of everyday living with which he is confronted.

All learning should deal with aspects of the society in which the child lives and ways in which these aspects are important to him. The child's experience should be related directly to his environment, and thus enable him to acquire the tools he will need as he continues to grow.

THE NONGRADED CURRICULUM

The curriculum in a nongraded school should assume that the particular group of children for which it is planned are human; the program must be broad and flexible to meet the challenge of ability and interest of all of the students, as humans in being.

The heart of the curriculum should be the development of a child's mental thought process while the body of current knowledge should serve only as the vehicle.

Whenever there is a sequence of instructional skills, it should be followed.

Opportunity for self-acceptance and self-discovery is the essence for making the curriculum real and meaningful.

In planning the curriculum to focus on the individual learner, the following guidelines should be kept in mind:

- there are differences as well as similarities among individuals.
- learning is evidenced through a change in behavior.
- the most meaningful learning takes place through the process of discovery of one's potency.

- individuals draw relationships from their background of experiences.
- individuals react to a stimulus and initiate action at their own rate and depth.
- learning takes place best when the individual has the freedom of choice.
- each child is in the continual process of individual growth.
- each child has rights and responsibilities as an individual.
- each child has rights and responsibilities as a member of a group.
- there is a direct relationship between meaningful learning and amount of intra-personal involvement.
- learning situations need to be provided at many levels in a variety of groupings.
- the school environment must be one which encourages a feeling of belonging.
- each child must have opportunities to think and work as an individual as well as a member of a group.
- learning takes place best when an individual assumes responsibility for his own program of instruction.

The curriculum, then, becomes an organized series of experiences which have been decided upon in terms of the needs of the learner and which provide for his continuous growth and development toward desirable goals or behavioral objectives.

The purpose of these learning activities is to enable the child, under the direction of the school, to acquire and develop skills, abilities, understandings and attitudes which will help him live effectively and happily in his environment.

THE TEACHER IN A NONGRADED SCHOOL

The learning activities of each child and the way he undertakes them enables the teacher to discover his difficulties, analyze his progress, and guide him in achieving desirable goals.

The free reading which a child does gives the teacher an opportunity to appraise his interests, likes and dislikes, and the deficiencies in his reading skills so that she can intelligently guide his future reading activities.

The child's performance in using numbers should reveal his grasp of number concepts and mathematical processes. From his progress and achievement in the various areas of schoolwork, the teacher can discover where each pupil needs assistance.

The teacher in a nongraded school must assume much responsibility in helping each child with problems such as building confidence in himself, developing greater independence in work and play, gaining better control of his emotions, and getting along better with his peers.

In a nongraded school the teacher must have faith in children. Children are not born wicked, ill-mannered, and irritable; they are reflections of the adults they know; their attitudes and behaviors are caused by the environment which adults have created and which children are expected to "fit into." Every delinquent is the result of the failure of many adults including his parents, teachers and neighbors.

It is important for the teacher to see each child as a unique human being, neither good nor bad except as his living makes him that way. The teacher must see each child as having purposes of his own and a pattern of growth which he must follow in order to develop *his* feelings and *his* attitudes because *his* living demands this.

The teacher must have an insight into each child's background so that she may understand why he behaves as he does. She must learn to know and accept his feelings about himself, about adults, and about what he has experienced. The wise teacher listens when a child talks and watches as a child works and plays alone or with others. The teacher needs to meet children on a one-to-one basis as in Figure 1-1.

Figure 1-1

Typically, a teacher assumes her role to be only that of challenging each child to learn. This cannot be accomplished by simply presenting a group of skills and concepts and expecting the child to "learn."

The teacher must recognize each child as a unique individual, different from all others. Each child needs to be considered differently; each needs to "do his own thing." The teacher should not expect children to conform to standardized procedures and graded materials because there is no such thing as a standardized child. Many schools have been treating growing human beings as clearly labelled packages to be run through the same assembly line for so long that these aggressions felt in school by children have been taken out during the rest of their living. Hence, we have damage to school buildings, fighting, drop outs, burning of draft cards, riots and disorders of every kind.

Children are not objects, they are human beings and should be treated as such. The teacher in a nongraded school should be an adult who is interesting, understanding, sympathetic, and one to whom a child may relate confidentially. The teacher should be a close friend of each child.

Since the nongraded school is an extension of the way of living for the children who attend, then it is the role of the teacher to see that children get a "fair shake" in the neighborhood. The teacher knows the needs of the children, and she should help the community provide wholesome activities and recreational facilities which make up an environment conducive to successful child growth and development. (A discussion of a community school project is found in Chapter 10.)

THE PRINCIPAL IN A NONGRADED SCHOOL

The principal in a nongraded school is the key to providing more significant learning for children. He must have faith in the staff and free them of unnecessary pressures so that they may carry out their important responsibility to the children.

The principal sets the "tone" of the school; the atmosphere which he creates must be relaxed. The principal, as the educational leader in the school, must enthusiastically accept the responsibility of creating an atmosphere which will free teachers so that they may contribute to the leadership process. The whole school must be filled with the cooperative approach to common problems, those which affect the "way of life" in the school and the community.

Cooperative leadership-necessitates interaction within the school. All those who are concerned and affected by the decisions should share in the making of the decisions. A nongraded school needs the leadership of values and ideas rather than the leadership of authoritarian position or job title.

The morale of each staff member is strengthened when he feels that his ideas and suggestions are welcomed and respected. School policies should be thought of as "ours" rather than "his." The behavior of a teacher is controlled by the values which are shaped by her experiences; therefore, she is more likely to work creatively with children when the school is permeated with the cooperative approach.

The principal should approach change enthusiastically, but also carefully so that teachers' security will not be threatened. Often, his role in initiating change is determined by the readiness of the staff to assume its share of responsibility in the change process.

The principal must possess skill in leading group discussion, and know how to work honestly and sincerely with others so that the creative power of each is freed to make contributions to the goals of the group. He must be sensitive to the attitudes, values, and needs of each.

It is the responsibility of the principal to conduct himself in such a way that he exemplifies desirable educational values. His behavior should reflect sound human values, a well-adjusted personality, and a positive outlook on life. He should be enthusiastic in his role as the educational leader in a nongraded school. Nongrading must be his "way of life."

THE PUPIL IN A NONGRADED SCHOOL

Almost every child comes to school as a curious and energetic human being. In a nongraded school this little bundle of energy should have many activities and experiences which keep him "turned on."

He does not need to sit down at a desk to "learn." All of his experiences, and particularly his first, should be ones in which he can see that teachers trust him and have faith in him. He should see at the very beginning that learning is not separate from living, but rather that he learns as he lives, at school as well as at home and in the community.

The pupil needs to feel important and that his questions are welcomed. He needs to know that the purposes of this nongraded school are to meet his needs and concerns, to help him overcome his fears and anxieties, and to satisfy his curiosities.

Children need to work together, to help each other, and to learn from each other. It is both natural and normal for children to talk and discuss their everyday problems. They speak each other's language and, therefore, much learning takes place as these little humans socialize. Grown-up humans talk with each other; it seems to satisfy their needs.

The child needs to share the leadership responsibility; he needs to be a part of the decision making, to help set up his own goals and to evaluate his own progress. Children learn to play games, ride bikes, walk, run, and so on without adult teachers telling them every move to make. They learn by doing. Many children need only for the teacher to "free" them to teach themselves. They will ask for help from adults when they need it.

Not only does the pupil need to be a part of a group, but also he needs to feel that his uniqueness is important and respected. The philosophy of nongradedness is enhanced by tolerating and encouraging diversity and creativity. Through this encouragement, the individual child has a chance to be himself without coercion from others. A diversity of groups and activities in school gives him the opportunity to find himself at ease in the groups that satisfy his needs. He needs a variety of activities and a variety of groups. His way of living is multi-directional; he cannot survive if directed into uniformity.

However, there is a need for each child to learn to live with some conformity. There are some rules and regulations which govern our society. (For instance, a red light means STOP; or DANGER — KEEP OUT means one is not to trespass.) Conformity in these areas does not infringe upon individual freedoms and rights; they are necessary for the welfare of the society. In schools, children need to conform to certain things in respect to other people. This kind of conformity makes for a better life for all. If the child does

The child needs physical activity (Figure 1-2).

He needs time to work alone (Figure 1-3).

He needs creative activities (Figure 1-4).

He needs to have some large group experiences (Figure 1-5).

not experience this kind of conformity, then the school is not fulfilling its obligation.

THE SCHOOL BUILDING FOR A NONGRADED PROGRAM

Many educators are reluctant to initiate a nongraded, team-teaching program of elementary education because they say that the flexibility required in such a program is not possible in a traditional building. This is just an excuse, not a reason. Some of the best nongraded programs I've seen or read about are housed in traditional facilities.

The organizational patterns of nongrading and team teaching, which are flexible arrangements to permit individualized instruction and promote the philosophy of continuous growth, are enhanced by modern school plants. However, a modern building is not a prerequisite to nongrading. The building is far less important than the human element.

Innovations grow out of the involvement of teachers in planning; by sharing ideas and responsibility, creativity is stimulated. If you have a conviction that the nongraded concept is what is needed in your situation, then develop a commitment to the philosophy and approach the change with competence.

GOALS AND OBJECTIVES OF A NONGRADED PROGRAM

In a nongraded school, the total staff must be involved in a sharing of ideas and in formalizing the philosophy of the school; together they should work out the specific goals and objectives of their program. Planning should be a cooperative venture.

Some of the purposes for adapting a nongraded program of elementary education should be:

- to provide an opportunity for every child to learn according to his own growth pattern.
- to establish for each child a pattern of success in school experiences.
- to eliminate artificial grade barriers so that the faster-moving child will not have to mark time.

- to permit the slower-moving child to progress with satisfaction and success at his own rate.
- to permit each child to be taught at his best learning level.
- to provide for each child a curriculum adapted to his growth pattern.

These purposes should lead to the establishment of the following specific goals of a nongraded school:

1. To help each child find satisfaction in learning.
2. To help each child realize that subject matter skills are tools he should use in meeting and solving problems.
3. To help each child develop self-confidence.
4. To help each child think imaginatively and openly explore his ideas.
5. To help each child free himself to explore the resources of the school, both human beings and materials, as well as his own resources.
6. To help each child assume responsibility for his own learning.
7. To help each child to become self-directed and self-disciplined.

All of these purposes, goals, and objectives can be fulfilled in a nongraded program by simply creating an atmosphere which promotes the philosophy that school is an extension of everyone's style of living. The success of a nongraded school is not measured by remembering and reviewing; it is evaluated in terms of how well each person is being and becoming human.

SUMMARY

The most important characteristic of a nongraded school is the "human" element. Everyone needs to be needed. Each needs to be respected as an important individual. You probably have heard these sayings: "I've got to be me!" and "I've got to do my own thing!" This is what nongrading is all about; each must develop a positive self-concept.

Each child is "human" and should be treated as such rather than as a piece of furniture or some other object. Childhood is a time of adventure and activity; children need to be kept active in school.

The teacher is the human resource to the child. She needs to be interesting, understanding, and sympathetic to each child. She must be a true friend of each child.

One must look at the staff of a nongraded school as a community of educators, each sensitive to the needs, feelings, and attitudes of all the others. They plan, work and evaluate cooperatively.

The principal of a nongraded school must set the "tone" and create a relaxed atmosphere which will free teachers and students from unnecessary pressures and allow them to develop their creative potential.

The major purpose of the curriculum in a nongraded school should be to enable each child to acquire and develop skills, understandings, attitudes, and values which will help him live effectively and happily in his environment.

The nongraded school must be a "fun" place — not a place where you go to do your pain for five hours a day and then have your pleasure. School should be a continuation of one's style of living. Learning must be kept alive. Children learn as they live. Nongrading is a way of life.

2

TEACHING FOR
SELF-DIRECTION
AND SELF-DISCIPLINE

In the nongraded school, teachers must provide many opportunities for a growing, responsible independence, with each child gradually accepting more responsibility for his own learning and assuming greater self-direction. Emphasis should be placed on the personal development of the individual and on self-understanding.

A child's development of a positive self-concept, of attitudes and values, and of standards of behavior is influenced by the atmosphere and the environment in which he lives and learns. A well-developed human being is one who has self-respect, because this is a basic need of all humans. A major task of the teacher is to help each child develop and maintain self-respect.

The activities of a child are directed toward satisfying his needs. His growth pattern affects his behavior and he has problems when he cannot satisfy his needs. In order to help each child find satisfaction in learning and develop self-confidence, the nongraded school should plan a program to help children live a better and richer life in school.

GENERAL GUIDELINES FOR TEACHERS

The following suggestions are offered to teachers to help them provide for the mental, social, physical and emotional needs of children.

The classroom environment is a great factor in the learning process. The mental needs of a child cannot be met unless an intellectual environment is created in the classroom. The teacher should employ practices which encourage children to learn. The teacher can meet the physical needs of the children by providing a variety of activities to break up the monotony of long, quiet sitting periods. The emotional needs can be met by showing love for every child. The teacher should develop a personal relationship between every child and herself. To meet the social needs of the children, the teacher should provide a democratic leadership and teach the children the democratic way of life. This would give each a sense of responsibility and help him to fit into the group.

The teacher should strive to help each student to become self-disciplined; that is, to apply himself at all times to the best of his ability toward achieving his aims or goals. This type of discipline cannot be imposed on the individual, but rather, it is the achievement of the individual himself. In teaching this type of discipline, the teacher should provide activities which are suitable to the child's ability and of interest to him. If he is interested in his activity and if it is within his range of ability, he will want to discipline himself in order to get the most from the activity. This method of getting self-discipline also applies to group work. If individuals are interested in the activity and it is within their range of ability, the group will discipline itself so that each member may achieve the best possible results.

The teacher should do some long-range planning so that she can organize her thinking in relation to the broad units of work which are to be considered. She should consider any purposes that the children might have and plan a program which will stimulate their interests and challenge their abilities.

The teacher should stimulate the interests of the children so that they begin to volunteer their ideas about what could be done in relation to the unit of work in question. The children should sit in an informal way with the teacher and talk about their purposes and goals, plan who is going to do what, form their committees, and get started. Then the teacher should work with each group to see that their group plans are workable and that everyone has been included in the activities of the group.

The teacher should include in her plans a complete list of sources of a variety of materials which will be needed to develop fully every individual and group activity that is to be undertaken. There are basically two types of materials necessary — those which are used primarily to help the individual child and those which are used to help a group of children to understand important things which come up in group activities. In selecting this material the teacher should make certain that it will benefit those using it by helping them to grow. There must be consistency; there should not be excellent materials for use in teaching math and no art materials at all. There must be a balance of instructional materials selected to better meet all the needs of the children, and thus develop them into well-rounded individuals.

Discussion experiences are necessary to give the children an opportunity to analyze their problems and decide what the group must do to solve them. Through discussion, each child gets an understanding of how everyone else in the group feels about the situation, and conclusions can be drawn about what they are going to do.

Teachers need to provide sharing experiences, which can be, for example, in the form of informal oral reporting. All the children of the group should be given an opportunity to present group ideas as well as individual ideas. A sharing experience should be a report of some type where every member of the group takes part in presenting to the others the results of the group work and activities.

During their group work all children should have some research experiences. After the group has discovered what it is that they need to know, they should use research materials and learn to think critically to sort out the important from the unimportant and thus be better prepared to report their findings.

The teacher should provide for independent work experiences for those who complete their part of the group work first. Independent work should be purposeful and functional and should contribute in some way to the work of the whole group. Some types of worthwhile independent work experiences could be creative writing, creative art work, recreational reading, room and school duties such as student council reports, practice on skills, working with concrete materials to help build concepts in arithmetic, or research reading. There are some kinds of independent work experiences which are best accomplished when given as homework assignments.

Some of these might include simple scientific experiments, making scrapbooks, making collections, using research materials, or locating materials such as pictures and magazine articles and newspaper clippings. A specific example: in order to extend the concept of area in mathematics, a child could be given the homework assignment of drawing the floor plan of his home to scale and figuring out how many square feet of living space there are. This assignment could take several weeks. Both independent work at home and at school is of little value unless it is shared with the group. Only through their continual contributions to the group can children develop a feeling of being a necessary part of a group.

A good program should definitely include evaluation experiences. Groups and individuals should be given opportunity frequently to look at their work and activities to see how well they have accomplished their purposes and goals. Children should participate in the planning by helping set up the goals and objectives. When the interest of the group begins to lag, then it's time for an evaluation period to see if the activities are of any value in helping to solve the problem. Children like the compliments and praise which come from the evaluation period. Evaluation should not only be for praise, but also for discussion of questions such as these: How could we do a better job next time? What further steps can we take to more completely solve this problem? What improvements can we make in our group process to best solve our future problems?

PROVIDING A VARIETY OF EXPERIENCES

The philosophy of nongradedness is enhanced by the encouragement of diversity. Since each child is unique and since his way of living is multi-directional, he needs to have a variety of educational experiences from which to choose. Through his selection he will have many opportunities to satisfy his many and various needs.

Since a child learns as he lives, probably the most important kind of activity is the direct, first-hand experience — real experience from his environment. These kinds of experiences are relevant to the child because he has a particular need at this particular time.

For example, a child can readily learn to use the card catalog in the library (Figure 2-1) when she wants to find a book about a subject in which she is currently interested. In this situation, learning to use the card catalog is relevant to the child because she can use this system to locate a book which will give her more information about her interest. If all children are taught how to use the card catalog because it is planned for "fourth grade," many children will not see the value of this "learning" because it is irrelevant to them at this time. They are not looking for a particular book or particular information.

Figure 2-1

Another example: an excellent time for boys to learn percentage is when they are playing little league baseball and want to keep a record of their batting averages. This learning is relevant now because they need to know how to figure their individual averages. This experience will satisfy their immediate need.

There are many times when a teacher should provide experiences such as films, maps, charts, graphs, or recordings to substitute for or supplement the direct, first-hand experiences. As an example, the teacher working with the little leaguers in the preceding paragraph might suggest clippings from the sports section of the newspaper (Figure 2-2) to help the youngsters see how the professional batting averages are recorded.

Figure 2-2

Children need to have on-going experiences. Since no study is ever completely finished, provisions should be made to guide children in adding new meaning to a previously developed concept through the correlation of a new experience.

All learning grows out of experience. When a situation confronts a child, he draws from his background of experiences to help him solve the problem at hand. New ideas, new skills, new concepts, in order to be meaningful, must make sense to the child. In order to make sense there needs to be a correlation between the old and the new. He learns as he lives.

A successful nongraded program must include experiences which help the child develop aesthetic values. He needs to have creative outlets in drama, singing, dancing, painting (Figure 2-3), drawing, writing, etc. In addition to these opportunities to express himself, he needs to share the creative works of his peers, his teachers, and the "masters." He needs to hear good music, good stories and poetry, and see the masterpieces of art.

Figure 2-3

Children need experiences in critical thinking. They need to examine many sources of information and tear ideas apart in order to learn to think critically before reaching conclusions. They need to question the answers, not answer the questions; they need to discover ideas, not cover the content.

The various types of experiences suggested here need to be provided in a variety of situations. The child needs opportunities to be a member of large groups as well as small groups; he needs to work at times with children of his own age and at other times with children younger and/or older than he; he needs to work at times with children of the same sex and at other times with children of the opposite sex. The size of the group and the nature of those in the group with whom he works depend on his interest, ability and the purpose of the activity. In addition to group work, he needs many opportunities to work alone. The nongraded school must provide for all of these needs through various experiences in a variety of groupings.

PROVIDING SECURITY FOR CHILDREN

In the nongraded school each child needs to have security. He needs to feel that he belongs because, as he is, he is important, needed and valued by everyone with whom he lives and learns.

The teacher can help establish this security by being friendly. Each child needs to see the teacher as a kind, understanding, and sympathetic adult interested in his well-being.

The teacher must sensitively recognize each child's uniqueness and constructively build upon his differences instead of expecting him to fit into the same identical mold.

A permissive atmosphere must be in existence throughout the school, for such an environment will free each child to be himself. He needs to know that the teacher respects his individuality and has faith in him and in his potential. Teachers must take time to listen to a child as he talks about his experiences, presents his problems, and asks his questions.

An understanding teacher should show, by her enthusiasm, that she enjoys each child with whom she works. She should plan the activities with the children in a democratic manner so that every one of them knows that his contributions are respected and important.

All children should be given equal respect. Praise for achievement should be honest and should be related in terms of the goals and objectives previously established.

Finally, the teacher must recognize aggressiveness, withdrawal, or anti-social behavior as acts of insecurity and find ways other than punishment to help the child become secure.

THE TEACHER IS THE HUMAN RESOURCE

The greatest human resource to a child is his teacher. This important adult must show a genuine affection for his pupils. I'm not implying that we need to baby the child by hugging and kissing.

I'm suggesting that the teacher should be "warm" toward children. Act like a human being. Live with the children; play with them (Figure 2-4); work with them; learn with them.

Figure 2-4

Instead of acting out the stereotyped authoritarian role by giving all the orders and commands, assume the role of one of the members of the group; get in the children's camp, so to speak (Figure 2-5). Actions speak louder than words. Children see the teacher through her behavior. Through requests and suggestions as a member of the group, a teacher will reap higher rewards than through authoritarian commands.

Figure 2-5

In the nongraded school the teacher must take time to talk and listen to each child. This is a realistic way of showing a sincere affection, and it makes the child feel that he can always confide in a true friend.

ENCOURAGING CHILDREN TO SOCIALIZE

The social climate in a nongraded school should be such that each child and each group is encouraged to be self-directed and self-disciplined. Self-direction and self-discipline will not happen overnight. Children need to be taught how to effectively utilize their freedom.

To establish this kind of climate in a school, the teacher should help the children by starting with small group work. She must be patient and be willing to allow more time for these cooperative activities to show results.

In organizing these small groups (4-8 children), those with similar interests should work together. Children who are already friends should be in the same group. The teacher must help each group set its goals and understand the purposes of the activity. She should help each child to see what he can do in helping the group reach the goal. Continuous evaluation of the group work will help accomplish the desired results.

As children develop skill as contributing members of small groups and as they become more secure in their feelings toward themselves as well as others, then larger group activities should be planned. At this point it may be well to indicate that group work is not the only method of helping children acquire self-direction and self-discipline. Many tasks must be undertaken on an individual basis. A group activity should be planned when there is a common need which could best be satisfied through a cooperative effort.

Children need to work together, to help each other, and to learn from each other. It is quite normal for children to talk over their experiences. It is also natural for children to talk with adults. Teachers should expect children to interact as they live together at school. Children should not be expected to sit down and keep quiet in order to learn.

In a nongraded school the social climate should be such that the children are encouraged to participate in group planning, to think critically, and to initiate activities. Children's problems are solved by questioning, evaluating, and pooling of the ideas of the various members of the group. In such an environment the role of the teacher is that of a guide. She is the resource person — the "expert" in group leadership, but not necessarily the group leader.

THE GROUP PROCESS

Group unity does not just happen; it must be achieved. This group spirit will come as the result of everyone working and playing together — that is, "living" at school. This unity is not something concrete that you can put your hands on; it is something you can sense, feel, experience, and enjoy. It is the "style of living" in a nongraded school.

This group spirit is not an end in itself. Through the group process each child will continuously improve his methods of operation as an effective member of the group; he will continue to find satisfaction in the achievements of the group; he will continually realize and appreciate the values of togetherness in the activities of the school.

The teacher should provide many experiences which can best be accomplished by the group. By sharing the leadership role with different children, the group will derive satisfaction and pride in accomplishments. Guide children to plan their own activities and to put their own plans into action. Children should share the responsibility for keeping their school neat, clean, and attractive. Their art work should be displayed all the time.

Committees should be responsible for planning social functions such as parties and assemblies. When children are responsible for these things that are important to them, they will respond with appropriate behavior. If the group process is utilized in activities and experiences which are relevant to children, then children will become self-directed and self-disciplined. As a specific example of this kind of experience I'm suggesting the organization of some kind of student government.

STUDENT GOVERNMENT AND SELF-DIRECTION

The activities of a student government (Figure 2-6) can help children to recognize the needs of the group (the whole school), and to learn to contribute to the common purposes which have been established. Sometimes the contribution is made individually, sometimes in small groups, and sometimes as a member of the total group.

Figure 2-6

Our school paper, *On the Level* (Figure 2-7), is the result of one of the Student Council projects at South Frederick Elementary School. The children worked cooperatively on this project. I'd like to refer you to page 5 of the paper to read a child's explanation of how this particular council was organized. After the election of officers, each room then elected two representatives to serve on the council. Other articles describe some of the activities which were planned, organized and implemented by children.

ON THE LEVEL

Vol. I No. 1   SOUTH FREDERICK ELEMENTARY   May 1968

SPRING CONCERT SCHEDULED

Our combined chorus and band are to present an Annual Spring Festival.

When the chorus begins to sing under the direction of Mrs. Henson, and the band begins to play, under Mr. Storm's direction, the audience knows it is in for a treat.

South Frederick students will be entertaining parents and friends at Frederick High School, on Tuesday, May 7th at 7:30 p.m.

Linda Long
Room 15

ART FESTIVAL COMING SOON

May 15, 1968, an Art Festival at the Governor Thomas Johnson High School will be held from 7 o'clock to 8 o'clock p.m.

People who have been asked to represent our school and give art demonstrations are to report to Mrs. Jones, Wednesday May 8th, 1968. These people are to have their own transportation.

Carol Crouse
Room 15

STUDENTS OF ROOM 15 TAKE TRIP

On April 19th Mrs. Lippy's sixth year students took a bus trip to Washington, D. C. and Mt. Vernon, Va. They found their trip very interesting, enjoyable and educational.

Their first stop was at the Washington Cathedral. A Cathedral is a very important type of church which is used by many people of different religions and beliefs.

The Gothic architecture with its towers of marble and stained glass windows was one of the highlights of the Cathedral.

Although the Cathedral is only 3/4 of the way completed it is still very interesting as well as educational.

The class also visited the Bishop's garden which is on the Cathedral grounds. The winding paths, grottoes, fountains, and its many flower beds all added to its beauty.

(Continued on next page)

Figure 2-7

(continued from previous page)

Their next stop was at the United States Supreme Court Building. It ranks as the highest court in the country. At the Supreme Court Building the group joined a guided tour and was seated in front of the chairs of the nine judges. They listened to a very educational lecture and description of the building and the operation of the court.

Another highlight of the trip was a tour of the Bureau of Engraving and Printing. In this building our entire supply of paper currency is printed. Printing of postage stamps in different colors and designs could also be observed. Other items are printed in this building, also.

Next they traveled to Mt. Vernon, Va. There they observed George Washington's home and colonial life in that time. They also observed the many houses outside of the mansion where many kinds of work was done. Some of the things they observed at Mt. Vernon were the gardens, the museum, the antique furnishings, and George Washington's tomb.

By Room 15
    Jennifer Boward, Linda Long
    Barbara Etzler, Carol Crouse,
    Tracy Crisp

EDITORIAL

STEPS IN THE RIGHT DIRECTION

It is time now for each of us to take steps to keep the front lawn neat and attractive. Steps? Yes, I said steps. It will take a few extra steps by each and every one of us who travel the front way, to walk on the sidewalk instead of going across the grass. Many of us feel that these few extra steps are very worth while.

Mud has it's proper place but we don't think that place is in front of the building.

If we each took a few extra steps in the right direction it would keep down the mud and help up the grass.

We know that any lawn or yard can look more attractive when surrounded by pretty green grass.

We can have a pretty green lawn here at South Frederick school if each little girl and boy and if each big girl and boy and each adult would take a few steps in the right direction. That direction is off the grass and on the pavement.

****

Page 2
Figure 2-7 *(Continued)*

INTERVIEWS WITH FIRST YEAR STUDENTS

Patricia Williams

On April 29, 1968, Patricia Williams, age seven, of Mrs. Fascaldo's room was interviewed during her art period.

Patricia answered the questions as she liked. Patricia was asked if she liked the nongraded schooling. She reported that she did, because she liked to do many different things.

The most important things she has learned this year were mathematics and reading. She said that she likes to do homework, also.

Patricia's favorite subject is art. During the art class she was making a gingerbread man out of clay.

Patricia likes music and the songs Mrs. Henson picks for them to sing.

Mrs. Dorsey's class was interviewed April 29th, 1968 during their Math period.

The children were working quietly with their papers.

In science they were observing what the sky looks like in the evening and in the morning.

They had different art activities on the bulletin board.

The children wrote stories and pictures to illustrate their stories. The stories were typed and put into booklets.

Pamela Grove

WEATHER EVERY MORNING

Some children in room 15 have been studying Weather. Every morning someone will post a chart in the front hall which tells the forecast. If you are interested in what the weather will be for the day, go down the front hall and look to the right or look to the left as you come in the front door.

Phyllis Amorello
Room 15

MELISSA AND THE FLEA

Melissa had a little flea.
She caught it from a dog,
She put it on a little pig,
And now it's on a hog.

Brenda May
Room 18

ON THE LEVEL — STAFF

Editor in Chief —
Jenifer Boward

Reporters
Steve Barger — 11
Tyrone Bowie — 12
Kathy Brode — 13
Ronnie Younkins — 14
Linda Long — 15
Kathy Toms - 16
Tammy Stull — 17
Brenda May — 18
Shelly Baggett — 19
Beverly Warnock — 20
Shirlene Roberts — 21
Charlene McKnight — 22

Page 3

Figure 2-7*(Continued)*

ROOM 1 GOES FISHING

On April 23, 1968 Miss Browne's first year class went on a fishing trip.

They spent the morning fishing. Several of the children caught fish.

For lunch they traveled to Cunningham Falls. After lunch they played games. Then they went to the playground for more fun.

Finally it was time for them to leave. On the way home the children sang songs.

Jennifer Boward
Room 15

I woke up on Tuesday morning. I remembered that my class was going on a fishing trip. So I got ready to go. I walked to school. We waited for the bus. By and by the bus came. My daddy and I got on the bus. The bus went. When we got on the highway we sang songs and played games. Soon we were there. Mr. Powers was in charge. He got the fishing poles. Darrell was my partner. We spread ourselves around the pond. Darrell caught one fish and I caught two. Later we stopped fishing. Then we went to Cunningham Falls. We ate lunch. Then we played a game called the "Lion Hunt." Then we went to the playground. I went on the snake sliding board. Then we went back to school. My daddy got a sunburn, but we all had a good time.

Richard Koogle

First we came to school. Then we got parents to look after the children. Then we got on the bus. We sang songs and played games. Soon we were there. We got our fishing poles. We got ready to fish. Then we started. I caught four fish. Five was the highest number. Then we had to stop. We had to put our fish in a basket. We got back on the bus. We soon got to Cunningham Falls to eat our lunch. Boy, we had a good lunch. Then we went on a "Lion Hunt." That was fun. Then we went to the playground. We had fun. We got on the bus. Then we went back to school. We gave out some fish. Then we lay on the mats. Then we went home. It sure was a fun day.

Carol Warnock

My partner was Sonya. The person who watched me and Sonya was Dr. Thompson. I did not catch any fish. But I got one from Jay. We sang songs on the bus. We played games, too. We ate lunch. Then we went to the playground. We went on the snake sliding board. We went in the boxes. We went on the monkey bars. And we went on the logs. Then we went on the bus. We took the bus to school. When we got to school we took the mats out. We rested on the mats. We took our fish home. Mothers cooked the fish. We ate them at home.

Denise Scherer

Page 4

Figure 2-7 *(Continued)*

STUDENT COUNCIL

The reason we have a newspaper is because the Student Council thought of one, so you should know how the newspaper came to be.

After Christmas vacation, Mr. Smith announced that he would like us to have a Student Council for our school. Everyone thought this was a good idea. The first step was to have the people who wanted to run for the office of: President, Vice-President, Secretary, Assistant Secretary to pass around a petition to those who wanted to sign it. The people who wanted to run for an office were required to have at least 10 names of approval signed on their petition.

After the petitions were turned in these people gave speeches. At this election all of the candidates were presented. The purpose of this election was to eliminate some of the candidates so that there wouldn't be so many people running for one office. The candidates elected at the primary election would then be the ones who were going on to the general election.

During the next several weeks the candidates were busy campaigning. They gave speeches, put up posters and passed out buttons.

A few days before the election Mr. Smith called a meeting of the people who had been appointed as the election committee. These were the ones to conduct the election day going down to the Materials Center where the election was held. Plans were made.

Finally the election day came. All day the students of our school were voting. At 2:00 the poll closed. The committee went to the Material Center and counted the votes. The results were as follows: Raynard Scott, President; Bobby Myers, Vice-President; Holly Burke, Secretary; Jennifer Boward, Assistant Secretary.

Since then, every Wednesday or almost every Wednesday there has been a Student Council meeting from 2:00 to 3:00. So far, the Student Council has been a success and has helped to solve some of the biggest problems around our school.

Tracy Crisp

PLAY DAY, AN APPROACHING EVENT "COMING ALONG SMOOTHLY"

Play Day which was put in action by the Student Council, is to be held May 27, 28, 29 or on the last school week in June, (one day only) all depending on the weather.

Mr. Patterson, and a committee have met and are now making plans.

Events such as high jumps, soft ball throws, dashes and three-legged races are to take place.

We hope this day will turn out to be fun-filled and a big success for much time and effort has already been put into it.

Pam Grove

Page 5

Figure 2-7 (Continued)

SOCIAL STUDIES

In fourth-year Social Studies
we have been learning about the
early explorers and discoverers of
the United States. We wanted to
find out who these people were and
why they came to the region that is our
country today.

We each read a trade book about
one of these famous people. Some
of us read about the same person.
We talked in our small groups. Then
we grouped ourselves together to
learn about men from the same
country. We compared our books and
checked to see if our information
agreed and if we could depend on it
being the truth. Sometimes we had to
check more books and use filmstrips
and encyclopedias.

We found out the main reasons
why these people came to America.

We also found out that the explorers were not all the same kind
of people. Some were good and nice.
Some were brave but bad. Many were
disappointed in the new land and
never came back again. Many told
their kings and queens about America.
If they had not wanted to come back
we might not be living here today.

Social Studies is more fun when
you read about the people. You
learn that these people are like us.
Maybe we will be famous someday, too.

Beverly Warnock
Room 20

THE BIG OUTDOORS

When I finish my bun
    I go out under the big bright
    sun
I sit under a tree with a big
    fat bee
When I see all the girls
    I pull their curls
And all the boys
    Sit down with their toys
I saw a mouse
    That ran into the house
In the grass was a pair of oars
    So that ends my poem of
"The Big Outdoors"

Theresa Heller
Room 14

THE LITTLE GREEN HORNET

There used to be a hornet
that was black and yellow.
All the other hornets were
green. The little hornet was
very sad because he wasn't
green. All the other hornets
made fun of the little hornet.
He would just go back to his
house, and go to his room and
cry. The little hornet's mother
and father tried to cheer him
up, but they couldn't.

So one Saturday morning the
little hornet went out to watch
his father paint the house green.
The little hornet was not watching
what he was doing and he knocked
over the paint and he was all green.

His mother tried to wash it off,
but she couldn't. So the little
hornet was finally green, and all
of his friends would play with him.

Lydia Buckles

Page 6

Figure 2-7(Continued)

EVERYTHING NEEDS SOMETHING

The flowers need showers,
The bees need trees,
The flys need the sky.
So everything needs something
you see.

Tammie Adkins
Room 18

"THINK"

Solve each of the following problems. Write what each represents.

1.   2.   L W E
               A Y R !

3. Every/ right/ thing   4. DKI

5. Tom   6. o()   7.

o o o o
o o o o

JOKES

1. I am green and I'm just a piece of paper. What am I?
2. What did the big fire-cracker say to the little fire-cracker?
3. What did the big chimney say to the little chimney?
4. Why do they have mirrors on candy machines?

CROSSWORD PUZZLE

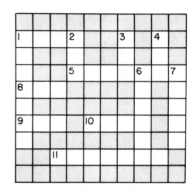

Timothy Harding
Room 14

Across

1. The red planet
5. The eighth planet from the sun
8. You ride in a ---
9. What the sun gives off
10. The earth's satellite
11. When the moon comes in front of the earth

Down

1. The hottest planet in the solar
2. The center of the solar system
3. If you don't stand you ---
4. Rhymes with sun and starts with F
6. The seventh planet from the sun
7. The planet we live on

Page 7

Figure 2-7(Continued)

TEAMWORK

What was the auditorium in building A is now two class-rooms.

One of the classrooms belongs to Mrs. Fuscaldo. The children in this class are planting seeds which will grow into flowers. These flowers will be taken home to the childrens' mothers for Mothers Day.

Also, the children in this class are putting on a puppet show prior to the play that they saw, which was "Jack and the Beanstalk."

The other classroom belongs to Mrs. Poole.

The children in this class care for the birds by feeding them.

Mrs. Poole will take her reading group to the C. Burr Artz Library on May 15th to learn how to use its facilities.

Both of these teachers teach 1st and 2nd year children. They teach as a team, and the children participate in different activities together.

MRS. TRUNK'S CLASS

The pupils of room 4, Mrs. Trunk's class, have had visits from a dear little friend of theirs, the cardinal. Both "Mr. and Mrs. Cardinal" have come to see them at least three times each day.

From these visits it has inspired the children to write stories.

Linda Cleveland has done just that. Here is her little story.

My Friend the Cardinal

One day when Mrs. Trunk was reading us a story, a cardinal came to the birdhouse outside the window and started to eat. We were very still for a few minutes, but he went away. I guess he went to his family, but I'm not sure. So she kept on reading until the end of the chapter, then she stopped. I kept on thinking about him while I was working. But I stopped thinking about him. The bell had rung.

BOOKLETS

You can use these little booklets as scrap books, hobbybooks, writing and drawing books, and as photograph albums.

Booklets:

What you need: Sheets of the same size. . . heavy thread or cord. . .darning needle. . . nail. . .scissors

What you do: Fold several sheets of paper down the center. Use nail to punch two holes on the fold through all thicknesses of the paper. Then, with a darning needle and heavy thread and beginning on the inside of the book push the needle through to the outside, leaving about three inches of thread inside the book. Bring the needle back through the other hole to the center. Pull the thread tight and tie in a knot.

Lynn Johnson
Room 20

Page 8

Figure 2-7(Continued)

FLORIDA

One day very early
  When the sky was pearly
I woke and rose from bed
  Still very sleepy and dizzy
In my head.
  I dressed and ate and set
About my early morning tasks.
  When I was done and quite awake.
I gathered up my suitcases and
  hurried to the car, and
  yelled "Lets go for goodness sake!"
We were off to Florida.
  We traveled most of the day
Stopping along the way
  For bites to eat and
dessert so sweet
  and that was the way
It went each day
  on the way to Florida
When we reached Florida
  I saw huge skyscrapers
That reached up to the sky,
  That when you looked up
you could see the rockets
  go wizzing by.
The ocean's the best of all
  a wave would come up
And then you would fall
  In the ocean you would find
Shells of many a different kind.
  Sometimes on the beaches
you would find a jelly-fish or two
  And if you didn't watch
you would get a sting or two.
  Soon it was time to leave
Florida.

Cindy Wood
Room 21

BARNABY BUNNY

The students of Mrs. Dodd's class may enjoy playing during class with Barnaby Bunny, the class pet.

Barnaby Bunny is a gray rabbit which was given to the class three weeks before Easter.

Mrs. Dodd allows Barnaby to hop around the room during classes. If Barnaby comes to a student, the student may pick him up and play with him.

The children love Barnaby. He is the only pet in the class.

Some of the childrens thoughts of Barnaby can be found below.

Carol Crouse
Room 15

We have a little Bunny. His name is Barnaby Bunny. He hops in the waste basket and he is gray with a little white nose. He is my friend.

Anthony Smallwood

THE LITTLE BUNNY

I know a fantastic bunny named Barnaby. He lives in our school. He has a very good cage. His cage is always clean. He has rabbit pellets and carrots to eat. Barnaby is a nice bunny. He is nice to everyone. He hops all aroun I think he has fun at school. He gets fresh water to drink. He is gray with som white in him. He is the best bunny you ha ever seen.

Kathi S. O'Bryan

Page 9
Figure 2-7 (Continued)

HEARD IN THE EAST HALLS

All was silent in the east corridors. Teachers were hammering on skills C, D, E, F,G,H,I,J,K,L,M,N, and O. Suddenly in the dead silence came a peep, peep, peep, peep. What was it? Baby chicks in room eleven, of course.

Then all was quiet once more. Teachers start from where they left off, students sigh and go back to work.

Tramp! Tramp! Tramp! A yellow dog runs past the windows hurrying to get home.

All of a sudden music starts pouring in, in eight different tunes of Bingo. "B-i-n-g-o, B-i-n-g-o, B-i-n-g-o and Bingo was his name O!" This goes on for awhile and then everyone goes back to work.

One morning before 9:00 a.m. rock'n roll music is heard across the hall. People go to see what it is and find children were dancing to a dance no one had ever seen or heard.

Occasionally people passing by can hear in room 15 someone strumming a guitar and a few humming and singing "Blowin' In The Wind." Once more all is quiet and people begin their day's activities.

On another occasion some of the boys in room 15 were taking a device they had made to the art room to paint.

It has a "burglar alarm", flashing lights, fans and many other things.

The halls were crowded with students that day and so the boys just turned on the "burglar alarm" to clear them.

The people got right out of the way because they thought that they were sent out to clear the halls.

These are just some of the sounds heard in the east halls.

Linda Long
Room 15

"ODDS AND ENDS" OF NEWS

ATTENTION!

All boys between the ages of 7 and 8 can expect a visit within one week from a gentleman that is talking about Cub Scouts.

Pam Grove

INTERVIEWS WITH FIRST YEAR STUDENTS

Patrick Moore

April 29, 1968, Patrick Moore, of Mrs. Fascaldo's room was interviewed during his art class.

Patrick's favorite subject is Physical Education. He likes the ball handling skills best.

Patrick likes music. He likes most of the songs Mrs. Henson picks out for them to sing.

Patrick likes the idea of nongraded schools, because he enjoys doing the types of things he does.

Carol Crouse
Room 15

Page 10

Figure 2-7*(Continued)*

INDIANS

We also studied about the Indians in the Americas. We tried to find out where they came from long ago and how they got what they needed to live. We tried to learn how they are living today.

We learned that the Indians lived by fishing, hunting, seed gathering, following the buffalo, and raising corn, beans and squash. They also raised sheep.

Today many Indians live on reservations. Many Indians live just like the other people in the United States, too.

Did you know that —
1. The Indians may have lived in America 30,000 years ago?
2. The Indian population is increasing in the United States
3. The Indians and all other people today live wherever they can find food, clothing and shelter for their families.

Mark Everly
Room 20

THE APACHES

The Apaches lived in the Southwest. Some of them did not like to stay in one place, so they wandered around and raided the other Indians. Some good Apaches were like Cochise and raised crops. Geronimo was an Apache who went on raids.

Richard Keeney
Room 20

FLOWERS

Flowers are pretty all red and blue. But no flower is as cute as you.

Tammie Adkins
Room 18

THE TRAIN

I have a train on a tiny track.
It runs away,
And comes right back.

ANSWERS FROM "THINK"

1. A fat lady doing a dive
2. A crooked lawyer
3. Right in the middle of everything
4. Mixed-up kid
5. Tomatoes
6. Ohio
7. Tennessee

JOKES

1. A piece of money
2. My pop is bigger than your pop
3. You're too young to smoke
4. So you can see how you look when the candy doesn't come out.

CROSSWORD PUZZLE

Down	Across
1. Mercury	1. Mars
2. Sun	5. Neptune
3. Sit	8. Car
4. Fun	9. Ray
6. Uranus	10. Moon
7. Earth	11. Eclipse

Page 11

Figure 2-7 *(Continued)*

ARBOR DAY PROGRAM

An Arbor Day program was presented by the students of Room 13, on Friday, April 26th, at 1:30 p.m. The program lasted about a half an hour and was very enjoyable.

The program consisted of a welcome, the pledge to the flag, and the song "America". There were original poems and songs. There was also, an original skit called, "A Martian Discovers Arbor Day", by Michael Kelley.

After the program a Flowering Crabapple Tree was planted in the courtyard in celebration of Arbor Day. The tree was donated by the Jr. Women's Club of Frederick.

Linda Long
Room 15

ROOM 8 TO GIVE PLAY

Some students from Mrs. Sterling's class are going to give the play, "Cinderella". The children are working on this activity without help from the teacher. The play will be given in about one week.

NEW "FRIEND" AT SCHOOL

In Room 2, Miss Cronise's class, the children are going to have a new tadpole. His name is Charlie. Terry Kennedy is going to bring it in. The children are going to watch it grow and care for it.

SFE WELCOMES NEW STUDENTS

The pupils and faculty of South Frederick Elementary School welcome the new children who have come or will be coming to A — building this year. In the first year, John Roop has come from Columbus, Georgia. He is in Miss Weedy's class. In Miss Cronise's first year class, a new girl will be coming in on May 1st or 2nd. Her name is Sabre Ripple. In the second year class, Robert Young from Florida has come into Mrs. Price's room.

We hope that these children will be happy in our school.

Holly Burke
Room 15

LEARNING THROUGH FUN

Sixth year girls are having a very educational and enjoyable Home Economics Club on Wednesdays and Fridays after school. The class lasts from 3:30 until 5:00.

Miss Boyles, the teacher, is a student at Hood College who enjoys teaching and working with the girls.

In this class the girls are learning to sew, cook, and many other things will be taught in future classes.

Linda Long
Room 15

Page 12

Figure 2-7(Continued)

SUMMARY

The teacher is the most important single factor in the development of a school environment which will promote the philosophy of nongradedness. Children look to the teacher as an example. They see how she lives more than they hear what she tells them to do. Nongrading must be the teacher's "style of living."

Children look to teachers for guidance in the solution of their everyday problems; they expect teachers to be able to understand and help solve the problems of group living. That's what school is all about.

Children look to the teacher as the "expert" in human relations. The teacher should guide children in making decisions which will result in higher qualities of living and provide experiences which will lead to higher levels of thinking.

This "expert" should see her role as a resource person; she should provide guidance in group activities of planning, fulfilling and evaluating the total program; she should help children interpret the values and attitudes which are developed through "living" together at school.

3

TEAM TEACHING
IN NONGRADED LEARNING CENTERS

Team teaching is an organizational pattern which promotes flexibility and permits and encourages individualization of instruction. There are many different schemes in operation. A school should not try to adopt any particular one, but rather should be selective and use the parts of existing plans which best meet that school's specific needs.

VARIOUS CONNOTATIONS OF TEAM TEACHING

There are many definitions and descriptions of team teaching. Quite a few have been printed in various educational magazines and textbooks. To many, team teaching means only the using of large and/or small group instruction. Others see it as a hierarchy of personnel having a designated team leader with other teachers as subordinates, each with a different function in the area of his special competence. To some it means two or more teachers working together with equal responsibility.

PROS AND CONS OF TEAM TEACHING

The advantages claimed for team teaching are many. Some of the advocates of team teaching tell us that research and experience have shown that grade level grouping in self-contained classrooms for all learning is both ineffective and inefficient. They state that some lessons can be taught better in a large group, and that a group of teachers, working together to share the responsibility of a large group of children, can better meet the needs of all children. In many schools the children and teachers have been divided into teams spanning more than one grade level and the schedules arranged so as to permit children to work in another team when their doing so seems advantageous.

Also pointed out on the positive side of team teaching was the fact that elementary school teachers who had been finding it impossible to keep abreast of new knowledge in all areas of the curriculum, now were able to do this with teammates sharing the total responsibility. Each teacher on a team assumes the major responsibility for one or two areas of the curriculum and keeps the others up-to-date. For example, one teacher is responsible for math; he does professional reading and other study in this area, condenses material, and explains it to co-workers. This same teacher assumes the major role in planning for instruction in math for the entire team. He is the "math expert." In this manner these teachers are able to keep curriculum revision continuous in terms of present needs.

Teachers have reported that they find team teaching stimulating because they have the opportunity to watch other teachers at work. This arrangement also gives the individual teacher some time to himself while other team members are teaching in a large group situation.

Still others contend that the organizational scheme allows the teacher more time to give individual help to students who need it. Team teaching has been found helpful in working with dis-advantaged children because teachers have more time to give attention to children with specific problems.

Some children have been motivated just by the change of rooms and teachers. Children get the advantage of the skilled teacher for part of the day instead of being with the inexperienced all day long.

It was also reported that pupils are able to spend more time working with a teacher, because when they are divided into small groups there is more opportunity for the teacher to work with each group.

Teachers in schools with team-teaching programs report that they feel they know their pupils better and, therefore, can give more individual attention. They feel that team teaching provides more individualization of instruction.

The major disadvantages are not within team teaching itself, but rather within the lack of modern school facilities with built-in flexibility that would provide rooms of the right size for large group as well as small group work. Also lacking are offices for teachers and clerical assistants to take care of routine paper work.

Another drawback to team teaching is that some teachers do not want to work on a team. They prefer to work in a self-contained classroom and they don't want to be observed by other teachers.

CHARACTERISTICS OF A TEAM-TEACHING PLAN

In a typical team-teaching school one might see the following organization. The pupils are grouped heterogeneously for Social Studies and Science. Variances in the capabilities of children are taken care of by the wide range of texts and other materials provided for them, instructional tasks at various levels of difficulty, and opportunities to explore their own interests.

For the skill subjects (Language Arts and Mathematics) the pupils are grouped on the basis of past achievement and on suggested levels by previous teachers. They are then regrouped as their needs change. This regrouping means close coordination and continuous planning by teachers.

The team plans for comprehensiveness, sequence, improved methods, meeting individual needs, preparation of creative materials, and opportunities for large and small group instruction.

There is no predetermined arrangement for teachers to combine classes for large group instruction; rather, such occasions are dictated by the development of the curriculum as appropriate learning opportunities are planned.

For skill subjects teachers usually work in separate classrooms with their particular groups. However, occasionally one teacher will take part of another teacher's class for an activity in literature while the other teacher helps a smaller group with a special project.

Often teachers plan to co-teach every day. In this case, the two teachers organize all the pupils at several learning stations, such as a listening station or skill table, and then move from group to group.

Within the framework of the various groupings continuous evaluation of pupils takes place. No one group is static. During the course of the year pupil groupings will vary. At times pupils will be members of fast-moving, high achievement groups in certain phases of the program. At other times they will be members of groups designed to meet specific developmental needs in the skills. Interaction between the teachers and pupils and teachers with teachers are vital aspects of evaluation in a continuous progress plan.

A PRACTICAL APPROACH TO TEAM TEACHING

In several nongraded programs now in existence the following statement is used: "We define a team as a group of two or more teachers who assume the common responsibility for the total instructional program for two or more classrooms of children."

This definition implies that the children as well as the teachers make up the team and that there is a close working relationship between teachers of a team. Teachers group and regroup pupils frequently to satisfy the instructional needs of each pupil. This team organization provides for more productive planning and sharing of the instructional process, and thus leads to more efficient and more interesting ways of presenting educational experiences.

Since the teachers are concerned more with concepts and generalizations than they are with facts, the team approach helps students "uncover" the subject matter, rather then have the teachers "cover it." This promotes the idea of having children question the answers rather than answer the questions.

In these nongraded programs the pupils are assigned to homerooms on a multi-age, heterogeneous basis. The children are placed in instructional groups within the team. For Language Arts,

Figure 3-1

children are grouped according to reading levels and skills (Figure 3-1); in Mathematics, they are similarly grouped and regrouped according to changing skills and needs.

By grouping students in this manner, each child has a better opportunity to work on his own achievement level at his own rate, and the overall range of achievement within a room is narrowed. In homerooms, heterogeneous grouping (different ages and different levels) is used for science, social studies, and other areas of the curriculum.

Each teacher on the team attempts to help the children assigned to her begin their work at their different levels and makes as much progress as she can with each. At the end of the school year, not all of the children will have done the same work or completed the same books. After summer vacation, each child begins where he left off in the spring.

TEAM ORGANIZATIONS

As indicated in Figure 3-2, teachers of rooms 11, 12, and 16 have 3rd and 4th year students. They have levels A, B, C, D, and G for Language Arts. When they regroup, all of level A and part of Level B are in one room; the rest of Level B and all of Level C are in another; the third teacher takes all of Levels D and G. For Mathematics they regroup again: one teacher has Level C; another has Level D; and the other teacher has Level G. They use the homeroom grouping for all other subjects.

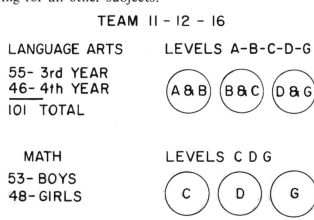

TEAM II – 12 – 16

LANGUAGE ARTS   LEVELS A-B-C-D-G
55- 3rd YEAR
46- 4th YEAR
101 TOTAL

A & B   B & C   D & G

MATH   LEVELS C D G
53- BOYS
48- GIRLS

C   D   G

Figure 3-2

HOMEROOM GROUPS FOR ALL OTHER SUBJECTS.

The XYZ team of third, fourth, and fifth year students use the block of time between 10:30 A.M. and 2:40 P.M. each day for Mathematics and Language Arts. They teach the content subjects to their multi-age, heterogeneous homeroom and regroup for Language Arts and Math to meet individual needs (Figure 3-3).

XYZ TEAM

TEACHER X	TEACHER Y	TEACHER Z
7-3rd year students	11-3rd year students	16-3rd year students
24-4th year students	20-4th year students	13-4th year students
31-Total	31-Total	1-5th year student
		30-Total
16 Boys; 15 Girls	15 Boys; 16 Girls	16 Boys; 14 Girls

Reading	Math	Reading	Math	Reading	Math
3-Level 4	3-Level 5	4-Level 5	4-Level 5	2-Level 3	4-Level 5
5-Level 5	12-Level 7	3-Level 6	8-Level 7	1-Level 5	14-Level 7
1-Level 6	16-Level 9	8-Level 7	19-Level 9	4-Level 6	12-Level 9
4-Level 7		6-Level 8		3-Level 7	
8-Level 8		3-Level 9		10-Level 8	
3-Level 9		5-Level 10		1-Level 9	
6-Level 10		2-Level 11		7-Level 10	
1-Level 11				2-Level 11	

Each teacher works with her heterogeneous homeroom group in Social Studies and Science. At 10:30 A.M. each day the students are redeployed for Mathematics to the classrooms and subgrouped as indicated:

TEACHER X · · · · | 11 - Level 5 | | 12 - Level 7 |

TEACHER Y · · · · | 11 - Level 7 | | 11 - Level 7 | | 11 - Level 9 |

TEACHER Z · · · · | 12 - Level 9 | | 12 - Level 9 | | 12 - Level 9 |

At 1:00 P.M. each day the students are redeployed again for Language Arts to the classrooms and subgrouped as indicated:

TEACHER X · · · | 10 - Level 5 | | 12 - Level 8 | | 12 - Level 8 |

TEACHER Y · · · | 3 - Level 4 | | 8 - Level 6 | | 15 - Level 7 |

TEACHER Z · · · | 2 - Level 3 | | 7 - Level 9 | | 18 - Level 10 | | 5 - Level 11 |

Figure 3-3

Teachers of the ABC team operate basically with their heterogeneous homerooms of third, fourth, and fifth year students. However, they redeploy students each day at 1:00 P.M. for Mathematics because they recognize that even when pupils are arranged into more teachable reading groups, a variety of mathematical levels is inevitable (Figure 3-4).

ABC TEAM

TEACHER A	TEACHER B	TEACHER C
6-3rd year students	11-4th year students	12-4th year students
25-4th year students	19-5th year students	19-5th year students
31-Total	30-Total	31-Total
17 Boys; 14 Girls	13 Boys; 17 Girls	16 Boys; 15 Girls

TEACHER A		TEACHER B		TEACHER C	
Reading	**Math**	**Reading**	**Math**	**Reading**	**Math**
11-Level 7	6-Level 7	8-Level 7	3-Level 4	13-Level 5	7-Level 5
9-Level 8	25-Level 9	13-Level 8	2-Level 7	9-Level 6	3-Level 6
11-Level 9		9-Level 11	7-Level 8	9-Level 11	6-Level 7
			8-Level 9		5-Level 8
			1-Level 10		2-Level 9
			9-Level 11		8-Level 11

Each teacher works with the three levels in her homeroom for the Language Arts. At a specified time each day, the students are redeployed for Mathematics to the classrooms and subgrouped as indicated:

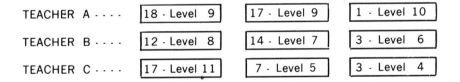

TEACHER A · · · ·	18 - Level 9	17 - Level 9	1 - Level 10
TEACHER B · · · ·	12 - Level 8	14 - Level 7	3 - Level 6
TEACHER C · · · ·	17 - Level 11	7 - Level 5	3 - Level 4

Teachers B and C also regroup for the Social Studies and Science. This is done on the basis of interest as well as need. Often it is done by year in school as indicated:

TEACHER B	TEACHER C
23 - 4th year students	38 - 5th year students

Figure 3-4

In addition to regrouping within the team there is some regrouping between teams. There is occasional swapping of individual students to better meet specific needs as they are recognized. Teachers analyze the needs and work with other teachers to arrange redeployment for part of a day for individual children.

TEAM PLANNING TIME

Planning time for teachers is scheduled on school time throughout the week. Pictured in Figure 3-5 is one team as they study the material available. They are planning several learning experiences to meet the needs of the children in their team.

Figure 3-5

There are many times when the principal or vice-principal is asked to join a team planning session. In Figure 3-6 the principal is making a suggestion to this teaching team. As a follow-up of a planning session sometimes new materials are suggested by the vice-principal (Figure 3-7).

Figure 3-6

Figure 3-7

One of the most important tasks in the business of school administration and organization is the scheduling of specialists. Schedule making in the traditional graded elementary school does not present any great difficulties. It consists simply of determining that each teacher in each self-contained classroom conform to the time limits for each subject as directed and that the specialists conduct lessons as scheduled.

However, in a nongraded program flexibility must be included with scheduling. All of the specialists are scheduled on a regular basis by the week, but classroom teachers, teams of teachers, and specialists may change this routine as needed and as frequently as desired. Teaching time is often traded by the special teachers. Often several specialists work together with classes or groups on specific projects. There is some unscheduled time to allow the specialists extra time for working with individual children and large or small groups to meet specific needs.

There are many times when the classroom teacher feels that she needs to use the regularly scheduled time for some other purpose and so she simply notifies the special teacher. There are other times when the classroom teacher feels the need for more aid from the specialist than the regular schedule will permit. Together they plan for this larger time block to accomplish the task before them.

Occasionally, teams of teachers need to have a specialist work with all the children within the team at the same time. The extra time allotments permit this type of large group activity.

In setting up the regular schedule for the specialists in Art, Library, Music, and Physical Education, a "back-to-back" plan provides teams of teachers opportunity during the school day for planning, team conferences with pupils or parents, and evaluation of individual progress. (See Figure 3-8).

TEAM SCHEDULE

TIME	MON	TUES	WED	THUR	FRI
9:00	11-LANGUAGE ARTS 12- " 16- "	" "	******************** ******************** ********************		
10:40	11-ART 12-LIB 16-MUS (PLAN)	PE ART LIB (PLAN)		LIB MUS PE (PLAN)	MUS PE ART (PLAN)
1:00	MATH **				
2:00	SOCIAL STUDIES OR SCIENCE **********************				

Figure 3-8

The master schedule (Figure 3-9) shows how specialists are scheduled to provide planning time during the week. Each team has four planning periods 45 minutes in length while their classes are taught by the specialists. The shaded areas indicate unscheduled time which is used for special projects and individual help.

In addition to the changes already discussed, the classroom teacher can plan and trade scheduled times with other classroom teachers. This unscheduled time provides the flexibility to allow limitless possibilities of arrangements which can be made to better meet the specific needs of individuals, small groups, and whole teams.

This flexibility makes close coordination and teamwork in planning a necessity. This teamwork promotes continuous evaluation and regrouping to meet the needs of children.

SPECIAL TEACHERS – MASTER SCHEDULE

	ART					LIBRARY					MUSIC					PHYSICAL EDUCATION				
	Mon	Tues	Wed	Thur	Fri	Mon	Tues	Wed	Thur	Fri	Mon	Tues	Wed	Thur	Fri	Mon	Tues	Wed	Thur	Fri
8:30–9:15	21	22		23		22	21	11		23	23		17	21	22	13	23	12	22	21
9:30–10:15	12	16	13	11	14	16	12	14	17	13	14	11	16	13	12	15	17		14	16
10:30–11:45	18	19	15	20		19	18		15	20	20	15		18	19		20		19	18
12:15–1:00	6	7		8	9	7	6		9	8	8	9		7	6	9	8		6	7
1:10–1:55	1	2		4	5	5	1		2	4	4	5		1	2	2	4		5	1
2:10–2:55	17	10		3		10	3				3				10	11			10	3

Figure 3-9

THE LEARNING CENTER APPROACH

The goals and purposes of a nongraded program could best be served by open-space learning centers and the use of disciplinary teaching teams. By placing students and teachers in one area where they could work together easily, give suggestions to each other, hear each other and help each other, all would benefit.

Students would be involved in planning for meeting their own needs. Teachers would plan together to create the best possible learning atmosphere. All teachers would have their personal work areas located in a central room. I feel this would enhance interstaff communication, not only in terms of a particular child's situation, but the general "togetherness." The staff, while not necessarily having to have congruent ideas in implementation, must feel good about and unthreatened by each other.

Each teacher would be an implementer in his field and would not be expected to be a specialist in another field in which he is less competent. Each teacher could concentrate his study and preparation in the area for which he is responsible. This, per se, is not departmentalization in that all subjects are not viewed as such, but are rather a body of knowledge in process. Furthermore, each child's schedule will be unique to him. Classes should not be scheduled from center to center and period to period.

I view the learning center approach as a consistent variation of the basic nongraded philosophic tenets, in that a center is an actual geographic location where a child can work independently with a series of related activities which are designed to promote independent understanding of certain concepts. The teachers would assist students where needed in the selection of appropriate centers and activities. Ultimately, the child would develop the ability to schedule himself and discipline himself to carry out his own scheduled activities.

This would include self-directed movement throughout the building to appropriate learning areas according to schedules that have been formed by the child the previous day. His progress would be recorded in each learning center and codified among home teachers. A period of time at the beginning of each day should be used for planning and a period of time at the end of each day should be used for evaluation.

There should be some type of homeroom organization to handle administrative matters and to provide for identification with a smaller peer group and with a teacher even though pupils will be moving into various groupings throughout the day (large group activity, small group activity, individualized instruction, independent study, and so on).

Children would need a period of time (probably several months) to understand and utilize fully the freedom of moving from center to center and learning to form personal responsibility for large periods of time during the day. Some children would probably be able to handle this type of freedom almost immediately, while others probably will always need some guidance. Teacher-pupil conferences should be fully utilized in guiding pupils to choose the best experiences for meeting their needs. A good deal of the scheduling for the centers will be done by instructional groups and planned with the teachers in the centers. Children need to be taught how to use their freedom wisely.

LEARNING CENTER TEAMS

A learning center is an actual geographic location in the school where each child can work independently or with a group. All learning should deal with aspects of the society in which the child lives and with the ways in which these aspects are important to him. The child's experiences must be related directly to his environment, and thus enable him to acquire the tools he will need as he continues to grow.

Each learning center should house all the books, materials, equipment, and other resources (including the human resource of teachers, aides, and other personnel) which pertain to the particular discipline of the center.

In each learning center the teaching team would be charged with the responsibility of planning all the activities of its center. These plans would include analyzing the needs, prescribing the activities, and evaluating the progress.

For example, the math team would arrange for instruction and guidance of all the children who would come to the math center. The experiences and materials should be so varied that any child could come to the center with any math-related problem and find the necessary activity to help him solve his problem in such a way that the learning experience would be relevant to him.

In each center the teaching team would provide many activities which would be self-directing. A child could come to the center and proceed independently with pre-arranged instructions. One teacher could be working with a group on a particular skill which is a common need of those in the group; another teacher could be involved in a one-to-one conference with a child; another teacher could be engaged in professional reading or preparation of future "center" activities; an aide could just be available to those children working on independent activities; a group of children could be viewing a film — the possibilities are limitless and could all be happening simultaneously. The center would be alive with activity. Instead of doing meaningless busy work, children would be seeking relevant solutions to real problems.

INDIVIDUALIZED SCHEDULES

Since each child's growth pattern is different from all others, his schedule should be unique to him and his needs. One child may complete an activity in 15 minutes while another child may require an hour to do the same task. Because of this diversity I would suggest the use of a modular schedule. That is, divide the school day into 15-minute blocks of time. This would allow each child to schedule himself for the length of time that he feels would be necessary for him to complete an activity.

A child may wish to plan a project which would last several weeks. With this type of scheduling he could plan time each day to pursue this particular interest. For example, he may want to make a puppet with paper maché. This would require a short period of work time each day with an overnight drying time.

Another child may wish to concentrate on a special project and he could schedule himself for an afternoon or perhaps an entire day for his activity. For example, the editor of the school paper may wish to spend a day setting up the "dummy" and making arrangements for the printing of the paper.

If a child is very much interested in music, he may schedule himself for more activities in the music center than would another child who would prefer more art work. With modular scheduling each child would have more opportunities to pursue his major interests. Modular scheduling would certainly promote self-direction and self-discipline because each could plan his own time to meet his own needs, to satisfy his own curiosities, and to develop more depth in his area of major interest. School activities would be relevant.

Once again, I'd like to emphasize the importance of the teacher-pupil conferences. During the planning and evaluation periods, the teachers would carefully guide each child so that he would not schedule himself too heavily in one area at the neglect of another. For example, the teacher might say to the child during the conference, "I see on your schedule that you have not been to the music center this week. Don't you think you should plan for this next week? Let's put it on your schedule now."

The teacher needs to have faith in the child. Assume that he will utilize his time wisely and give him the freedom to plan his schedule. If and when you find that he needs guidance, help him to make a well-rounded schedule. Don't do it for him. Don't *tell* him what to do and when, but help him to see the value of wise use of his time.

A sample of a child's schedule is shown in Figure 3-10. The time blocks with the "X" mark on them indicate the parts of the schedule which were planned during a teacher-pupil conference, or because of the on-going experiences of her instructional group, or because of the specific times allocated for certain activities (i.e., instrumental music must be scheduled when the band teacher is available, or student council meets each Friday at 12:15). The schedule for Monday is completely planned. The child would plan for the unscheduled modules day by day as needs dictated for the rest of the week.

STAFF PLANNING TIME

I would like to suggest that the school day be lengthened by a half hour on Monday, Tuesday, Thursday and Friday. This would provide an additional two hours for school activities. The children could then be dismissed at noon on Wednesdays without any loss of school time. As a result, the teaching staff could use every Wednesday afternoon for total staff planning, center team planning, individual teacher planning, parent conferences and other professional activities.

MODULE	MONDAY	TUESDAY	WEDNESDAY	THURSDAY	FRIDAY
8:30	Plan	Plan	Plan	Plan	Plan
8:45	Plan	Plan	Plan	Plan	Plan
9:00	S.S. Center	Lang. Arts Center	Art		
9:15	S.S. Center	Lang. Arts Center	Art		
9:30	I.M.C.		Art		
9:45	S.S. Center				
10:00	Seminar				
10:15	Seminar			S.S. Center	
10:30	Math Center	Math Center		Large Group Film	
10:45	Math Center	Math Center		Seminar	
11:00	Math Center			Seminar	Music
11:15	Math Center				Music
11:30	Math Center	Lunch			Music
11:45	Lunch	Lunch	Evaluation	Lunch	I.M.C.
12:00	Lunch	P.E.		Lunch	Lunch
12:15	I.M.C.	P.E.			Lunch
12:30	I.M.C.		Activities		Student
12:45	Instrumental			Instrumental	Council
1:00	Instrumental		(Teacher	Instrumental	
1:15	Sci. Center		Planning)		
1:30	P.E.				
1:45	P.E.				
2:00	P.E.				
2:15	Lang. Arts Center				
2:30	Lang. Arts Center			P.E.	P.E.
2:45	Lang. Arts Center			P.E.	P.E.
3:00	Evaluation	Evaluation		Evaluation	Evaluation
3:15	Evaluation	Evaluation		Evaluation	Evaluation

Figure 3-10

For those children whose parents work as well as for those who wish to stay at school on Wednesday afternoons, I'd like to suggest that recreational activities and the like could be planned and supervised by aides and parent volunteers. Scout leaders and dance studios could be encouraged to schedule their sessions on Wednesdays. Individual students could also use this additional time to pursue their independent projects and special interests. Some of the special teachers may wish to conduct club activities such as Glee Club, Creative Dance, or Tumbling Club at this time.

FACILITIES FOR LEARNING CENTERS

Many educators claim that team-teaching programs which promote continuous progress of children can be conducted only in a modern building because of the flexibility required. I would agree that such a program could be initiated and developed more easily in an open-space building with a large instructional materials center and large, open areas with acoustical ceilings and floor coverings.

The goals and purposes of a nongraded program, which uses disciplinary teaching teams in learning centers, could best be served by an open-space building. However, a modern facility is not a prerequisite to such a program. The building is far less important than the human element. Traditional buildings can be renovated by taking out some walls and by adding acoustical treatment.

Learning centers can be established in traditional buildings even without renovation. Each center could be a geographical section of a building and include several classrooms (with four walls around them). Although it would not be as convenient and expedient in permitting children to move freely from center to center throughout the building, it is possible to utilize an old "egg crate" school in a more effective manner. The success of a program should be evaluated in terms of what is happening to children, rather than what kind of facility is being used.

SUMMARY

The most important characteristic of team teaching and the learning center approach is the "human" element. In this chapter it has been shown that through the utilization of learning centers a child can work independently with a series of related activities which are designed to promote understanding of certain concepts and how, ultimately, a child will develop the ability to schedule himself and discipline himself to carry out his own scheduled activities.

Included here are sample schedules of special teachers as well as a sample of an individual child's schedule and an explanation of modular scheduling.

Discussion of school facilities is included to illustrate that a staff does not need the most modern plant and the most ideal situation to initiate team teaching in learning centers. To reiterate an old saying, "Where there's a will, there's a way." The program is far more important than the facility.

4

TEACHING IN
THE LANGUAGE ARTS
NONGRADED LEARNING CENTER

Instruction in the Language Arts Nongraded Learning Center should be planned with activities and experiences which will help each child improve in reading, speaking, listening and writing. The child must see the need for and the value of this instruction; it must be relevant; there must be a real purpose for the activity.

In order for instruction in the skills of communication to be interesting and meaningful, individual differences in ability to learn and in previous experience must be considered. A new skill should be built on the successful development of the skills which preceed it. Instruction should proceed from the familiar to the new; from the concrete to the abstract; from the easy to the more difficult.

GUIDELINES FOR TEACHING LANGUAGE ARTS

The following is a list of some of the guidelines for teachers to consider in planning, conducting, and evaluating the activities in the Language Arts Nongraded Learning Center:

- The language arts skills should be organized in a sequential order.
- Children's interests and present needs should be considered.
- The language arts activities should be relevant to the rest of the school program of instruction.
- There should be a variety of activities and a variety of materials available.

- There should be some learning activities in which all children may participate.
- There should be differentiated activities to provide for individual differences.
- There should be many opportunities for meaningful practice for individuals to overcome deficiencies.
- Evaluation of progress must be continuous.

GOALS AND OBJECTIVES

All of the activities and experiences in the Language Arts Nongraded Learning Center should be integrated with the total school curriculum. The major goal of language arts instruction should be to help each child to improve *his* communication (both oral and written) of *his* ideas to others in school as well as outside of school.

The objectives of reading activities should be to enable children to read more efficiently and to enjoy reading. The specific objectives of the reading program should be to help each pupil achieve in reading. This can be accomplished by identifying positive needs; setting realistic goals; establishing a teaching program for word recognition mastery, comprehension skills, critical thinking and study habits; promoting a desire to read for pleasure; and evaluating the progress continuously.

Reading instruction should fit the needs of individual children and should be based on their achievement. As a result of a sequential program of reading the child should be able to read and understand a variety of materials. If reading activities are made meaningful and interesting, the child should learn to read different kinds of things for different purposes. Reading experiences should help him to be successful in reading textbooks, research materials, newspapers and magazines. He should learn how to read for information as well as for pleasure. If the purpose of reading is to enable the child to read only from a basal reader, then let's forget all about reading instruction.

The teaching of oral and written communication skills must be integrated with the total school program. Many traditional schools teach all children to write simply because they are in a certain grade. I say that children should be taught to write when they are ready for it — that is, when their muscle coordination has developed sufficiently and when they see the need of writing in order to communicate their ideas.

Children will learn to improve their speech and word usage, build a vocabulary and a pattern of sentence structure, and capitalize and punctuate when these things become necessary in order for them to share their ideas with each other through written communication. They will develop and improve their listening skills and speaking skills as they work and talk with others. This is a growth pattern which comes naturally to children as they "live" together.

TEACHING TECHNIQUES FOR LANGUAGE ARTS

A sound instructional program for Language Arts should be based on pupil's needs. The teachers should be responsible for knowing just where the pupil is having trouble and for directing specific skills to alleviate the problem.

Sound teaching directs itself toward eliminating one problem at a time. Skills are developed in a sequence from context material. Good teaching in Language Arts is sequential and systematic. The functional approach should be used in selection and organization of activities and experiences in the Language Arts Nongraded Learning Center.

Much of the scheduling of children for this center should be by instructional groups — that is, eight, ten or fifteen children who are progressing at about the same rate and who have similar needs at the same time. Whenever a child's needs cannot be satisfied through the activities planned for his instructional group, then he should be scheduled individually. There will be times when the child could profit from the activities of another group. Flexibility is the rule — make changes whenever and as often as necessary.

All of the experiences should be planned as "activities-of-daily-living." For example, such reading skills as selecting, organizing and evaluating information can best be developed in reading activities related to social studies or science. All these experiences should be the result of problems which develop as children "live" together at school. There should not be separate periods for instruction in reading, writing, spelling, speaking, composition and literature; all these should be integrated.

The Language Arts Center should provide various types of activities; there should be experiences for large groups, instructional groups, and small groups as well as individualized activities. Children should have many opportunities for one-to-one conferences with an adult, independent study, seminars, specific lessons guided by a teacher, interest group discussions, and large group activities — some with a teacher and others without. Variety is needed.

The activities of the Language Arts Center should include: reading experience stories, basal readers, programmed materials, textbooks, trade books, poetry, magazines, newspapers, encyclopedias, maps, graphs; telling and listening to stories; listening to records; talking informally with peers and/or adults; making tape recordings; discussing and planning interest activities; making speeches and reports; participating in choral reading; participating in meetings; giving directions; making announcements; writing experience stories; keeping records; writing reports; making signs and titles for bulletin boards; writing letters; writing creatively (stories, poetry, plays).

MATERIALS FOR LANGUAGE ARTS

The Language Arts Nongraded Learning Center should be provided with a variety of materials and equipment. The center should house all the basal reading series books, trade books, programmed materials such as the SRA Labs, magazines, newspapers, encyclopedias, tape recorders, record players, listening stations (head phones), film strips, projectors and viewers, phonics kits, puppets, typewriters, etc.

There should be places within the center for children to be more relaxed for reading or for creative activities. A "living room" corner with appropriate furniture would be great.

Following is a suggested list of materials and places where they may be obtained with approximate costs:

American Book Company, 300 Pike Street, Cincinnati,
      Ohio
    The Reading Round Table . . . . $ 125.00
Barnell Loft, LTD., 111 South Centre Ave., Rockville
      Centre, N. Y.

(10 books) Specific Skill Series, Level 4
            with answer key and work sheets 7.90
(10 books) Specific Skill Series, Level 5
            with answer key and work sheets 7.90
(10 books) Specific Skill Series, Level 6
            with answer key and work sheets 7.90

Benefic Press, 1900 N. Narragansett Avenue, Chicago,
        Ill. 60639
    5 sets World of Adventure Series (Bamman & Whitehead)
            Number 326908 @ $12.00 . . . .   60.00
    24 World of Adventure Series Activity Work Text
            Number 326001 @   .80 . . . .   19.20

California Test Bureau, Division of McGraw-Hill Book Company,
        Bridge Street, New Cumberland, Pa.
    Lessons for Self-Instruction in Basic Skills
            Reading Comprehension, Jr. Assortment 45.00
    12 English Language Sentence Patterns, Level C & D 12.00
    12 English Language, Verbs, Level C & D 12.00
    12 English Language, Punctuation, Level C & D 12.00
    12 English Language, Capitalization, Level C & D 12.00

Coronet Instructional Films, 65 East S. Water Street,
        Chicago, Ill. 60601
    6 David Discovers the Dictionary @ $1.50 . . . .   9.00

Educational Developmental Laboratories, Inc., 284 Pulaski Road,
        Huntington, N. Y. 11744
    1 Study Skills Library Kit C 10.50
    1 Study Skills Library Kit D 10.50
    1 Study Skills Library Kit E 10.50
    1 Study Skills Library Kit F 10.50

Encyclopaedia Britannics Press, Inc., 425 North Michigan Avenue,
        Chicago, Ill. 60611
    1 Literature Sampler, Code No. 80010 . . . .   45.00

Follett Publishing Company, 508 Glen Avenue, Laurel
        Springs, N. J. 08044
    1 set Individualized English Set J 66.00
        (Includes items 0301 through 0308)

Ginn & Company, 72 Fifth Avenue, New York, N.Y. 10011
    10 Basic Word Study Skills for Middle Grades,
            Part I, The Letters and Sounds in Words
            (Paperback — for self-instruction) @ .64 . . . .   6.40
    10 Basic Word Study Skills for the Middle Grades,
            Part II, Words and Their Parts
            (Paperback — for self-instruction) @ .64 . . . .   6.40
    10 Invitations to Writing and Speaking Creatively @ .96 . . . .   9.60

Harcourt, Brace & World, 7555 Caldwell Avenue,
    Chicago, Ill.
    Language for Daily Uses Series
        5 each level................................ 79.20
        1 each level (Poetry Record)................. 36.00
Lyons & Carnahan, 407 East 25th Street, Chicago, Ill.
    10 Programmed Vocabulary........................... 10.00
Macmillan Company, Front & Brown Streets, Riverside,
    N. J. 08075
    1 Spectrum of Skills, No. 25030..................... 78.00
    10 Learning How to Use the Dictionary No. 19544........ 14.80
    10 Dictionaries...................................... 27.90
    1 set A — Reading Spectrum.......................... 33.00
    1 set B — Reading Spectrum.......................... 39.00
    15 Oral & Written Composition Book 3................ 45.00
    15 Oral & Written Composition Book 4................ 45.00
    15 Oral & Written Composition Book 5................ 45.00
    15 Oral & Written Composition Book 6................ 45.00
    Set of Hand Puppets................................. 15.00
Charles E. Merrill Book Company, Inc., 1300 Alum
    Creek Drive, Columbus, Ohio 43216
    1 Kit Building Reading Power, No. 7700.............. 35.00
    15 Skilltext, Uncle Ben, Gr. 4, No. 6540........... 10.80
    15 Skilltext, Tom Trot, Gr. 5, No. 6550........... 10.80
    15 Skilltext, Pat, the Pilot, Gr. 6, No. 6560...... 10.80
    1 set Skilltapes, No. 2240......................... 80.00
    1 set Skilltapes, No. 2250......................... 80.00
    1 set Skilltapes, No. 2260......................... 80.00
Prentice-Hall, Inc., Englewood Cliffs, N. J.
    Thinking and Writing Series
        1 Text, No. 31791 — 7 (Chart Book)........... 34.80
        2 teacher's edition No. 31792 — 5.............. 3.76
        10 Level A, No. 96445 — 2.................... 11.60
        2 teacher's editions No. 96446 — 0............. 4.32
        10 Level B, No. 13617 — 6.................... 16.80
        2 teacher's editions No. 13618 — 4............. 4.32
        10 Level C, No. 19903 — 4.................... 17.60
        2 teacher's editions No. 19904 — 2............. 4.32
        10 Level D, No. 07345 — 2.................... 18.00
        2 teacher's editions No. 07346 — 0............. 4.32
        10 Level E, No 29564 — 2.................... 18.80
        2 teacher's editions No. 29565 — 9............. 4.32
Reader's Digest Service, Inc., Pleasantville, N.Y. 10570
    20 each Level 4, 5, 6 Reading Skill Builders @ .60.......... 36.00
    2 each Level teacher's manual for Reading Skill Builders

Science Research Associates, 259 East Erie Street,
    Chicago, Ill. 60611
    1 Reading Laboratory 11C, No. 3-1900 . . . . $56.50
    24 Student Record Books, No. 3-1910 . . . . 10.80
    3 Specimen Set, No. 3-1901 . . . . 3.00
    1 Spelling Word Power Lab 11A, No. 3-7500 . . . . 59.50
    10 Student Record Books, No. 3-7510 . . . . 3.80
    1 Spelling Word Power Lab 11B, No. 3-3000 . . . . 59.50
    10 Student Record Books, No. 3-3010 . . . . 3.80
    1 Spelling Word Power Lab 111A, No. 3-7700 . . . . 59.50
    10 Student Record Books, No. 3-7710 . . . . 3.80
    1 Pilot Library 11A, No. 3-5400 . . . . 52.50
    10 Student Record Books, No. 3-5475 . . . . 4.30
    1 Pilot Library 11C, No. 3-200 . . . . 52.50
    10 Student Record Books, No. 3-274 . . . . 4.30
    1 Organizing & Reporting Skills Kit, No. 3-4100 . . . . 82.50
    15 Pupil Booklets, No. 3-4110 . . . . 6.75
    1 Penskill II Kit 49.50
    10 Student Books 4.30
    1 Reading for Understanding Kit 29.50
    20 Student Books 5.40
    SRA Comprehensive Reading Series
    10 Each Level — G, H, I, J, K, L 1183.20
    2 each Teacher's Handbook for above 28.68
    1 workbook for each level above 6.00

Teacher's College Press, Teachers College, Columbia
    University, 525 West 120th Street,
    New York, N. Y. 10027
    1 Gates-Peardon Reading Exercises, Gr. 4
        assortment 19.50
    1 Gates-Peardon Reading Exercises, Gr. 5
        assortment 20.50
    1 Gates-Peardon Reading Exercises, Gr. 6
        assortment 21.00

ACTIVITIES IN THE LANGUAGE ARTS CENTER

In this center one might see the following activities happening
simultaneously: one teacher working with an instructional group on
a particular skill which is a common need of all those in this group;
another teacher having a one-to-one conference with a child to help
him plan his time in this center for the next few days; a group of
children listening to a story record with headphones; another
teacher working with a group involved in a discussion of various

readings on a particular topic; an aide sitting with a group as they share library stories; a child typing his own story; another teacher working with an instructional group on a specific skill; several children writing letters; others working independently at stations with programmed material; a teacher working with a group of children in the "living room" corner on the creative writing of poetry; some children reading just for pleasure — the activities are limitless.

A child might complete several activities during one visit to this center. He would have the freedom to choose and move from station to station within the center as his needs changed or as he completed an activity. Each day would be different — each activity would be different — but all of these experiences would be meaningful because they would be real to each child, rather than just busy work.

LANGUAGE ARTS SKILLS AND EVALUATIONS

Although some educators strongly oppose the establishment of levels in the skill area of Language Arts, it seems to me to be an intermediate step toward nongrading. Many teachers would be insecure without any structure or guidance. Ultimately, I think the levels could be replaced by a continuum of behavioral objectives.

If in each school situation one could be highly selective in employing only the best-trained teaching staff and could choose the student population by screening the background of each child and his parents, and if pupil-teacher ratio were kept low, then perhaps it would not be necessary to use levels.

However, until we reach this point the majority of educators want to have some organized plan for teaching the skills of communication. I suggest that the levels approach is the most *practical* approach to nongrading.

In the Language Arts center each child would have his own skill sheet which would be kept accurate and up to date. As he completed a task and/or developed an understanding of the skill, his record sheet would so indicate. Whenever all the skills for a particular level would be checked, the child would be evaluated to see if there were any deficiencies which might require further study prior to his moving on to the next level. Each would move at his own rate and as his needs changed.

It is suggested that one person be designated to do the evaluations so that she may become the "expert" in performing this very important task. Children would be moved from level A to level B without an evaluation. Suggested lists of language arts skills organized in a series of levels, A through O, as well as some of the evaluations used for several levels are included here.

LANGUAGE ARTS — LEVEL A

Name_____

Emphasis on Looking and Listening

_____ 1. Hears likenesses and differences of sounds and words

_____ 2. Sees likenesses and differences in pictures, words, and letters

Emphasis on Speaking

_____ 1. Enumerates list of items in pictures

_____ 2. Is able to interpret what is happening in picture

_____ 3. Predicts what will happen next in picture

_____ 4. Speaks in a clear, natural voice

_____ 5. Speaks loudly enough to be heard

_____ 6. Speaks words correctly

_____ 7. Uses appropriate phrasing of sentences

_____ 8. Takes turns in speaking

Emphasis on Listening

_____ 1. Uses records, earphones, tape recordings, radio and television to develop listening skills

_____ 2. Participates in audience situations (programs, etc.)

_____ 3. Listens to poetry and stories read by teacher

_____ 4. Follows oral directions

_____ 5. Provides endings to stories read by teacher

_____ 6. Recognizes the speaker in stories

_____ 7. Has developed left to right progression

Emphasis on Writing

_____ 1. Prints name legibly

_____ 2. Maintains correct posture for writing

_____ 3. Maintains correct position of hand for pencil and of paper on desk

LANGUAGE ARTS — LEVEL B
(Those children building sight vocabulary)

_____ 1. Dictates experience stories to build sight vocabulary

_____ 2. Can copy and reproduce words from the dictated stories

_____ 3. Recognizes main idea of selection

_____ 4. Recalls story sequence

_____ 5. Finds details in story

_____ 6. Can draw inferences

_____ 7. Understands pronoun references

_____ 8. Predicts events in a story

_____ 9. Recognizes rhyming words

_____10. Identifies characters

_____11. Reads orally to answer specific questions

_____12. Recognizes letters and sounds of these beginning consonants

_____ (a)   M T B H P N

_____ (b)   D W G C J

_____ (c)   F L R S

_____ (d)   K Q V X Z Y

_____ (e)   Recognizes vowels

_____13. Identifies capital and small letters

_____14. Reads to express feelings of characters

_____15. Uses picture and context clues to get meaning

_____16. Illustrates stories

_____17. Predicts outcomes on basis of previous experience

_____18. Uses table of contents

_____19. Uses punctuation marks at ends of sentences

_____20. Recognizes opposites

_____21. Recognizes singular words and plural words ending in _s_

_____22. Participates in informal conversations

_____23. Interprets material through dramatic play

_____24. Recognizes and uses variant endings — _s, ed, ing_

_____25. Shows improvement in manuscript writing

_____26. Knows how to attack a new word by:

_____ (a)   Using picture clues

_____ (b)   Reading to the end of a sentence and making a guess

_____ (c)   Checking that guess by use of phonetic clues — beginning and ending

_____ (d)   Using structural clues

_____ (e)   Checking himself by asking the teacher

EVALUATION — LEVEL B

STORIES

Run and Play. 3

Up and Down. 11

We Go to School. 15

A Ride on the Bus. 18

We Go to the Farm. 24

Work and Play. 29

A Little Kitten. 33

Directions

1. Find a story that begins on page 11. Draw a line under the name of that story.
2. Find a story that begins on page 24. Draw a line under the name of that story.
3. Find the story — *A Ride on the Bus.* Draw a ring around the page it begins on.
4. Find the story — *Run and Play.* Draw a ring around the page it begins on.

Draw a ring around the words in each line that mean more than one.

1. cows	pig	horse	cats
2. barn	balls	birds	friends
3. animals	homes	zoo	day

Rhyming Words

Draw a ring around the word in each row that rhymes with the first word in each row.

1. pet	run	get	saw
2. no	on	for	go
3. too	good	zoo	look
4. not	our	own	hot
5. can	cane	car	ran

Opposites

Draw a ring around the word that is the opposite of the first word in the line.

1. yes	stop	is	no
2. day	morning	said	night
3. down	blue	up	have
4. come	go	run	walk
5. big	blue	little	help

Read the story below and draw a picture of the story. Use another piece of paper.

Tip is a big dog.
He is black and brown.
He has a long tail and long ears.
He plays with a red ball.
He lives in a yellow house.
The house has a fence around it.

Recognition of Alphabet

Draw a ring around letter in each line called by teacher.

1. c	d	E	f	14. d	a	l	g
2. f	A	g	h	15. C	l	i	n
3. p	q	R	s	16. v	a	h	q
4. w	x	o	v	17. c	e	T	s
5. z	e	g	j	18. m	a	v	x
6. l	a	c	i	19. c	Z	e	g
7. s	t	i	v	20. f	o	l	d
8. z	l	o	k	21. c	e	m	d
9. m	n	v	r	22. O	a	h	n
10. s	n	o	v	23. p	u	m	j
11. p	b	k	u	24. l	a	c	y
12. c	l	b	v	25. x	o	v	w
13. k	p	n	x	26. d	m	c	j

ORAL READING — LEVEL B

A TRIP

One day the children went to a park.
They went on the school bus.
It was a big orange bus.
The children saw big green trees at the park.
They had rides on a seesaw.
It was little.
They played on a swing.
The boys and girls had fun at the park.

Pronoun Referents

1. What do the underlined words refer to?

LANGUAGE ARTS — LEVEL C

Name _____

_____ 1. Reads for meaning
_____ 2. Finds facts and sequence in story
_____ 3. Extends concepts
_____ 4. Alternates story endings
_____ 5. Groups and classifies words and facts in categories
_____ 6. Re-reads orally for specific reasons
_____ 7. Detects imaginary ideas
_____ 8. Follows written directions
_____ 9. Identifies sentences that do not belong
_____ 10. Listens to make comparisons
_____ 11. Supplies titles for sentence groups
_____ 12. Predicts outcomes
_____ 13. Evaluates titles after reading
_____ 14. Recognizes digraphs — th, sn, sl, sc, sk, sm, sp, sw
_____ 15. Recognizes blends
_____   *(a)*   st, sn, sl, sc, sk, sm, sp, sw
_____   *(b)*   br, fr, cr, tr, pr, dr, gr
_____   *(c)*   cl, fl, pl, gl, sl, bl
_____ 16. Recognizes and knows meaning of contractions with one letter
         omission
_____ 17. Recognizes final consonant sounds

_____18. Recognizes compound words and can build compound words

_____19. Knows alphabetical sequence

_____20. Understands words that tell *who* and *what*

_____21. Speaking

_____ *(a)* Can make introductions and give greetings

_____ *(b)* Can carry on telephone conversation

_____ *(c)* Participates in choral speaking

_____22. Writing

_____ *(a)* Writes original stories and poems

_____ *(b)* Copies sentences correctly

_____ *(c)* Puts periods and question marks at ends of sentences

_____ *(d)* Completes sentences with appropriate words

_____23. Is improving in ability to answer questions that are:

_____ *(a)* Concrete

_____ *(b)* Creative

_____ *(c)* Abstract

_____24. Uses evaluative criteria in self-selection of reading material

_____25. Knows how to attack a word by:

_____ *(a)* Using pictures for clues

_____ *(b)* Reading to the end of a sentence and making a guess

_____ *(c)* Checking that guess by use of phonetic clues (beginning and ending sounds)

_____ *(d)* Using structural clues

_____ *(e)* Checking himself by asking the teacher

_____26. Can write examples of comprehension skills

EVALUATION — LEVEL C

Sequence of Alphabet

Put in the missing letters

A _ _ D _ _ _ H _ J _ _ M _ _ _ Q _ _
T _ _ _ X _ _

Following Directions

Draw the pictures on your paper.

1. Draw one line under the ball.
2. Draw a line around the one that we eat.
3. Put X on the star.
4. Draw two lines under the toy we fly.
5. Draw a line through the one we ride.

Contractions

Write the two words each contraction is made from.

1. it's
2. he's
3. isn't
4. I'll
5. that's

Sentence That Does Not Belong

Circle the number of the sentence that does not belong in this story.

1. The moon is in the sky.
2. Light comes from the moonlight.
3. The moon makes moonlight.
4. It was a pretty day.
5. The tree stops the moonlight.
6. The house makes a shadow at night.

Make Compound Words of the Following

1. bus   _____   a. got
2. police _____   b. man
3. for   _____   c. one
4. some   _____   d. way
5. mail   _____   e. stop
6. birth   _____   f. down
7. count   _____   g. day
8. any   _____   h. box

Classifying Words

Put 1 by all words that name people.
Put 2 by all words that name animals.
Put 3 by all words that name ways to travel.

1. people	2. animals	3. ways to travel
____mother	____motorcycle	____rabbit
____boat	____boys	____truck
____cow	____puppy	____bus
____bicycle	____twin	____elephant
____dog	____kitten	____scooter
____monkey	____brother	____deer
____train	____airplane	____rocket

THE TRIP

(Read silently)

Mother and Father went away on a trip. They went on an airplane. Jack and Alice did not go. They had never been on an airplane. They wished that they could go. They stayed with Grandmother.

Mother said, "I will bring you a toy airplane. You will have fun with it."

"When?" asked Jack and Alice.

"When I come back," their mother said.

The children could not wait. They asked, "Is Mother coming home today?" Grandmother said, "Not today." The next day they asked Grandmother, "Is Mother coming home today?" She told them, "No. She will be home tomorrow."

The Grandmother thought and thought. She gave the children a new game.

Alice and Jack played and played.

Soon Grandmother called, "Come to dinner!"

The children ran into the house. There was a letter from Mother and Father. It had a picture of an airplane on it. How happy the children were.

EVALUATION — LEVEL C

Number the events in the correct order.

_____ Mother said that she would bring a toy airplane.
_____ They got a letter from Mother.
_____ Alice and Jack's father and mother took a trip.
_____ The children played a game.
_____ The children kept asking when Mother was coming home.
_____ The children went to Grandmother's to stay.

1. The children wished that they _____ _____ with Mother and Father.
2. The children had _____ been on an airplane.
3. Grandmother gave the children a new _____.
4. Grandmother called the children to come to _____.
5. The letter had a picture of an _____ on it.

always   never   airplane   book   game   could
          train   dinner   breakfast   go

Auditory Discrimination of Two-Letter Blends

Directions: Examiner call words. Pupils write the first two letters.				
1. sled	2. fly	3. gloves	4. plate	5. clown
6. blocks	7. globe	8. flour	9. clock	10. slide
1. tray	2. brush	3. dress	4. track	5. drum
6. cracker	7. broom	8. triangle	9. crocodile	10. bracelet

PRONOUN REFERENCES — LEVEL C

Underline the word or words that mean the same as the *italicized* word.

1. Jack said, "See, Don.
   See *my* big ball."
   Don   Jack   Ned

2. Mary and Alice said, "*We* can not go, Ann.
   Ask Jane to go."
   Mary and Alice   Jane and Alice

3. "Here *we* are," said Dick and Jane.
   "We will see Joe and Jerry here."
   Jerry and Joe   Dick and Jane

4. "Look at *me,* Tom," said Jack.
"I am big and tall."
Jack   Tom   Dick

5. "Throw the ball to *me,"* said Jerry.
"Throw me the big ball."
Jane   Alice   Jerry

LANGUAGE ARTS — LEVEL D

Name_____

Comprehension Skills

_____ 1. Interprets figurative language
_____ 2. Discriminates between fact and fancy
_____ 3. Makes judgments from given facts
_____ 4. Extends concepts — conceives alternate endings
_____ 5. Senses characters' feelings
_____ 6. Notes relevant and irrelevant facts
_____ 7. Follows written directions
_____ 8. Skims for information
_____ 9. Distinguishes inferences
_____10. Notes cause and effect
_____11. Compares facts
_____12. Visualizes situations
_____13. Understands parts that tell *who, when, where, how* and *what*
_____14. Uses new words in sentences
_____15. Classifies phrases
_____16. Recognizes shifts of meanings caused by using words in different context
_____17. Makes use of enrichment materials and activities
_____18. Finds word pictures and illustrates them
_____19. Is improving in ability to answer questions that are:
_____ *(a)*   Concrete
_____ *(b)*   Creative
_____ *(c)*   Abstract
_____20. Uses evaluative criteria in self-selection of reading materials

Word Attack Skills

_____ 1. Hears syllables
_____ 2. Hears word endings
_____ 3. Recognizes and uses consonant blends
_____ 4. Discriminates words that are similar in form
_____ 5. Recognizes compound words
_____ 6. Uses context clues to aid in word recognition and meaning
_____ 7. Chooses correct verb forms
_____ 8. Recognizes double medial consonants
_____ 9. Makes substitutions of initial consonants to form new words
_____10. Hears and recognizes vowel sounds
_____11. Attacks new words independently
_____12. Knows how to attack a word by:
_____ (a) Using pictures for clues
_____ (b) Reading to the end of a sentence and making a guess
_____ (c) Checking that guess by phonetic clues
_____ (d) Using structural clues
_____ (e) Checking himself by asking teacher

Language Skills

_____ 1. Reads easy poems with understanding
_____ 2. Writes own name and address
_____ 3. Writes sentences from dictation
_____ 4. Copies short letters and poems
_____ 5. Writes original stories and poems
_____ 6. Can write samples of the comprehension skills

Spelling Skills

_____ 1. Distinguishes the sounds that letters make in words (vowel and consonants)
_____ 2. Connects specific sounds with letters that spell them: _C_ or _K_ spells the _K_ sound; _S_ spells the _s_ and _z_ sound of _bus_ and _is_
_____ 3. Recognizes and knows meaning of digraphs: _wh, th, ch, sh, ng_
_____ 4. Connects specific vowel sounds with letters which spell them (Applies generalizations as an aid for vowel sounds)
_____ 5. Knows sounds of _ow_ and _ou, er, oo,_ and _ay_
_____ 6. Makes plurals by adding _s_ or _es_ to most words
_____ 7. Makes past tense of some verbs by adding _d_ or _ed_

_____ 8. Adds _s_ to verbs when needed

_____ 9. Recognizes syllables in words

LANGUAGE ARTS — LEVEL E

Name_____

Comprehension Skills

_____ 1. Interprets figurative language

_____ 2. Discriminates between fact and fancy

_____ 3. Makes judgments from given facts

_____ 4. Extends concepts — conceives alternate endings

_____ 5. Senses characters' feelings

_____ 6. Notes relevant and irrelevant facts

_____ 7. Follows written directions

_____ 8. Skims for information

_____ 9. Distinguishes inferences

_____10. Notes cause and effect

_____11. Compares facts

_____12. Visualizes situations

_____13. Understands parts that tell _who, when, where, how_ and _what_

_____14. Uses new words in sentences

_____15. Classifies phrases

_____16. Recognizes shifts of meanings caused by using words in different context

_____17. Makes use of enrichment materials and activities

_____18. Finds word pictures and illustrates them

_____19. Is improving in ability to answer questions that are:

_____ _(a)_   concrete

_____ _(b)_   creative

_____ _(c)_   abstract

_____20. Uses evaluative criteria in self-selection of reading materials

Word Attack Skills

_____ 1. Recognizes multiple meaning of words
_____ 2. Substitutes initial and final consonants
_____ 3. Recognizes roots of words (Also "ing" words as *riding*)
_____ 4. Recognizes short vowel sounds in words
_____ 5. Recognizes effect of final *e* on previous vowel in one-syllable word
_____ 6. Knows sound of *oo* as in *food* and *woods*
_____ 7. Knows influence of *r* on vowels
_____ 8. Attacks new words independently
_____ 9. Can attack new words by:
_____ *(a)* Using pictures for clues
_____ *(b)* Reading to the end of a sentence and making a guess
_____ *(c)* Checking that guess by phonetic clues
_____ *(d)* Using structural clues
_____ *(e)* Checking himself by asking the teacher

Language Skills

_____ 1. Can complete a rhyme with correct word
_____ 2. Can write rhyming words
_____ 3. Can write samples of the comprehension skills

Spelling Skills

_____ 1. Distinguishes the sounds that letters make in words (vowels and consonants)
_____ 2. Connects specific sounds with letters that spell them: *c* or *k* spells the *k* sound; *s* spells the *s* and *z* sound of *bus* and *is*
_____ 3. Recognizes and knows meaning of digraphs: *wh, th, ch, sh, ng*
_____ 4. Connects specific vowel sounds with letters which spell them (Applies generalizations as an aid for vowel sounds)
_____ 5. Knows sound of *ow* and *ou, er, oo,* and *ay*
_____ 6. Makes plurals by adding *s* or *es* to most words
_____ 7. Makes past tense of some verbs by adding *d* or *ed*
_____ 8. Adds *s* to verbs when needed
_____ 9. Recognizes syllables in words

EVALUATION — LEVEL E

Root Words

Write the root or base word for each word below. Be sure to spell the base word correctly.

1. singer   _____
2. hoping   _____
3. hopping _____
4. playing _____
5. lived   _____

6. carried   _____
7. eaten   _____
8. laughing   _____
9. stopping   _____
10. broken   _____

Long, Short, and Silent Vowels

Copy the words. Mark the vowels.

1. gave	6. came	11. fish	16. cup
2. sat	7. boat	12. tree	17. feed
3. legs	8. home	13. gold	18. king
4. hope	9. ate	14. reach	19. sails
5. no	10. wife	15. wait	20. time

Write the words in each row that do not rhyme with first word.

1. top	stop	cat	chop	mop	pop	duck	hop
2. cap	tap	fan	lap	map	gate	nap	rap
3. lip	tip	rip	dip	flip	car	hop	nip
4. cross	moss	zoo	toss	boss	goose		
5. bus	muss	must	fuss	hippopotamus			
6. bug	rug	boat	chug	dug	hug	bed	jug
7. grass	glass	pass	mass	post	bass	lass	

Multiple Meanings of Words

Read these meanings and the sentences below them. Choose one meaning to fit each sentence.

A. *run*   *a.* to be in charge of

                   b. to flow

                   c. to go from one place to another

____1. Why does the paint *run* all over the floor?

____2. The bus *runs* between here and Baltimore.

____3. Jane's father *runs* the store.

B. *spring*   *a.* to leap or jump

b. season after winter

c. a small stream of water coming from earth.

_____ 1. Flowers come out in *spring.*

_____ 2. He will *spring* from the board.

_____ 3. The frog jumped in the *spring.*

Final Endings

1. The girls are _____ with dolls. (playing   played)
2. Sometimes Ann _____ alone. (plays   playing)
3. The children _____ for their cat. (looked   looking)
4. The boat _____ out to sea. (sailed   sailing)
5. Sue _____ clean the house. (helping   helps)

Final Consonants

1. The girl has a (hal - hat - haj).
2. Do you like (jab - jan - jam) on your bread?
3. There are seven days in one (weed - week - weel).
4. The cat (mets - mels - mews) at the door.
5. Does the shoe (fit - fis - fiz)?

Vowels — r Influence

Write the key words: *car   fur   corn   care*

Write the following words under the key word that has the same sound.

north - burn - star - her - forty - third - share - warm - where - park - air - arm

Write these key words: *moon   book*

Write the following words under the key words that have the same sound.

poor - root - hook - soon - took - wood - roof - noon - stood - wool - cool - good - food - shoot

Rhymes

Jack put on his coat
And jumped in the _____.

The small green toad
Hopped down the _____.

Three little goats
Ate from a field of green _____.

The man with a hoe
Hit his big _____.

Visualizing — Illustrating

Read and illustrate the one assigned by the teacher.

1. Dumpy is a short clown.
   His suit has big orange and purple dots on it.
   He has a tall hat with red feathers.
   He has a big yellow flower in his hand.

2. This clown has big ears and a big nose.
   His suit has red and blue stripes.
   His hat is flat and green.
   He is riding a bicycle.

THE LITTLE PINE TREE

This is the story of a nice little pine tree that lived in a big, big forest. It was in a good place. It had what it needed to grow. The air was fresh and the ground was soft and damp. There were many big trees in the woods. They had big trunks. There were pine trees, cedar trees and fir trees.

All the trees were happy except the little pine tree. It was not happy at all. It wanted to be big and tall. It wanted to grow fast. It wanted to be proud.

The little tree grew but not very fast. In a few years it was seven feet tall. You can tell how old a standing tree is by the shoots it has.

The big trees were much taller and bigger. They could see the stars, sun, clouds and the moon.

In summer the birds flew in and out of the trees. In winter snow covered the trees. Woodcutters cut down the larger trees with big saws. The saws made a buzzing sound. The trees were put on big sleds and the horses pulled them out of the woods.

Number from 1 to 10. Circle the numbers of sentences that are true about the story.

1. The little pine tree lived in the forest.
2. The little pine tree was very happy.
3. It was very proud.
4. One can tell by the leaves how old a tree is.
5. The little pine tree wanted to grow fast.
6. Woodcutters cut the trees in the spring.

7. Trees were put on sleds after they were cut.
8. The little trees could see more than the big trees.
9. Trees have trunks.
10. Trees live well in damp ground.

LANGUAGE ARTS — LEVEL F

Name _____

Comprehension Skills

_____ 1. Interprets figurative language
_____ 2. Discriminates between fact and fancy
_____ 3. Makes judgments from given facts
_____ 4. Extends concepts — conceives alternate endings
_____ 5. Senses characters' feelings
_____ 6. Notes relevant and irrelevant facts
_____ 7. Follows written directions
_____ 8. Skims for information
_____ 9. Distinguishes inferences
_____ 10. Notes cause and effect
_____ 11. Compares facts
_____ 12. Visualizes situations
_____ 13. Understands parts that tell *who, when, where, how,* and *what*
_____ 14. Uses new words in sentences
_____ 15. Classifies phrases
_____ 16. Recognizes shifts of meanings caused by using words in different context
_____ 17. Makes use of enrichment materials and activities
_____ 18. Finds word pictures and illustrates them
_____ 19. Is improving in ability to answer questions that are:
_____ *(a)* concrete
_____ *(b)* creative
_____ *(c)* abstract
_____ 20. Uses evaluative criteria in self-selection of reading materials

Word Attack Skills

_____ 1. Recognizes silent vowels in words
_____ 2. Uses comparative words correctly
_____ 3. Has improved in recognition and use of consonant digraphs
_____ 4. Recognizes and knows sound of dipthongs (*ou, ow, oi, oy*)

_____ 5. Recognizes the variant sounds of vowels as *a* before *l*, *a* before *r*, and *a* as in *paw*.

_____ 6. Uses phonetic clues to recognize words

_____ 7. Discriminates definite and indefinite words

_____ 8. Has increased recognition of vowel digraphs — *ee*, *ea*, *ay*, *au*, *aw*, *ow*

_____ 9. Knows when to double the final consonant before adding *ing*

_____ 10. Attacks new words independently

_____ 11. Can attack new words by:

_____ *(a)* Using pictures for clues

_____ *(b)* Reading to the end of a sentence and making a guess

_____ *(c)* Checking that guess by phonetic clues

_____ *(d)* Using structural clues

_____ *(e)* Checking himself by asking the teacher

Language Skills

_____ 1. Can write riddles

_____ 2. Can write a one-sentence news item

_____ 3. Uses *saw* and *seen* correctly

_____ 4. Can keep to the main idea in a discussion

_____ 5. Can write samples of comprehension skills

Spelling Skills

_____ 1. Distinguishes the sounds that letters make in words (vowels and consonants)

_____ 2. Connects specific sounds with letters that spell them: *c* or *k* spells the *k* sound; *s* spells the *s* and *z* sound of *bus* and *is*

_____ 3. Recognizes and knows meaning of digraphs: *wh*, *th*, *ch*, *sh*, *ng*

_____ 4. Connects specific vowel sounds with letters which spell them (Applies generalizations as an aid for vowel sounds)

_____ 5. Knows sound of *ow* and *ou*, *er*, *oo*, and *ay*

_____ 6. Makes plurals by adding *s* or *es* to most words

_____ 7. Makes past tense of some verbs by adding *d* or *ed*

_____ 8. Adds *s* to verbs when needed

_____ 9. Recognizes syllables in words

LANGUAGE ARTS — LEVEL G

Name_____

Comprehension Skills

_____ 1. Finds factual information

_____ 2. Groups and classifies facts

_____ 3. Expands and illustrates concepts

_____ 4. Identifies characters by pantomime, role-playing, and dramatization

_____ 5. Notes details to main events (sub-sentences)

_____ 6. Has increased in ability to draw and make inferences

_____ 7. Makes comparisons

_____ 8. Has increased in ability to find sources of information

_____ 9. Notes clues

_____10. Is able to interpret author's purpose

_____11. Recognizes plot structure (problem)

_____12. Extends social attitudes

_____13. Main ideas

_____ *(a)* Selects titles

_____ *(b)* Selects sentences which express main ideas

_____ *(c)* States main ideas in own words

_____14. Can read simple charts, maps, graphs, tables, and diagrams

_____15. Participates in the reading of good literature

_____16. Is improving in ability to answer questions that are:

_____ *(a)* concrete

_____ *(b)* creative

_____ *(c)* abstract

_____17. Uses evaluative criteria in self-selection of reading materials

Word Attack Skills

_____ 1. Has increased skill in using vowel digraphs

_____ 2. Understands and knows meaning of prefixes *un* and *re*

_____ 3. Has developed auditory discrimination of polysyllabic words
and accent

_____ 4. Understands *er* as agent

_____ 5. Understands *er* as comparative

_____ 6. Understands use of suffix *ly*

_____ 7. Can attack words by:

_____ *(a)* Using pictures for clues

_____ (b)   Reading to the end of the sentence and making a guess
_____ (c)   Checking that guess by phonetic clues
_____ (d)   Using structural clues
_____ (e)   Checking himself by asking the teacher

Language Skills

_____ 1.   Uses capital letters to begin:
_____ (a)   Names of days of the week
_____ (b)   Names of holidays
_____ (c)   Names of streets and roads
_____ (d)   Names of special places and special groups of people
_____ (e)   First letter of first word and first letter of all important words in a title

_____ 2.   Capital for letter *I*

_____ 3.   Recognition of groups of words that are sentences

_____ 4.   Uses *did, done, ran, run*, correctly

_____ 5.   Has acceptable slant in cursive writing

_____ 6.   Letters used in cursive writings are of acceptable size

_____ 7.   Can write samples of comprehension skills

Spelling Skills

_____ 1.   Connects specific consonant sounds with the letters which spell them
_____ (a)   Knows that the sound of *s* is often spelled with *c*
_____ (b)   Knows the *ks* sound is often spelled with *x*
_____ (c)   Knows the sound of *f* in the final position is sometimes spelled with *gh*

_____ 2.   Recognizes combinations to look for in spelling vowel sounds
_____ (a)   Knows that *er* ending is usually spelled *er* but sometimes it is spelled *or*
_____ (b)   Knows that in words spelled with *ar*, the sound of *a* when followed by *r* is different from the *a* of *hat* or *rain*

_____ 3.   Understands and uses the following structural generalizations:
_____ (a)   Forms plural or past tense of many words which end with *y* by changing *y* to *i* before adding *es* or *ed*
_____ (b)   Makes new words by adding *ing*
_____ (c)   Doubles the final consonant of many words before adding *ing*
_____ (d)   Forms the past tense of some verbs by changing the spelling
_____ (e)   Makes new words of many words by adding *r, er, st, or, est*
_____ (f)   Counts the syllables in a word by counting the vowel sounds

_____ (g) When words have two consonants between vowels, tries
first to divide the word between consonants

_____ (h) When words have one consonant between vowels, first
tries to divide the word before the consonant

_____ (i) For long words which are made up of two short words,
spells the words first and writes them together

_____ 4. Uses an apostrophe to show that letters have been omitted in
contractions

EVALUATION — LEVEL G

"er" as Agent

Write the word for each blank.

1. A man who farms is a _____.
2. A person who walks is a _____.
3. A girl who runs is a _____.
4. The man who keeps store is a store_____.
5. One who talks a lot is a _____.

"er" Comparative

1. The pool is deep. The lake is _____ than the pool.
2. The moon is bright. The sun is _____ than the moon.
3. This candy is sweet. The candy is _____ still.
4. The pillow is soft. The blanket is _____ than the pillow.
5. Jack is six years old. Jane is seven years old so she is _____
    than Jack.

"un" as a Prefix

Write the meaning of these words.

1. unkind _____   4. untrue _____
2. unable _____   5. unfriendly_____
3. unhappy_____

"re" as a Prefix

Write the meaning of these words.

1. rewrite _____   4. reheat _____
2. rewind _____   5. rebuild_____
3. revisit _____

Add "ly," "er," "est" to the Word

Write the word.

1. The sun was shining very bright_____.
2. The tiger moved careful_____.
3. The boys were near_____the door than the girls.
4. This is the deep_____lake in the country.
5. Mark dropped the pan quick_____.
6. The work was only part_____finished.
7. The rain started very sudden_____.
8. Jack is old_____than May.
9. That is the tall_____tree in the yard.
10. The monkey is small_____than the bear.

Put *did* or *done* in the correct blank. Do not write the sentence.

1. She has _____ her work.
2. She _____ it in a few minutes.
3. We _____ our work this morning.
4. Have you _____ this before?
5. The men had _____ their work by noon.

Put *ran* or *run* in the correct blank.

1. She _____ all the way home.
2. I have _____ all the way home.
3. She was tired because she had _____ a long way.
4. We _____ a race.
5. The horse _____ in a race today.

Number the paper from 1 to 6. Put *X* by the numbers of groups of words that are sentences.

_____ 1. The Indian's head moved up and down.
_____ 2. Reached for their guns.
_____ 3. All the small boys.
_____ 4. Judy stood in front of the store window.
_____ 5. Mother squirrel looked at her twins.
_____ 6. Returned to the apple tree.

Rusty was a big friendly dog who lived in the city. The only animals that Rusty knew about were animals he saw in the city like cats, squirrels and birds. These animals were not friendly.

One summer Rusty's owner took him on a camping trip in the Big Woods. Rusty went for a walk alone. He met a little animal. It looked friendly. It was black with a broad black stripe down its back. Rusty ran up to it and barked. The animal raised its furry tail and ran away. Oh! Rusty barked and ran away. The

animal had covered him with something that had an awful smell.
Rusty rolled over and over, this way and that. He rolled in the
dirt. He rubbed his head in the grass. He ran home. His owner
laughed and said, "Rusty, you have been near a skunk."

1. What is this story about?
   1. What happened when a man met a skunk
   2. What happened to a city dog
   3. What happened when a skunk went to the park
2. What would be the best title for this story?
   1. Why Skunks Have a Bushy Tail
   2. Why Skunks Have a Smell
   3. A Big Surprise

GENERAL STORE

A general store is an interesting place to visit. I stopped at one
while on a bus trip one summer. It was called the Red Door
Country Store. The door was a bright cheery red.

Inside were all kinds of things that are in grocery stores —
cans of vegetables, soup, crackers, soap and candy. There were
barrels with sour pickles.

In one corner of the store there were shoes, boots, belts and
handbags.

The storekeeper was a little stout man with a shiny bald head.
He used a ladder to reach things on tall shelves.

The storekeeper was also the postmaster. People came to the
store to buy stamps and mail packages and to get their mail.

In winter, men from the village gather around the wood-
burning stove to tell jokes, play checkers and talk about the
weather.

Number from 1 to 10. Circle numbers of sentences that are true.

1. A general store sells only vegetables.
2. The storekeeper was fat.
3. The stove in the store burns coal for fuel.
4. Men enjoy gathering at the store.
5. You can buy stamps at the store.
6. Sour pickles were in jars.
7. There are many general stores in cities.
8. A general store sells many things.

9. This store was in a big city.
10. The door was painted red.

Name five things sold at this store.

PEANUTS

Do you call the peanut a nut? It is really a vegetable that grows on a vine and belongs to the same family as peas and beans. The plant is a bush. It is different from peas because the pods of peanuts ripen under ground. We call the pods shells.

The farmers dig up the peanuts in the fall and let them dry in the field. People think the peanut came from South America.

Peanuts are good to eat. We eat them at picnics, ball games and at the circus.

Some peanuts are made into peanut butter. Some are salted, roasted or put in candy bars. The skins and stems are used for cattle food.

Other names for peanuts are goobers, ground peas, earthnuts and groundnuts.

Circle the letters of three answers for each question.

1. What are three names for peanuts?
   a. roasted   b. earthnuts   c. food
   d. goobers   e. groundnuts   f. peas
2. What are three things peanuts are used for?
   a. candy bars   b. beans   c. cattle food
   d. peas   e. peanut butter   f. fruit
3. How are peanuts like peas?
   a. have pods   b. grow on vines   c. are green
   d. are big   e. are salty   f. are little

This sheet for teacher only

Auditory Discrimination of Syllables

Letter your paper from A to J. Teacher will call word. Write the number of syllables you hear in each word.

A. excitement   F. anticipate
B. spice   G. motel
C. spectator   H. carpenter
D. potato   I. teacher
E. tree   J. consider

> ### Accented Syllables
>
> Letter paper from A to J. Teacher will call same words as above. Children write number of syllable that is accented.

Copy the words in each sentence that should be capitalized.

1. her birthday is on sunday.
2. it will soon be christmas.
3. she lives on pine street.
4. the japanese cookie was very good.
5. oranges grow in california.
6. the name of the book was ann and the red umbrella.
7. the doctor and i had a long talk.
8. we have vacation at easter.
9. do you know jane jackson?
10. mr. and mrs. brown are at home.

LANGUAGE ARTS — LEVEL H

Name_____

Comprehension Skills

_____ 1. Finds facts
_____ 2. Groups and classifies facts
_____ 3. Expands and illustrates concepts
_____ 4. Identifies characters by pantomime, role-playing, and dramatization
_____ 5. Notes details to main events (sub-sentences)
_____ 6. Has increased in ability to draw and make inferences
_____ 7. Makes comparisons
_____ 8. Has increased in ability to find sources of information
_____ 9. Notes clues
_____ 10. Is able to interpret author's purpose
_____ 11. Recognizes plot structure
_____ 12. Extends social attitudes
_____ 13. Main ideas
_____ (a) Selects titles

_____ *(b)* Selects sentences which express main ideas
_____ *(c)* States main ideas in own words
_____14. Can read simple charts, maps, graphs, tables, and diagrams
_____15. Participates in the reading of good literature
_____16. Is improving in ability to answer questions that are:
_____ *(a)* concrete
_____ *(b)* creative
_____ *(c)* abstract
_____17. Uses evaluative criteria in self-selection of reading materials

Word Attack Skills

_____ 1. Can alphabetize — first and second letters
_____ 2. Is familiar with elementary dictionary usage
_____ 3. Recognizes three-letter blends
_____ 4. Understands homonymns and synonymns
_____ 5. Knows contractions *she'll, he'll, we'll*
_____ 6. Understands the use of the apostrophe for ownership
_____ 7. Can hear the three basic syllable generalizations
_____ 8. Can attack new words by:
_____ *(a)* Using pictures for clues
_____ *(b)* Reading to the end of a sentence and making a guess
_____ *(c)* Checking that guess by phonetic clues
_____ *(d)* Using structural clues
_____ *(e)* Checking himself by asking the teacher

Language Skills

_____ 1. Can write addresses
_____ 2. Can write letters of invitation and thank-you using simple form
_____ 3. Understands abbreviations *Mr.* and *Mrs.*
_____ 4. Understands how to write initials
_____ 5. Can use the following words correctly:
_____ *(a)* *went gone*
_____ *(b)* *ate eaten*
_____ *(c)* *is are*
_____ 6. Can write samples of comprehension skills

Spelling Skills

_____ 1. Connects specific consonant sounds with the letters which spell them
_____ *(a)* Knows that the sound of *s* is often spelled with *c*
_____ *(b)* Knows the *ks* sound is often spelled with *x*

_____ *(c)* Knows the sound of *f* in the final position is sometimes spelled with *gh*

_____ 2. Recognizes combinations to look for in spelling vowel sounds

_____ *(a)* Knows that *er* ending is usually spelled *er* but sometimes it is spelled *or*

_____ *(b)* Knows that in words spelled with *ar*, the sound of *a* when followed by *r* is different from the *a* of *hat* or *rain*

_____ 3. Understands and uses the following structural generalizations:

_____ *(a)* Forms plural or past tense of many words which end with *y* by changing *y* to *i* before adding *es* or *ed*

_____ *(b)* Makes new words by adding *ing*

_____ *(c)* Doubles the final consonant of many words before adding *ing*

_____ *(d)* Forms the past tense of some verbs by changing the spelling

_____ *(e)* Makes new words of many words by adding *r, er, st, or, est*

_____ *(f)* Counts the syllables in a word by counting the vowel sounds

_____ *(g)* When words have two consonants between vowels, first tries to divide the word between consonants

_____ *(h)* When words have one consonant between vowels, first tries to divide the word before the consonant

_____ *(i)* For long words which are made up of two short words, spells the words first and writes them together

_____ 4. Uses an apostrophe to show that letters have been omitted in contractions

LANGUAGE ARTS — LEVEL I

Name_____

Comprehension Skills

_____ 1. Finds facts

_____ 2. Groups and classifies facts

_____ 3. Expands and illustrates concepts

_____ 4. Identifies characters by pantomime, role-playing, and dramatization

_____ 5. Notes details to main events (sub-sentences)

_____ 6. Has increased in ability to draw and make inferences

_____ 7. Makes comparisons

_____ 8. Has increased in ability to find sources of information

_____ 9. Notes clues

_____10. Is able to interpret author's purpose

_____11. Recognizes plot structure

_____12. Extends social attitudes

_____13. Main ideas

_____ *(a)* Selects titles

_____ *(b)* Selects sentences which express main ideas

_____ *(c)* States main ideas in own words

_____14. Can read simple charts, maps, graphs, tables, and diagrams

_____15. Participates in the reading of good literature

_____16. Is improving in ability to answer questions that are:

_____ *(a)* concrete

_____ *(b)* creative

_____ *(c)* abstract

_____17. Uses evaluative criteria in self-selection of reading materials

Word Attack Skills

_____ 1. Can attack two-syllable words

_____ 2. Recognizes silent letters — *gh, h, k, l, w, gn,* and *b* as in *climb*

_____ 3. Recognizes open and closed syllables as an aid in word attack

_____ 4. Understands that *f* is changed to *v* before *es*

_____ 5. Understands that *y* is changed to *i* before *er* or *es*

_____ 6. Understands that prefixes and suffixes are syllables

_____ 7. Knows the generalizations for dividing words into syllables:

_____ *(a)* V/CV

_____ *(b)* VC/CV

_____ *(c)* *le* principle

_____ 8. Can attack words by:

_____ *(a)* Using pictures for clues

_____ *(b)* Reading to the end of a sentence and making a guess

_____ *(c)* Checking that guess by phonetic clues

_____ *(d)* Using structural clues

_____ *(e)* Checking himself by asking the teacher

Language Skills

_____ 1. Is improving in ability to write stories

_____ 2. Uses good beginning sentences for stories

_____ 3. Indents paragraphs

_____ 4. Keeps to the main idea in stories

_____ 5. Is adequate in ability to give reports

_____ 6. Using the following words correctly

_____ *(a)*   gave   given
_____ *(b)*   was   wasn't
_____ *(c)*   weren't
_____ 7. Can write samples of the comprehension skills

Spelling Skills

_____ 1. Connects specific consonant sounds with the letters which spell
          them
_____ *(a)*   Knows that the sound of *s* is often spelled with *c*
_____ *(b)*   Knows the *ks* sound is often spelled with *x*
_____ *(c)*   Knows the sound of *f* in the final position is sometimes
                 spelled with *gh*

_____ 2. Recognizes combinations to look for in spelling vowel sounds
_____ *(a)*   Knows that *er* ending is usually spelled *er* but sometimes
                 it is spelled *or*
_____ *(b)*   Knows that in words spelled with *ar*, the sound of *a* when
                 followed by *r* is different from the *a* of *hat* or *rain*

_____ 3. Understands and uses the following structural generalizations:
_____ *(a)*   Forms plural or past tense of many words which end with
                 y by changing *y* to *i* before adding *es* or *ed*
_____ *(b)*   Makes new words by adding *ing*
_____ *(c)*   Doubles the final consonant of many words before adding
                 ing
_____ *(d)*   Forms the past tense of some verbs by changing the
                 spelling
_____ *(e)*   Makes new words of many words by adding *r, er, st, or,
                 est*
_____ *(f)*   Counts the syllables in a word by counting the vowel
                 sounds
_____ *(g)*   When words have two consonants between vowels, tries
                 first to divide the word between consonants
_____ *(h)*   When words have one consonant between vowels, first
                 tries to divide the word before the consonant
_____ *(i)*   For long words which are made up of two short words,
                 spells the words first and writes them together

_____ 4. Uses an apostrophe to show that letters have been omitted in
          contractions

EVALUATION — LEVEL I

Copy the words and cross out the silent letters.

1. know   4. calf
2. night   5. knew
3. climb   6. knight

7. sack   9. often
8. write   10. dollar

Copy and draw a ring around the open syllables.

1. ho   tel
2. go   pher
3. ba   na   na
4. cu   bit
5. li   brary

Add *es* to these words. Be careful!

1. city   6. lily
2. life   7. wolf
3. country   8. candy
4. hurry   9. knife
5. calf   10. bounty

Add *er* to these words. Be careful!

1. happy   6. heavy
2. carry   7. easy
3. lazy   8. sleepy
4. merry   9. lovely
5. busy   10. lofty

Fill in the blanks with one of the words at the end.

1. The teacher has _____ them some work to do. (gave - given)
2. We _____ here yesterday. (weren't - wasn't)
3. That _____ my paper. (weren't - wasn't)
4. Mother _____ me some candy to eat. (gave - given)

Divide these words into syllables. (Why?)

1. remove   1. provide
2. sparkle   2. vacant
3. trophy   3. gamble
4. zebra   4. cactus
5. display   5. tiny
6. target   6. orbit
7. mistreat   7. unhappy
8. soda   8. rewrite
9. zipper   9. predawn
10. bamboo   10. lively

Write a sentence using each of these words.

gave   given   weren't   wasn't

LOLLIPOPS

BALLOONS

We can learn from pictures. Joe went to the store. He bought the lollipops and ballons you see above. How many more lollipops did he buy than balloons? ____

MAIN IDEAS

Mother Nature takes care of some animals so they can hide from their enemies. Some animals are smaller and weaker than other animals. A fawn or young deer is brown with white spots and if he stands still he can not be seen easily. The white spots look like small patches of sunlight.

Another animal, the chameleon, is a member of the lizard family. It can change color to match its background.

The snowshoe rabbit turns white when it snows and brown in summer.

Another animal that changes its color with seasons is the weasel. Its fur is white in winter and brown in summer.

Which sentence best gives the main idea of story?

  a. The color of some animals helps to protect them.
  b. Some animals are smaller than others.
  c. The chameleon is a member of the lizard family.

Which sentence does not belong? Draw a line under it.

  The children went to the zoo. They saw the bears, elephants and snakes. The airplane flew overhead. They saw beautiful birds. They had fun watching the monkeys.

  Jack Lee works as a cowboy on a ranch in the West. He has many jobs to do. He fixes fences to keep the cattle in. He rides around to see that everything is all right. He brushes the horses. He checks to see if there is water for the animals. He works from daylight to dark.

1.   A cowboy works
     a. long hours   *b.* in the afternoon   *c.* on a fence
2.   A cowboy must be able to
     a. walk   *b.* do many things   *c.* get water
3.   The ranch is in the
     a. North   *b.* East   *c.* West

GEORGE WASHINGTON'S HOME

1. Mount Vernon is a beautiful place. It is the home of George Washington. There are many buildings there. You can see the beautiful river from the front porch. The furniture is the kind used when he lived.

2. Many, many people visit Mount Vernon every year. They visit the house, the outside kitchen and the gardens. They see coaches like those he rode in.

3. People do not live today as they did when George Washington lived. They had no cars, radios, airplanes or televisions.

Circle the letter of the idea that tells about each paragraph.

Paragraph 1.
    a.   The home of George Washington
    b.   George Washington, the man
    c.   Washington, the city

Paragraph 2.
    a.   How trees are planted
    b.   Things visitors see at Mount Vernon
    c.   The beautiful garden

Paragraph 3.
    a.   The way George Washington traveled
    b.   Life many years ago
    c.   The way Americans travel today

FREDERICK IN SPRING

It was springtime in Frederick, Maryland. The leaves on the trees were beginning to come out. Forsythia bushes were patches of gold against the clear blue sky. The white clouds looked like piles of cotton flung against the sky. Green, green grass covered the ground. Golden daffodils nodded in the breeze. The ground was soft and springy.

Boys played marbles on the sidewalks and girls played jacks on the steps. Many children jumped rope.

Joe, his hands in his pockets, had a faraway look in his eyes.

He was thinking of the days ahead. School would soon be closed. Then he and his family would go to the beach for the summer. He could go sailing in sailboats and dig sand crabs and clams. He could swim in the ocean. He could watch the motor boats in the harbor.

Joe's friends called to him. He ran to them as he thought of spring. Summer was yet to come but it was springtime in Frederick now and there were many wonderful things to do right now.

1. Write two colorful expressions from the first paragraph.
2. Write the name of the season that had just passed.
3. Write three signs of spring told about in the story.
4. Write three things that Joe could do in the summer.

Table of Contents

Francis Scott Key...................................... 3

Elmer, the Poodle..................................... 10

A Secret Hideaway.................................... 17

The Magic Wand...................................... 24

The Golden Hen...................................... 46

Jungle Animals....................................... 52

Winter Wonderland................................... 59

Lilac Time.. 63

A Funny Television Show............................. 65

The Bamboo Doorway................................ 72

Up, Up, and Away................................... 79

The Magician and the Hat............................ 88

The Red-Nosed Tiger................................ 101

1. Which story will you be reading on page 60?_____
2. Which story will you be reading on page 51?_____
3. What will be the last page of the story *Elmer, The Poodle?*_____

Seeing Relationships

1. When I listen, I use my ears.
When I smell, I use my_____ .

2. Tuesday follows Monday.
   Friday follows_____.

3. Deer are fast_____.
   Fish are fast_____.

LANGUAGE ARTS — LEVEL J

Name_____

Comprehension Skills

_____ 1. Sets reasonable purposes based on concrete, abstract, and creative questioning

_____ 2. Is able to integrate facts of selection read

_____ 3. Can investigate facts

_____ 4. Uses figurative language

_____ 5. Can note and recall story facts and significant details

_____ 6. Extends and classifies concepts

_____ 7. Is improving in ability to state sequence of events

_____ 8. Can interpret motives and actions of characters

_____ 9. Is able to think critically about ideas that have been met in reading

_____10. Continues to recognize plot structure

_____11. Uses the following reference aids

_____ *(a)* index

_____ *(b)* table of contents

_____ *(c)* glossary

_____ *(d)* dictionary

_____ *(e)* atlases

_____ *(f)* encyclopedias

_____12. Is continuing following oral and written directions

_____13. Paces reading rate according to purpose and material being read

_____14. Is learning to withhold judgment until more information has been gained

_____15. Can do simple outlining and summarizing by:

_____ *(a)* Matching text paragraphs to main heads and subheads

_____ *(b)* Completing outline by supplying subheads

_____16. Is improving in use of charts, graphs, tables, maps and diagrams

_____17. Is improving in recognition of shifts of meanings caused by use of words in different context

_____ 18. Understands meaning of nouns and verbs

_____ 19. Continues to understand inferences

_____ 20. Compares and associates facts and stories

_____ 21. Is able to study a situation and make conjectures in keeping with circumstance

_____ 22. Continues to use punctuation as a guide to sentence meaning

_____ 23. Recognizes and knows the use of signal words (and, or, except, still, but, furthermore, especially, in this way, such as, on the other hand, etc.)

_____ 24. Participates in reading of good literature

_____ 25. Is able to gather material to solve a problem by using at least two periodicals, a textbook and a trade book

_____ 26. Is improving in ability to answer questions that are:

_____   *(a)* concrete

_____   *(b)* creative

_____   *(c)* abstract

_____ 27. Uses evaluative criteria in self-selection of reading materials

Word Attack Skills

_____ 1. Knows the vowel combinations *oo* and *ou*

_____ 2. Recognizes and uses all parts of the dictionary

_____ 3. Perceives stressed and unstressed syllables

_____ 4. Understands placement of accent marks

_____ 5. Recognizes open and closed syllables

_____ 6. Can divide suffixed and prefixed words into syllables

_____ 7. Knows when to drop final *e* before endings

_____ 8. Can attack new words by:

_____   *(a)* Using pictures for clues

_____   *(b)* Reading to the end of a sentence and making a guess

_____   *(c)* Checking that guess by phonetic clues

_____   *(d)* Using structural clues

_____   *(e)* Checking himself by using glossary, dictionary or asking the teacher

Language Skills

_____ 1. Has improved in skills of story writing - beginning and ending sentences

_____ 2. Knows how to punctuate sentences that are statements, questions, and exclamations

_____ 3. Knows parts and form of friendly letters and uses them when writing friendly letters

_____ 4. Can address envelopes

_____ 5. Knows meaning of singular and plural

_____ 6. Can give exact directions (making things, experiments, etc.)

_____ 7. Is beginning to take notes

_____ 8. Uses the following words correctly:

_____ *(a) took* and *taken*

_____ *(b) leave* and *let*

_____ *(c) teach* and *learn*

_____ *(d) grew* and *grown*

_____ *(e) was* and *were*

_____ 9. Uses comma to separate a series

_____ 10. Knows how to abbreviate and the punctuation to use

_____ 11. Is improving in writing

_____ 12. Can write samples of comprehension skills

Spelling Skills

_____ 1. Knows the spelling of the following consonant sounds:

_____ *(a)* The *ch* spelling of the *k* or *sh* sound

_____ *(b)* The *g* spelling of the *g* or *j*

_____ *(c)* The *ck* spelling of the *k* sound

_____ *(d)* The *c* spelling of *k* or *s*

_____ *(e)* The *x* spelling of the *ks* sound

_____ *(f)* The *wh* spelling of the *hw* sounds

_____ *(g)* The *qu* spelling of the *kw* sounds

_____ *(h)* The voiced and unvoiced *th* sounds

_____ *(i)* Silent consonants

_____ 2. Knows the following vowel sounds

_____ *(a)* The short sounds of medial vowels

_____ *(b)* The long sound in vowel-consonant-silent *e* words

_____ *(c)* The long sound in words with two words together

_____ *(d)* The long sound of open-syllable words

_____ *(e)* The *ou* and *ow* spelling of the *ou* sound

_____ *(f)* The *ow* spelling of the long *o* sound

_____ *(g)* The *oi* and *oy* spellings of the *oi* sound

_____ *(h)* The *y* spelling of the *i* sound

_____ 3. Understands the formation of irregular plurals

_____ 4. Understands the formation of plurals of nouns which end in *o*

_____ 5. Recognizes the number suffixes

_____ 6. Understands the suffixes which change the part of speech of the root word

_____ 7. Understands the use of the addition of prefixes to change meanings of root words

_____ 8. Recognizes and divides multisyllabic words

_____ 9. Uses devices to aid spelling recall such as remembering unexpected spellings, choosing the correct homonym and spelling part by part

_____ 10. Uses correct punctuation for contractions, possessives and abbreviations

LANGUAGE ARTS — LEVEL K

Name_____

Comprehension Skills

_____ 1. Sets reasonable purposes based on concrete, abstract and creative questioning

_____ 2. Is able to integrate facts of selection read

_____ 3. Can investigate facts

_____ 4. Uses figurative language

_____ 5. Can note and recall story facts and significant details

_____ 6. Extends and classifies concepts

_____ 7. Is improving in ability to state sequence of events

_____ 8. Can interpret motives and actions of characters

_____ 9. Is able to think critically about ideas that have been met in reading

_____ 10. Continues to recognize plot structure

_____ 11. Uses the following reference aids:

_____ *(a)* index

_____ *(b)* table of contents

_____ *(c)* glossary

_____ *(d)* dictionary

_____ *(e)* atlases

_____ *(f)* encyclopedias

_____ 12. Is continuing following oral and written directions

_____ 13. Paces reading rate according to material being read

_____ 14. Is learning to withhold judgment until more information has been gained

_____ 15. Can do simple outlining and summarizing by:

_____ *(a)* Matching text paragraphs to main heads and subheads

_____ *(b)* Completing outline by supplying subheads

_____16. Is improving in use of charts, graphs, tables, maps and diagrams

_____17. Is improving in recognition of shifts of meanings caused by use of words in different context

_____18. Understands meaning of nouns and verbs

_____19. Continues to understand inferences

_____20. Compares and associates facts and stories

_____21. Is able to study a situation and make conjectures in keeping with circumstance

_____22. Continues to use punctuation as a guide to sentence meaning

_____23. Recognizes and knows the use of signal words (and, or, except, still, but, furthermore, especially, in this way, such as, on the other hand, etc.)

_____24. Participates in reading of good literature

_____25. Is able to gather material to solve a problem by using at least two periodicals, a textbook and a trade book

_____26. Is improving in ability to answer questions that are:
_____ *(a)* concrete
_____ *(b)* creative
_____ *(c)* abstract

_____27. Uses evaluative criteria in self-selection of reading materials

Word Attack Skills

_____ 1. Understands plural exceptions (as, sheep, men, teeth, mice, etc.)

_____ 2. Understands and uses diacritical marks in dictionary

_____ 3. Uses respelling in dictionary as an aid to attacking and pronouncing new words

_____ 4. Understands *or, ist* and *ian* as agents

_____ 5. Can attack new words by:
_____ *(a)* Using pictures for clues
_____ *(b)* Reading to the end of a sentence and making a guess
_____ *(c)* Checking that guess by phonetic clues
_____ *(d)* Using structural clues
_____ *(e)* Checking himself by using glossary, dictionary or asking the teacher

Language Skills

_____ 1. Can use the telephone directory efficiently

_____ 2. Recognizes words that are nouns, verbs and pronouns

_____ 3. Knows form of business letter and can write a business letter

_____ 4. Knows correct usage of the following:
_____   *(a)* good   well
_____   *(b)* can   may
_____   *(c)* a   an
_____   *(d)* brought
_____ 5. Participates in choral speaking
_____ 6. Can write samples of comprehension skills

Spelling Skills

_____ 1. Knows the spelling of the following consonant sounds:
_____   *(a)* The *ch* spelling of the *k* or *sh* sound
_____   *(b)* The *g* spelling of the *g* or *j*
_____   *(c)* The *ck* spelling of the *k* sound
_____   *(d)* The *c* spelling of *k* or *s*
_____   *(e)* The *x* spelling of the *ks* sound
_____   *(f)* The *wh* spelling of the *hw* sounds
_____   *(g)* The *qu* spelling of the *kw* sounds
_____   *(h)* The voiced and unvoiced *th* sounds
_____   *(i)* Silent consonants
_____ 2. Knows the following vowel sounds:
_____   *(a)* The short sounds of medial vowels
_____   *(b)* The long sound in vowel-consonant-silent *e* words
_____   *(c)* The long sound in words with two words together
_____   *(d)* The long sound of open-syllable words
_____   *(e)* The *ou* and *ow* spelling of the *ou* sound
_____   *(f)* The *ow* spelling of the long *o* sound
_____   *(g)* The *oi* and *oy* spellings of the *oi* sound
_____   *(h)* The *y* spelling of the *i* sound
_____ 3. Understands the formation of irregular plurals
_____ 4. Understands the formation of plurals of nouns which end in *o*
_____ 5. Recognizes the number suffixes
_____ 6. Understands the suffixes which change the part of speech of the root word
_____ 7. Understands the use of the addition of prefixes to change meanings of root words
_____ 8. Recognizes and divides multisyllabic words
_____ 9. Uses devices to aid spelling recall such as remembering unexpected spellings, choosing the correct homonym and spelling part by part
_____10. Uses correct punctuation for contractions, possessives and abbreviations

EVALUATION — LEVEL K

Write the plurals of these words.

1.	dish	11.	cherry
2.	ax	12.	penny
3.	ox	13.	elf
4.	sheep	14.	thief
5.	tooth	15.	deer
6.	mouse	16.	foot
7.	child	17.	brush
8.	man	18.	policeman
9.	woman	19.	church
10.	guess	20.	glass

Fill in the blanks with the appropriate word.

1. A person who collects stamps is a stamp_____.
2. A person who inspects meat is a meat_____.
3. A person who runs the drug store is a_____.
4. A person who is born and lives in Italy is an_____.
5. A man who operates a machine is a machine_____.

Circle the letters of the respelling that fits each word.

1. beehive   (a) bē hiv'

             (b) bē' hīv

2. blindly   (a) blīnd le'

             (b) blīnd' le

3. blister   (a) blĭs' ter

             (b) blīs' ter

4. praise   (a) pra' zē

             (b) prāz

5. taught   (a) tôt

             (b) tūt

class	172	clear
clime	174	clothe

clear-cut	173	climb
clothes	175	coal

Use the guide words and page numbers above to indicate the page on which each of the following words could be found.

1. cluster____   5. clue____   9. clever____   13. cloister____

2. clean____   6. closet____   10. clause____   14. clutch____

3. clay____   7. cloak____   11. cleat____   15. clatter____

4. cliff____   8. cloud____   12. clog____   16. clerk ____

Write the following pairs of guide words on your page.

state — stay   *stead — stem*   *stem — stick*

Write these words alphabetically under the guide words.

steer	steadfast	stave	stern
statue	station	steak	staunch
sterling	steeple	stew	steward

Number your paper from 1 to 5 in two columns.

Arrange the letters of the names to show how they would be listed alphabetically in a telephone directory.

I	II
(a) Fox, Melvin	(a) Nelson, Anna
(b) Fox, Charles	(b) Neal, Jack
(c) Fox, Russell	(c) Nail, Edward
(d) Fox, Warren	(d) Nickel, Gladys
(e) Fox, Guy	(e) Norris, James

Write a business letter to Ebert's Dairy, Frederick, Md. Ask if your class may visit their dairy plant to see how ice cream is made.

Write all the nouns in these sentences on your paper.

1. The dog ate the meat.
2. The canary flew out of the cage.
3. There are three eggs in the nest.
4. She lives in Florida.
5. They will go on the first Friday in November.

Write all the verbs in these sentences.

1. We watched the games last night.
2. The boys lost the game.
3. Jack swam in the ocean last summer.
4. The light was bright.
5. The pine trees made a soft sound.

Write all the pronouns in these sentences.

1. She was here today.
2. The dog followed him to school.
3. I got it at the store.
4. This is their kitten.
5. His book is torn.

Write the correct word that goes in each sentence.

1. You have a_____bike. (good   well)

2. The little boy can write_____. (good   well)

3. He cannot ride as _____ as his brother. (good   well)

4. _____I get a book to read? (May   Can)

5. Please get me_____apple. (a   an)

6. That is_____big dog. (a   an)

7. Father_____ the boy to school. (brought   bought)

8. _____elf is a little man. (a   an)

9. She can jump rope_____. (good   well)

10. I_____it at the store. (brought   bought)

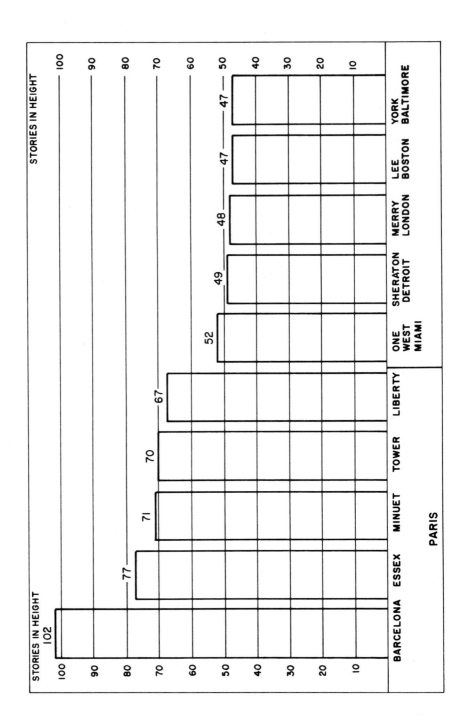

AMERICA'S SKYSCRAPERS

1. The graph shows the_____of some skyscrapers.
   (a) cost   *(b)* width   *(c)* height

2. Paris has the_____tallest skyscrapers shown on the graph.
   (a) five   *(b)* ten   *(c)* three

3. The tallest skyscraper in Paris is the_____building.
   (a) Essex   *(b)* Barcelona   *(c)* Liberty

4. The Barcelona is more than_____stories tall.
   (a) 100   *(b)* 150   *(c)* 200

5. The Sheraton is in_____.
   (a) Detroit   *(b)* London   *(c)* Baltimore

6. The graph shows skyscrapers in____cities other than Paris.
   (a) five   *(b)* three   *(c)* two

7. The tallest skyscraper outside Paris is in_____.
   (a) London   *(b)* Boston   *(c)* Miami

8. Four skyscrapers outside Paris are less than_____stories tall.
   (a) 10   *(b)* 30   *(c)* 50

9. The Minuet building is the____tallest skyscraper in Paris.
   (a) fourth   *(b)* third   *(c)* second

10. The Lee building has the same number of stories as the_____.
    (a) Essex   *(b)* York   *(c)* Sheraton

Read this story.

THE HOME OF A PRESIDENT

The third president of the United States was Thomas Jefferson. He was a man who could do many things. He built his home in Virginia. He started to build it in 1769 on Monticello, which was the highest hill on his plantation. Monticello means "little mountain."

Many people visit his home each year.

Thomas Jefferson was an inventor. Some of the things that he invented were a clock that told the hour and day of the week. He invented a swivel chair. He also invented a weathervane with a dial on the ceiling of the porch.

When he retired he lived at Monticello. Nearly every day he rode horseback over his large plantation and looked after his farms, cotton mill, flour mill, furniture shop, the smithy, and the nail factory.

Fill in the outline using information from the story above.

    I. The home of Thomas Jefferson

        A.

        B.

    II. Thomas Jefferson's inventions

        A.

        B.

    III. Thomas Jefferson's plantation

        A.

        B.

        C.

    IV. Thomas Jefferson, the man

        A.

        B.

Dictionary Page

Read the partial dictionary page.

Ia., Iowa

in-, a prefix that means: not; opposite from, without, as in *inaccurate, inactive, incapable.*

in., inch; inches

inc., incorporated.

In ca (ing′ kə), **1:** one of the persons of a race of Indians in South America: *The Incas ruled Peru before the Spanish Conquest.* **2:** the ruler of such a race. n.

in ci dent (in′ si dənt), **1:** an event. **2:** an unimportant happening. **3:** likely to happen; 1, 2, n., 3, adj.

in va lid (in′ və lid), **1:** a sick weak person. **2:** not well; weak and sick

I o wa (iə wə), a state located in the Middle Western United States. Abbreviation: Ia. n.

is land (i′lənd), **1:** a piece of land that has water on all sides. **2:** anything that resembles this. n.

joy less (joi′ lis), **1:** without joy; **2:** not prompting joy. adj.

leap (lēp), **1:** a jump or hop. **2:** space covered in a jump. **3:** jump: *a grasshopper leaps.* **4:** hop over, 1, 2 n., 3, 4 v. leaped or leapt, leaping.

le gal (lē′-gal), **1:** of law: legal knowledge **2:** of lawyers: legal advice

let's (lets), let us.

lightning rod, a rod, usually metal, attached to a ship or building for the purpose of guiding lightning into the water or earth.

lime (lim) **1:** a juicy fruit much like a lemon. **2:** the tree it grows on.

    1. How many words have more than one syllable?____

2. How many entries are abbreviations?____

3. How many meanings does leap have?____

4. Which syllable is accented in incident?_____

5. Which word is a contraction?_____

6. Which entry is made up of more than one word?_____

Following Directions

TOOTHPICK DARTS

Toothpicks make good little darts that are almost lighter than air. Near one end of a toothpick tie a piece of thread about twelve inches long. Hold the toothpick between your fingers. Then sail it through the air as you would a paper dart or airplane. You will find that the thread helps it to sail. Make eight darts with orange thread tails and eight with green, so that two people can play the game. Any two colors of thread can be used.

From heavy paper cut a twenty-inch circle for a target. With a crayon draw a small circle or bull's-eye in the center. Around the bull's-eye draw two larger circles about three or four inches apart. Lay the target on the floor and stand back at least six feet from it. Let the other player choose his color and try his luck. Then sail your eight darts at the target.

Score 1 point for darts landing in the outside circle. Score 2 points for the next circle, 3 for the next circle, and 4 points for those which land in the bull's-eye. If a dart lands on a circle line, count the larger score.

Follow these directions.

1. Draw a big circle for the target. Put in the bull's-eye, and color it red. Draw the other two circles.
2. In each circle you have just drawn, put a number to show how many points are scored there.
3. Put X's under your circle to show where the players stand. Write how far away it should be.
4. Write the names of two things used to make darts for this game.

TABLE OF CONTENTS

The Big Game • Mary Long........................... 3

The Pony Express • Jack Whitenton................... 10

The Great Giant • Thomas Jansen..................... 16

A Lovely Toadstool • June Hopewell.................. 23

An Earthquake • Ishum Burke........................29

The Girl Who Couldn't Talk • Lana Goode..............32
Detectives Who Help • David Green and Ivan Levine......38
The Glassbottomed Boat • Warren Lake................44
Daffodils on the Hill • Edward LeCoast................46
A Trip to India • Susan DeVoe.......................54
The Mystery of the Lake House • Raymond Stokes.......61

1. What story will you be reading on page 37?_____

2. What will be the last page of *A Trip to India?*_____

3. How many pages does the story *The Great Giant* have?_____

4. Which story was written by two people?_____

5. Which story did Warren Lake write?_____

6. Who wrote *Daffodils on the Hill?*_____

ESSEX HARBOR

Henry Hampton lived on the seacoast of New England, in a little town named Essex. Essex is a very old town, one of the oldest in our country. It was settled more than 300 years ago by people who came from England.

If you visited Essex you would know that it is very old by the many old buildings on the waterfront. The wharves are very old and they are not used as much as they were about a hundred years ago. At one time Essex was a great seaport. Famous clipper ships from all over the world sailed to and from her docks. The ships went to places in the Far East like China and Japan. They brought back articles such as beautiful silk cloth, dishes and spices.

Now those days are gone and large harbors of other cities on the East Coast get these and other materials from ocean liners and freighters. Essex harbor is not deep enough for these big ships, and her docks do not have the modern cranes that are needed to unload the modern ships that we have today. Since many of the old buildings are not used, they have sagged and rotted, and the old wharves have turned grey from the salt spray from the ocean, and weak from not being repaired.

One thing that has not changed is the sea. It is rough and cold in winter, but in summer it is smooth, calm, and blue. If you went there to visit, you could always buy fish along the wharves. You could go fishing for crabs, lobsters and clams.

Circle the letter of the correct ending to each sentence.

1. Henry Hampton lived near the
   (a) mountains   *(b)* plains   *(c)* seacoast.

2. Essex is a town that is very
   (a) old   *(b)* new   *(c)* big.
3. Essex was a great
   (a) city   *(b)* seaport   *(c)* seacoast.
4. About what year was Essex settled?
   (a) 1600   *(b)* 1700   *(c)* 1800
5. Into Essex's harbor once sailed famous
   (a) steamships   *(b)* ocean liners   *(c)* clipper ships

1. Write a sentence telling why the harbor is not as busy as it once was.
2. Write three things that ships once brought back from the Far East to the harbor of Essex.

LANGUAGE ARTS — LEVEL L

Name_____

Comprehension Skills

_____ 1. Is building concepts - aesthetic, associations, clarification, comparison, refining, historical, space, and time

_____ 2. Uses critical thinking skills - conjecturing, evaluating, judging, concluding, confirming, refuting, channelizing, reflecting

_____ 3. Makes use of study skills - extensive reading, locating information, note taking, outlining, summarizing, cross-reference, index, and appendix

_____ 4. Notes sequence - ideas, happenings, chronological sequence of events

_____ 5. Adjusts rate of reading to material and purposes

_____ 6. Distinguishes fact and opinion

_____ 7. Participates in oral reading

_____ 8. Is developing ability to discuss abstract meaning

_____ 9. Interprets meaning of figurative and idiomatic expressions

_____ 10. Is able to locate information as follows:

_____ *(a)* Skims for information

_____ *(b)* Uses encyclopedias and cross references efficiently

_____ *(c)* Uses index efficiently

_____ *(d)* Selects and evaluates information

_____ *(e)* Selects suitable information

_____ *(f)* Lists details pertaining to a topic

_____ *(g)* Recognizes relationships of ideas

_____ *(h)* Uses headings and topographical aids - italics, guide words, titles, and subtitles

_____ 11. Realizes author's point of view

_____12. Uses aids to retention of reading

_____13. Practices oral and written recall

_____14. Participates in dramatization

_____15. Perceives analogies

_____16. Is able to gather material to solve a problem by using at least two periodicals, a textbook and a trade book

_____17. Is improving in ability to answer questions that are:

_____   *(a)* concrete

_____   *(b)* creative

_____   *(c)* abstract

_____18. Uses evaluative criteria in self-selection of reading materials

Word Attack Skills

_____ 1. Continues the understanding of variant spelling of vowel sounds - *schwa* and *y* as a vowel

_____ 2. Is maintaining knowledge of phonetic principles and structural analysis of previous levels

_____ 3. Is maintaining knowledge of silent consonant letters - *kn, wr, b, gh, ph, wh,* etc.

_____ 4. Understands meaning of the following prefixes: *non, im, in, de, mid, super*

_____ 5. Can attack new words by:

_____   *(a)* Using pictures for clues

_____   *(b)* Reading to the end of a sentence and making a guess

_____   *(c)* Checking that guess by phonetic clues

_____   *(d)* Using structural clues

_____   *(e)* Checking himself by using glossary and/or dictionary

Language Skills

_____ 1. Uses correct punctuation in writing conversation

_____ 2. Uses commas to set off names of persons addressed

_____ 3. Uses commas to set off certain words at the beginning of a sentence, as *yes, no, oh, well,* etc.

_____ 4. Gathers information by:

_____   *(a)* Reading

_____   *(b)* Pictures

_____   *(c)* Movies

_____   *(d)* Television

_____   *(e)* Radio

_____   *(f)* Talking with people

_____   *(g)* Using his own eyes and ears

_____ 5. Uses verb forms correctly - present, past, and with helper

_____ 6. Uses these words correctly:

_____ *(a)* give   gave

_____ *(b)* sit   set

_____ *(c)* knew   known

_____ *(d)* threw   thrown

_____ 7. Enunciates clearly

_____ 8. Can write samples of comprehension skills

Spelling Skills

_____ 1. Knows the spelling of the following consonant sounds:

_____ *(a)* The *ch* spelling of the *k* or *sh* sound

_____ *(b)* The *g* spelling of the *g* or *j*

_____ *(c)* The *ck* spelling of the *k* sound

_____ *(d)* The *c* spelling of *k* or *s*

_____ *(e)* The *x* spelling of the *ks* sound

_____ *(f)* The *wh* spelling of the *hw* sounds

_____ *(g)* The *qu* spelling of the *kw* sounds

_____ *(h)* The voiced and unvoiced *th* sounds

_____ *(i)* Silent consonants

_____ 2. Knows the following vowel sounds:

_____ *(a)* The short sounds of medial vowels

_____ *(b)* The long sound in vowel-consonant-silent *e* words

_____ *(c)* The long sound in words with two words together

_____ *(d)* The long sound of open-syllable words

_____ *(e)* The *ou* and *ow* spelling of the *ou* sound

_____ *(f)* The *ow* spelling of the long *o* sound

_____ *(g)* The *oi* and *oy* spellings of the *oi* sound

_____ *(h)* The *y* spelling of the *i* sound

_____ 3. Understands the formation of irregular plurals

_____ 4. Understands the formation of plurals of nouns which end in *o*

_____ 5. Recognizes the number suffixes

_____ 6. Understands the suffixes which change the part of speech of the root word

_____ 7. Understands the use of the addition of prefixes to change meanings of root words

_____ 8. Recognizes and divides multisyllabic words

_____ 9. Uses devices to aid spelling recall such as remembering unexpected spellings, choosing the correct homonym and spelling part by part

_____ 10. Uses correct punctuation for contractions, possessives and abbreviations

LANGUAGE ARTS — LEVEL M

Name_____

Comprehension Skills

_____ 1. Is building concepts - aesthetic, associations, clarification, comparison, refining, historical, space, and time

_____ 2. Uses critical thinking skills - conjecturing, evaluating, judging, concluding, confirming, refuting, channelizing, reflecting

_____ 3. Makes use of study skills - extensive reading, locating information, note taking, outlining, summarizing, cross-reference, index, and appendix

_____ 4. Notes sequence - ideas, happenings, chronological sequence of events

_____ 5. Adjusts rate of reading to material and purposes

_____ 6. Distinguishes fact and opinion

_____ 7. Participates in oral reading

_____ 8. Is developing ability to discuss abstract meaning

_____ 9. Interprets meaning of figurative and idiomatic expressions

_____10. Is able to locate information as follows:
_____ *(a)* Skims for information
_____ *(b)* Uses encyclopedias and cross references efficiently
_____ *(c)* Uses index efficiently
_____ *(d)* Selects and evaluates information
_____ *(e)* Selects suitable information
_____ *(f)* Lists details pertaining to a topic
_____ *(g)* Recognizes relationships of ideas
_____ *(h)* Uses headings and topographical aids - italics, guide words, titles, and subtitles

_____11. Realizes author's point of view

_____12. Uses aids to retention of reading

_____13. Practices oral and written recall

_____14. Participates in dramatization

_____15. Perceives analogies

_____16. Is able to gather material to solve a problem by using at least two periodicals, a textbook and a trade book

_____17. Is improving in ability to answer questions that are:
_____ *(a)* concrete
_____ *(b)* creative
_____ *(c)* abstract

_____18. Uses evaluative criteria in self-selection of reading materials

Word Attack Skills

_____ 1. Recognizes vowel sounds in accented and unaccented syllables

_____ 2. Understands primary and secondary accents

_____ 3. Recognizes stems (base words)

_____ 4. Is adding more prefixes and suffixes (suffixes - *ant, ish, int*) (prefixes - *inter, intra*)

_____ 5. Recognizes parts of speech - nouns, verbs, adjectives, adverbs

_____ 6. Understands antonyms and heteronyms

_____ 7. Can attack new words by:

_____ *(a)* Using pictures for clues

_____ *(b)* Reading to the end of a sentence and making a guess

_____ *(c)* Checking that guess by using phonetic clues

_____ *(d)* Using structural clues

_____ *(e)* Checking himself by using glossary and dictionary

Language Skills

_____ 1. Is developing an enriched vocabulary

_____ 2. Shows improvement in choice of words

_____ 3. Understands words that are conjunctions and interjections

_____ 4. Understands singular and plural possessive forms of nouns

_____ 5. Can write samples of comprehension skills

Spelling Skills

_____ 1. Knows the spelling of the following consonant sounds:

_____ *(a)* The *ch* spelling of the *k* or *sh* sound

_____ *(b)* The *g* spelling of the *g* or *j*

_____ *(c)* The *ck* spelling of the *k* sound

_____ *(d)* The *c* spelling of the *k* or *s*

_____ *(e)* The *x* spelling of the *ks* sound

_____ *(f)* The *wh* spelling of the *hw* sounds

_____ *(g)* The *qu* spelling of the *kw* sounds

_____ *(h)* The voiced and unvoiced *th* sounds

_____ *(i)* Silent consonants

_____ 2. Knows the following vowel sounds:

_____ *(a)* The short sounds of medial vowels

_____ *(b)* The long sound in vowel-consonant-silent *e* words

_____ *(c)* The long sound in words with two words together

_____ *(d)* The long sound of open-syllable words

_____ *(e)* The *ou* and *ow* spelling of the *ou* sound

_____ *(f)* The *ow* spelling of the long *o* sound

_____ *(g)* The *oi* and *oy* spellings of the *oi* sound

_____ *(h)* The *y* spelling of the *i* sound

_____ 3. Understands the formation of irregular plurals

_____ 4. Understands the formation of plurals of nouns which end in *o*

_____ 5. Recognizes the number suffixes

_____ 6. Understands the suffixes which change the part of speech of the root word

_____ 7. Understands the use of the addition of prefixes to change meanings of root words

_____ 8. Recognizes and divides multisyllabic words

_____ 9. Uses devices to aid spelling recall such as remembering unexpected spellings, choosing the correct homonym and spelling part by part

_____ 10. Uses correct punctuation for contractions, possessives, and abbreviations

LANGUAGE ARTS — LEVEL N

Name_____

Comprehension Skills

_____ 1. Is continuing concept development - aesthetic, socio-economic, associating, clarifying, comparing, evaluating, extending, refining, concluding, scientific, geographical, historical

_____ 2. Is developing more skill in critical thinking

_____ 3. Is developing more skill in recognizing sequence of ideas and chronological sequence of events

_____ 4. Can interpret motives and actions of characters

_____ 5. Can make conjectures on basis of material

_____ 6. Maintains study skills begun on previous levels

_____ 7. Is increasing skill of pacing reading rate according to material and purpose

_____ 8. Reads well orally with expression

_____ 9. Uses newspaper and newspaper aids for information

_____ 10. Is able to read and use television tables

_____ 11. Is able to read and understand time tables

_____ 12. Uses card catalogue efficiently

_____ 13. Creative writing has improved

_____ 14. Reads good literature (balanced)

_____ *(a)* poetry

_____ *(b)* fact and fiction

_____ *(c)* fanciful and humorous

_____ *(d)* classics and modern

_____ 15. Understands writer's point of view

_____ 16. Understands author's purpose

_____ 17. Is able to gather material to solve a problem by using at least two periodicals, a textbook and a trade book

_____ 18. Is improving in ability to answer questions that are:

_____ *(a)* concrete

_____ *(b)* creative

_____ *(c)* abstract

_____ 19. Uses evaluative criteria in self-selection of reading materials

Word Attack Skills

_____ 1. Knows how to divide words at the end of the line

_____ 2. Uses primary and secondary accents correctly

_____ 3. Is maintaining skill in accenting words

_____ 4. Is adequate in changes of spelling of prefixes:

_____ *in* becomes *ir, il,* or *im*

_____ *co* becomes *cor, col*

_____ *ad* becomes *ag, al, an, as,* or *at*

_____ 5. Can attack words by:

_____ *(a)* Using pictures for clues

_____ *(b)* Reading to the end of a sentence and making a guess

_____ *(c)* Checking that guess by use of phonetic clues

_____ *(d)* Using structural clues

_____ *(e)* Checking himself by using glossary or dictionary

_____ 6. Understands meaning of common prefixes, as:

_____ *(a)* ad

_____ *(b)* circum

_____ *(c)* de

_____ *(d)* dis

_____ *(e)* im

_____ *(f)* in

_____ *(g)* inter

_____ *(h)* intra

_____ *(i)* mal

_____ *(j)* mis

_____ *(k)* pre

_____ *(l)* non

_____ *(m)* re

_____ *(n)* sub

_____ *(o)* trans

_____ *(p)* un

_____ 7. Is able to make verbs from other words by using *ify, ize, en*

_____ 8. Recognizes root words from affixed words

_____ 9. Understands combined forms to get meaning (Ex.: cosmo-world)

Language Skills

_____ 1. Recognizes and uses possessive form of singular and plural nouns

_____ 2. Uses correct punctuation for singular and plural possessive forms of nouns

_____ 3. Understands elementary parliamentary procedure

_____ 4. Is maintaining knowledge of parts of speech

_____ 5. Knows how to use these words correctly:
_____   (a) blew   blown
_____   (b) those   them
_____   (c) isn't   is
_____   (d) were   weren't
_____   (e) are   aren't

_____ 6. Is adequate in writing various forms of letters, using blocked and indented forms:
_____   (a) For information
_____   (b) For requests
_____   (c) For thank-you notes
_____   (d) In placing an order

_____ 7. Understands and recognizes subjects and predicates of sentences

_____ 8. Can write examples of comprehension skills

Spelling Skills

_____ 1. Knows the spelling of the following consonant sounds:
_____   (a) The *ch* spelling of the *k* or *sh* sound
_____   (b) The *g* spelling of the *g* or *j*
_____   (c) The *ck* spelling of the *k* sound
_____   (d) The *c* spelling of the *k* or *s*
_____   (e) The *x* spelling of the *ks* sound
_____   (f) The *wh* spelling of the *hw* sounds
_____   (g) The *qu* spelling of the *kw* sounds
_____   (h) The voiced and unvoiced *th* sounds
_____   (i) Silent consonants

_____ 2. Knows the following vowel sounds:
_____   (a) The short sounds of medial vowels
_____   (b) The long sound in vowel-consonant-silent *e* words
_____   (c) The long sound in words with two words together

_____ *(d)* The long sound of open-syllable words
_____ *(e)* The *ou* and *ow* spelling of the *ou* sound
_____ *(f)* The *ow* spelling of the long *o* sound
_____ *(g)* The *oi* and *oy* spellings of the *oi* sound
_____ *(h)* The *y* spelling of the *i* sound
_____ 3. Understands the formation of irregular plurals
_____ 4. Understands the formation of plurals of nouns which end in *o*
_____ 5. Recognizes the number suffixes
_____ 6. Understands the suffixes which change the part of speech of the root word
_____ 7. Understands the use of the addition of prefixes to change meanings of root words
_____ 8. Recognizes and divides multisyllabic words
_____ 9. Uses devices to aid spelling recall such as remembering unexpected spellings, choosing the correct homonym and spelling part by part
_____10. Uses correct punctuation for contractions, possessives and abbreviations

EVALUATION — LEVEL N

Make verbs from these words. Use *fy, ify, en* or *ize.*

1. terror_____
2. fright_____
3. drama_____
4. tight_____

Write the base words from which these words were made.

1. omission_____
2. curiosity_____
3. supplier_____
4. muscular_____
5. armful_____
6. crazily_____
7. scientific_____
8. productive_____
9. sanity_____
10. fanciful_____

Add the endings. Write the new word.

1. marry + age =
2. vary + able =
3. narrate + or =
4. lazy + ly =
5. fog + y =
6. fame + ous =
7. worry + some =

Number your paper from 1 to 10. Write the headings *S* and *P*.

From each sentence below copy the simple subject and predicate.

1. It was very cold.
2. Snow fell during the night.
3. Many cars were stranded.
4. Ice formed on the road.
5. Snowplows worked all day in the streets.
6. The vacation had been fun.
7. Our team won most of the games that we played.
8. Our families could ride together.
9. We studied the lesson yesterday.
10. They were at the fair three times.

Use these words in sentences. Draw a line under the word you are using in the sentence.

blew   blown   those   them   isn't   is   were   weren't   are   aren't

Match the meaning with the prefixes

_____ 1. circum   A.   together or with
_____ 2. com   B.   not
_____ 3. de   C.   between or among
_____ 4. dis   D.   bad
_____ 5. in   E.   before
_____ 6. inter   F.   away from or off; down; opposite of
_____ 7. intra   G.   not; in or within
_____ 8. mal   H.   not
_____ 9. mis   I.   across, on the other side of, or to the
                                 other side; through

_____10. pre   J.   beneath, below or under; lower in rank or importance; less than

_____11. non   K.   not; opposite of

_____12. re   L.   around

_____13. sub   M.   within

_____14. trans   N.   wrong; bad

_____15. un   O.   again; back

Write the words that these letters stand for. Then write the letters the schwas stand for in each word.

an′ ə melz _____

kuv′ ərd _____

hid′ ə n _____

bū′ tə fel _____

kam plēt′ le _____

Rules for Dividing Two-Syllable Words

A. V/CV

B. VC/CV

C. *le* principle . . consonant before *le* usually goes with *le*.

D. When *ck* comes before *le, k usually* goes with the first syllable.

E. Letters of digraphs and blends are not separated when a word is divided into syllables

F. Prefixes and suffixes are syllables.

Write these words in syllables. Put in the accent mark and write the letter of the rule that tells you how to divide the word.

_____ 1. daddy

_____ 2. donkey

_____ 3. hotel

_____ 4. around

_____ 5. weather

_____ 6. pirate

_____ 7. unfair

_____ 8. muscle

_____ 9. fiddle

_____10. trickle

NAME OF SCHOOL	ENROLL-MENT	CLASSROOM TEACHERS	PHYSICAL EDUCATION	ART	MUSIC
CLERMONT	789	23	I	I	I
OAKLEAF	1,124	38	2	I	2
PINE-CLIFF	874	26	I	I	2
WASHING-TON	981	33	2	I	I
MADISON	556	18	I	0	I
BLOOM-FIELD	849	30	2	I	I
PATAPSCO	1,006	40	2	2	2

1. The table illustrated here gives the _____ and _____ of each school.

2. The school with largest enrollment is_____.

3. The school with smallest enrollment is_____.

4. Oakleaf is about_____as large as Madison.

5. Altogether there are ____ art teachers, ____ music teachers and ____ physical education teachers.

6. Patapsco school has an average of ____ children in each room.

Following Directions

BIG BAD WOLF

When the weather is good, children like to play group games. At one school, different children choose and lead group games. Here is one that you may like to try. It is called "Big Bad Wolf." You will need ten or more children. Draw a large square. A 30-foot square is a good size. One child, "The Wolf," stands in the center of the square. The other children stand around the outside of the square. He yells, "I am the Big Bad Wolf. I am going to catch you. Are you afraid to come into my den?"

"No!" yell the other children.

The children start to run through the square. The wolf tries to tag as many as he can. All the children tagged stay in the square with the wolf and help him to tag the others. Children who get through the square without being tagged are safe. This goes on until all are tagged. The last child tagged becomes the wolf for the next game.

Follow these directions.

1. Draw a *large* square on your paper.
2. Suppose 15 children were playing this game. Draw stick figures to show where the children stand and use *W* for the wolf.
3. Draw arrows pointing in the directions the children run.
4. Imagine that the wolf has tagged seven children. Write a sentence telling what they should do now.
5. Write a sentence telling what happens when the last child has been tagged.

WATER TRAVEL IN EARLY AMERICA

In the early years of our country good roads like those we have today were unheard of. Since most roads were bad, people traveled by boats whenever they could. Boats were used to carry people and cargo. The early boats were flatboats made of logs. These boats had no power and had to go the way of the current so they always had to go downstream. This made traveling slow. The speed depended on the flow of the river. Most early settlers did not have sailboats.

The steam engine soon replaced the flat river boat. Robert Fulton was not the first to make a steamboat but his was the first to run one at a profit. His boat, the Clermont, made a trip up the Hudson River from New York to Albany. The steamboat did not need to depend on the wind. It was a faster way to travel and more cargo could be carried.

This was a great step in transportation. The United States benefited from the use of the steamboat. Trade between the eastern and western part of the United States was easier. Many more settlers moved westward. Men began to build factories in the east because they had better ways to ship their finished products. Farm products could be shipped to other parts of the country.

Using the above story, make an outline. The main headings are below.

   I. Early Travel in the United States

  II. Advantages of the Steamboat

 III. How the Steamboat Helped the United States

Write two letters.

1. Write a letter to:

The Frederick Milk Company, 433 Broadway, Frederick, Md. 19231. Imagine that you are studying food and would like some booklets and charts on milk for a report that you are going to give in class.

2. On the back of the letter, draw an envelope and address the letter to the company president, who is Mr. Jerome Burns.

3. Write a thank-you note to a friend or relative and thank them for a gift.

Use your home address in the heading.

LANGUAGE ARTS — LEVEL O

Name_____

Extension of Reading Experiences

_____ 1. Is extending concept development

_____ (a) Concrete concepts - objects and processes

_____ (b) Chronological concepts - hours, seasons and history

_____ (c) Spatial concepts - size, geometric shapes, distance

_____ (d) Social concepts - adjustment to the environment, cooperation, patriotism, justice, etc.

_____ (e) Interpretation of material - emotions, poetic language, etc.

_____ (f) Reading plays for concepts

_____ 2. Is continuing to build a more extensive vocabulary by:

_____ (a) Context clues

_____ (b) Phonetic analysis

_____ (c) Structural analysis

_____ (d) Syllabication

_____ (e) Summarizing

_____ 3. Is continuing to be flexible in rate of reading

_____ 4. Is continuing to read critically by:

_____ (a) Reading with discrimination

_____ (b) Reading for interpretation

_____ (c) Reading to analyze

_____ (d) Reading to visualize

_____ 5. Is maintaining and using study skills developed in lower levels:

_____ (a) Skimming

_____ (b) Outlining

_____ (c) Summarizing

_____ (d) Organizing ideas

_____ (e) Using the parts of a book

_____ (f) Using reference materials

_____ (g) Taking notes

_____ 6. Is able to use notes for study and review

_____ 7. Expresses thoughts in creative writing

_____ 8. Is developing an appreciation of literature by:

_____ (a) Relating and comparing selections which have similar characteristics

_____ (b) Contrasting selections which are distinctly dissimilar in form and content

_____ (c) Thinking of other ways in which an idea, a character, or an event might have been presented by the author

_____ 9. Takes part in research projects

_____ 10. Uses evaluative criteria in self-selection of reading materials

_____ 11. Can write examples of comprehension skills

_____ 12. Is able to gather material to solve a problem by using at least two periodicals, a textbook and a trade book

_____ 13. Can answer questions that are:

_____ (a) concrete

_____ (b) creative

_____ (c) abstract

Spelling Skills

_____ 1. Knows the spelling of the following consonant sounds:

_____ (a) The *ch* spelling of the *k* or *sh* sound

_____ (b) The *g* spelling of the *g* or *j*

_____ (c) The *ck* spelling of the *k* sound

_____ (d) The *c* spelling of the *k* or *s*

_____ (e) The *x* spelling of the *ks* sound

_____ (f) The *wh* spelling of the *hw* sounds

_____ (g) The *qu* spelling of the *kw* sounds

_____ (h) The voiced and unvoiced *th* sounds

_____ (i) Silent consonants

_____ 2. Knows the following vowel sounds:

_____ (a) The short sounds of medial vowels

_____ (b) The long sound in vowel-consonant-silent *e* words

_____ (c) The long sound in words with two words together

_____ (d) The long sound of open-syllable words

_____ (e) The *ou* and *ow* spelling of the *ou* sound

_____ (f) The *ow* spelling of the long *o* sound

_____ (g) The *oi* and *oy* spellings of the *oi* sound

_____ (h) The *y* spelling of the *i* sound

_____ 3. Understands the formation of irregular plurals

_____ 4. Understands the formation of plurals of nouns which end in *o*

_____ 5. Recognizes the number suffixes

_____ 6. Understands the suffixes which change the part of speech of the root word

_____ 7. Understands the use of the addition of prefixes to change meanings of root words

_____ 8. Recognizes and divides multisyllabic words

_____ 9. Uses devices to aid spelling recall such as remembering unexpected spellings, choosing the correct homonym and spelling part by part

_____ 10. Uses correct punctuation for contractions, possessives and abbreviations

SUMMARY

When planning the experiences and activities for the Language Arts Learning Center, teachers must remember that children are nongraded from the time of birth. An infant responds to objects and events in his home environment. Very early in life he hears, sees, touches, and manipulates. These experiences provide him with the background for organizing sounds into a sensible pattern of various sounds, which become words. These words associated with direct experience are soon spoken with meaning.

Noticing things and listening to correctly spoken words which describe them helps the preschool child to develop a vocabulary and speech. These direct experiences of seeing, hearing, feeling, and manipulating, listening and speaking lead quickly into reading, writing and spelling.

Teachers should plan to use many direct experiences with children in working with words. All children do not come from the same background or home environment, and they have not all had the same experiences. They do not all develop language abilities in the same sequence or at the same chronological age. One child does not read as well at age ten as another does at age seven.

Language arts activities must be made interesting and meaningful throughout the entire elementary program. For instruction to be most meaningful, teachers must consider individual differences in ability to learn and in previous experience. Instruction must proceed from the familiar to the new, from the easy to the more difficult.

At the beginning levels, concrete experiences should be used to help build meanings and to help the child learn basic sight words. In order for the child to achieve independence in learning new words and be able to read with meaning, the teacher must help him develop the skills of using context clues, phonetic and structural analysis.

As the child progresses and reaches the higher levels the major aim of reading instruction is to prepare him for reading particular materials and to establish independence in using the word analysis skills, deriving correct meanings, reading for specific purposes (textbook assignments, in locating, organizing and evaluating information, etc.).

Instruction in Language Arts should be planned with activities and experiences which will help each child improve in reading, speaking, listening, and writing. Teachers must continuously evaluate the progress of each child. The child must see the need and the value of this instruction; it must be relevant; there must be a real purpose for each activity; he must have need of the activity to help him improve *his* communication of *his* ideas to others at school and outside the school.

TEACHING IN
THE MATHEMATICS NONGRADED
LEARNING CENTER

Instruction in the Mathematics Nongraded Learning Center should be planned with experiences which will help each child to understand Mathematics through the application of math skills in the activities of daily living. The child needs to understand spoken and written expressions involving number relationships and mathematical concepts. The child must see the need and the value of this instruction; it must be relevant; there must be a real purpose for each activity.

In order for the instruction in the skills of Mathematics to be interesting and meaningful, individual differences in ability to learn and in previous experience must be considered. A new skill should be built on the development of the skills which precede it. Instruction should proceed from the familiar to the new — from the concrete to the abstract.

GUIDELINES FOR TEACHING MATHEMATICS

The following is a list of some of the guidelines for teachers to consider in planning, conducting, and evaluating the activities in the Mathematics Learning Center:

- Mathematics skills should be organized in sequential order.
- Children's interests and present needs should be considered.
- There should be differentiated activities to provide for individual differences.

- There should be some learning activities in which all children may participate.
- There should be a variety of activities and a variety of materials available.
- Mathematics activities should be relevant to the rest of the school program of instruction.
- There should be many opportunities for meaningful practice to help individuals overcome deficiencies.
- Evaluation of progress must be continuous.

GOALS AND OBJECTIVES

The activities and experiences in the Mathematics Learning Center should be integrated with the total school curriculum as much as possible. The basic objectives of the Mathematics program should be to help each child develop skill in logical reasoning and computation; to develop an understanding of the place of Mathematics in our society; to develop desirable work habits and attitudes from Mathematics; and to develop procedures for solving problems with the use of mathematical knowledge.

Each child must recognize that there is a definite mathematical vocabulary and that success in mastering the vocabulary will contribute to his mathematical competency. The development of this vocabulary is continuous and necessary for effective communication.

In the learning of new ideas, each child should have opportunities to make practical applications. When the child has a problem which is real to him and when he can see the value of an activity in math, then he will acquire the skill as he applies it in solving his problem. When such application is not immediately apparent, there should be a carry-over of the concept to a situation where it can be applied.

Since generalization plays an important role in the learning of Mathematics, each child should be encouraged to generalize. He should be encouraged always to check the validity of his result before he accepts it as being universally true.

Teachers should help each child to recognize the usefulness of estimation as a check on computation and as a practical tool for everyday living. The main purpose of estimating is to help children deal with numbers sensibly.

Abstraction is a recurring theme in Mathematics. As each child's ability dictates, he should progress through the cycle from manipulation of concrete materials, to various levels of abstract symbols, to the concrete realizations and applications of the abstractions.

Since Mathematics is a precise science, it is important that accuracy be considered a requirement in every phase of mathematical learning. The degree of accuracy that can be attained will vary with each child and with each activity.

Logical thinking should be an integral part of all Mathematics. Each child should be encouraged to use logical thinking as a basic tool to solve mathematical problems. The gaining of mathematical concepts should not be limited by textbooks or grade levels. Each child should be afforded opportunities to enrich and extend his mathematical concepts. As his knowledge of Mathematics increases he should be encouraged to investigate topics outside the basic curriculum.

TEACHING TECHNIQUES FOR MATHEMATICS

A sound instructional program for Mathematics should be based on pupils' needs. The teacher should be responsible for knowing just where each pupil is having trouble and for directing specific skills to alleviate the problem.

Sound teaching directs itself toward eliminating one problem at a time. Skills are developed in sequence. Good teaching in Mathematics is sequential and systematic. The activities and experiences in the math center should be selected and organized in a functional manner. The child should see the relevance of each activity. The teacher should provide a wide variety of life-like experiences in which numbers function directly. Mathematics activities will be more worthwhile and meaningful when they are integrated with the activities of daily living.

Much of the scheduling of children for this center should be by instructional groups — that is, eight, ten or fifteen children who are progressing at about the same rate and who have similar needs at the same time. Whenever a child's needs cannot be satisfied through the activities planned for his instructional group, he should be scheduled individually. There will be times when the child could profit from the activities of another group. Flexibility is the rule; make changes whenever and as often as necessary.

The Mathematics Learning Center should provide various types of activities; there should be experiences for large groups, instructional groups, and small groups as well as individualized activities. Children should have many opportunities for one-to-one conferences with an adult, independent study, seminars, specific lessons guided by a teacher, interest group discussions, and large group activities — some with a teacher and others without. Variety is needed.

The activities of the math center should include the following: problem-solving activities such as gathering information from various sources and experimentation with various manipulative materials to reach conclusions in solving a specific math problem; construction experiences such as making bulletin board displays, graphs, diagrams, etc.; creative activities such as inventing new methods or different ways to solve a particular problem or making up problems for others to experiment with; field trips to places such as a bus station to see how timetables are used in scheduling; practice activities such as using the number line to check completed work.

Each activity should be organized so that each child, at his own rate and working with his own goals in mind, can explore, manipulate and discover for himself.

MATERIALS FOR MATHEMATICS

The Mathematics Learning Center should be provided with a variety of materials and equipment which will aid teachers in making discovery the basic process. There needs to be enough variety to provide opportunity for children to have freedom of selection. This will meet individual needs without frustrating the slower child or limiting the faster-moving child.

The center should house several basic series of math textbooks, programmed materials, enrichment books and materials, sets of cubic measurements, perimeter area boards, fraction kits, Cuisenaire rods, fraction wheels, geometric designs, place value charts, metric scales, number lines, rulers, record players, filmstrips, viewers and projectors, tape recorders, thermometers, clocks, barometers, adding machines, cash registers, play money, play store with supplies, etc.

ACTIVITIES IN THE MATHEMATICS LEARNING CENTER

In this center one might see the following activities happening simultaneously: one teacher working with an instructional group on a particular skill which is a common need of all those in this group; another teacher having a one-to-one conference with a child to help him plan his time in this center for the next few days; a group of children buying and selling in a play store; another teacher working with a group involved in a discussion of the different ways they have discovered for solving a particular problem; an aide helping a group organize and make a bulletin board display about a math activity; a child experimenting with the Cuisenaire rods; several children viewing a filmstrip about uses of clocks and timetables; two children helping each other in review and drill work; many children working independently at stations with programmed material; and other children just experimenting at various interest centers.

A child might complete several activities during one visit to this center. He would have the freedom to choose and move from station to station within the center as his needs changed or as he completed an activity. Each day would be different — each activity would be different — but all of these experiences would be meaningful because they would be "real" to each child, rather than just "busy work."

MATHEMATICS SKILLS AND EVALUATIONS

Each child would have his own skill sheet which would be kept accurate and up to date. As he completed a task and/or developed an understanding of the skill, his record sheet would so indicate. Whenever all the skills for a particular level would be checked, the child would be evaluated to see if there were any deficiencies which might require further study prior to moving him on to the next level.

It is suggested that one person be designated to do the evaluations so that she may become the "expert" in performing this very important task. Suggested lists of mathematics skills organized in a series of levels, A through O, as well as the evaluation used for each level, are included on the following pages.

MATHEMATICS — LEVEL A

Name_____

_____ 1. Talks about sets.

_____ 2. Counts to find the number of members in a set (1 through 9).

_____ 3. Compares equivalent sets.

_____ 4. Uses terms *more than, number, less than, next, between, before, after, least.*

_____ 5. Demonstrates that the number tells how many members in a set.

_____ 6. Associates the numerals *1, 2, 3,* etc. through *9* with sets of one, two, three members, etc.

_____ 7. Writes the numerals *0, 1, 2, 3, 4, 5, 6, 7, 8, 9.*

_____ 8. Associates the numeral *0* and the word *zero* with an empty set.

_____ 9. Associates the words *one, two, three* with corresponding numerals and sets.

_____10. Identifies the cent sign (¢).

_____11. Demonstrates the value of a penny and a nickel.

DIRECTIONS FOR MATH   A

Evaluator: Check each child to be sure he does this correctly.

Samples
A. Put your finger on A at the left of the page. Look at the numerals on that line. Take your pencil and put an X on the numeral 1.
B. Put your finger on B. In the row of dots after the B put an X on the set with 3 dots in it.
C. Put your finger on C. In the row of pictures after C put an X on the set with the least in it.

EVALUATION — MATH A

Teacher _____   Name_____

Date _____

Beginning of Evaluation

D. Put an X on the set that has *more than* 5 members.
E. Put an X on the number that tells how many in one of the sets in D.
F. Put an X on the two sets that have the same number of members.
G. Put an X on the number of members shown in the set.
H. Write the *next* number in the blank spaces.
I. Put an X on the correct number as I read — 8 is *less than* which number?
J. I will read you a list of numbers. You put an X on the one that comes *next.* 1, 2, 3, 4
K. Put an X on the number that comes *before* 5.
L. Put an X on the number that comes *after* 7.
M. Put an X on the set which has 4 members.
N. Put an X on the number that tells how many in the set.
O. Put an X on the numeral that tells the number in the set.
P. Write the missing numerals in order.
Q. Put an X on the number that identifies an empty set.
R. Put an X on the one that *does not* belong.
S. Put an X on the one that means 5 ¢.
T. Put an X on the number that tells how many pennies in a nickel.

EVALUATION MATH A

Teacher _____   Pupil's Name _____

Date _____

A, B, C are sample items

A	7	3	2	1
B	..	::.	..	:.:
C	🌲🌲🌲	QQQQ	🛒

Beginning of Evaluation

D	.	.·.·	.·.	:.:
E	4	3	7	9
F	✶✶ ✶✶	o o o	△ △ △ △	▢
G	✶ ✶✶ ✶ ✶✶	5	3	6
H	1, ___, 3, 4, 5, ___, 7, ___, 9
I	4	2	9	7
J	1	6	5	8
K	3	4	8	7
L	2	5	6	8
M	△△	△△ △△△	△△△ △	△
N	QQQQ	Y	4	3
O	.·.·.	4 5 1	..	6 3 2	:.:	7 8 9
P	0, ___, ___, ___, 4, ___, ___, ___, ___, 9
Q	( )	1	0	2
R	⁴△⁴△⁴	4	five	5
S	five	5¢	5	|||||
T	9	4	3	5

MATHEMATICS — LEVEL B

Name_____

_____ 1. Uses ordinal numbers through tenth.

_____ 2. Chooses from among four sets the set having the greatest number of members.

_____ 3. Relates the penny, nickel and dime to what he buys.

_____ 4. Chooses from four numerals the one for the greatest number.

_____ 5. Identifies the number of tens and ones shown by a two-digit numeral.

_____ 6. Identifies the serial order of numerals through 10. (Finds numeral that belongs between two other numerals.)

_____ 7. Compares the value of coins with price tags.

_____ 8. Identifies corresponding geometric shapes.

_____ 9. Estimates length in inches.

_____10. Uses the language of definite and indefinite measurement.

_____11. Demonstrates the concept of one half of an object.

_____12. Tells time to the nearest hour.

_____13. Compares amounts of money (58¢, 47¢, 75¢, 39¢).

_____14. Identifies a set with a corresponding number word.

_____15. Identifies addition and subtraction facts with pictured sets.

_____16. Uses pictured sets to find how much greater one number is than another.

_____17. Identifies true and false number sentences.

DIRECTIONS FOR MATH B EVALUATION

A. By what name are these numbers known?

B. Draw an X on the set having the *greatest* number of members.

C. Draw an X on the set having the *most* money.

D. Draw an X on the numeral showing the *greatest* number.

E. Put an X on the number representing the *greatest* number of 10's in the ten's place.

F. Put an X on the number representing the *greatest* number of 1's in the one's place.

G. Write in the missing numerals.

H. Put an X on the set of coins you would need to pay for something that cost 50¢.

I.   Put an X on the name of the figure.
J.   This sheet of paper is about how long?
K.   Which of these is about a foot long?
L.   Which of these is about 2 feet long?
M.   Put an X on the figure showing ½ shaded.
N.   Put an X on the clock showing 11:00.
O.   Put an X on the number that represents the *most* money.
P.   Put an X on the number word that tells how many in the set.
Q.   Put an X on the number word that tells how many in the set.
R.   A + B = which set?
S.   What process is used in this problem?
T.   How much greater?
U.   Identify the one true number sentence on this line.
V.   Identify the true number sentence.

EVALUATION MATH B

Teacher _____   Pupil's Name _____

                                                      Date _____

A.   third,   fifth,   second,   ninth,   tenth,   first,   sixth,

     fourth,   eighth,   fifth,   seventh

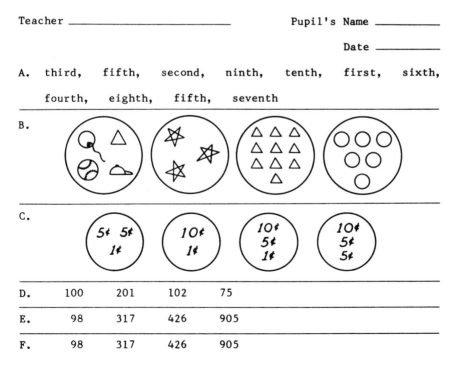

D.   100   201   102   75

E.   98   317   426   905

F.   98   317   426   905

G.   1, 2, ——, 4, 5, ——, ——, ——, ——, 10

H.

I.   [_____]   square,   triangle,   rectangle

J.   20 inches   11 inches   4 inches   7 inches

K.   dollar bill   towel rack   baseball bat   your bed

L.   15"   10"   24"   21"

M.

N.

O.   50¢   47¢   75¢   39¢

P.   50¢   47¢   75¢   39¢

Q.   nine   five   eight   four

R.

S.

T.   3   2   1   4

U.   7 > 4   6 > 7   1 > 3   2 > 2

V.   3 < 2   4 < 5   3 < 1   1 < 0

MATHEMATICS — LEVEL C

Name_____

_____ 1. Uses addition and subtraction facts with sums through 10.

_____ 2. Checks the addition of tens and ones.

_____ 3. Chooses the proper unit of measure (inches, cents, quarts, years).

_____ 4. Identifies a square corner (right angle).

_____ 5. Demonstrates the value of a penny, a nickel, and a dime.

_____ 6. Identifies the serial order of numerals through 100.

_____ 7. Chooses the two-digit numeral that represents a given number of tens and ones.

_____ 8. Uses linear measure for making sensible estimates of height.

_____ 9. Identifies the members in a number sentence family and chooses the one that does not belong.

_____10. Uses subtraction to find the other addend when the sum and one of the addends are known.

_____11. Identifies one half of a set.

_____12. Uses the symbols: $= + - < > \neq$

_____13. Adds and subtracts tens.

_____14. Finds the sum of three numbers to sum of 9.

_____15. Finds the number of 2's, 3's, 4's, and 5's in multiples of these numbers through 10. (Beginning multiplication & division.)

EVALUATION — MATH C

Teacher _____   Name_____

Date _____

1. $8 + 2 =$ ____ $9 +$ ____ $= 10$ $3 -$ ____ $= 3$

$5 - 3 =$ ____   ____ $+ 7 = 9$ $4 +$ ____ $= 5$

$4 - 1 =$ ____   ____ $- 2 = 7$ $7 +$ ____ $= 7$

$7 + 3 =$ ____ $6 -$ ____ $= 5$ $5 + 5 =$ ____

$2 - 1 =$ ____   ____ $+ 0 = 7$ $7 - 7 =$ ____

2. $11 + 13 =$ ____ $\begin{array}{r} 12 \\ + 10 \\ \hline \end{array}$

3. A _____ of milk costs 30 _____.
       (quart-inch-cent)   (years-cents-inches)

    The paper is ten _____ long.
          (years-cents-inches)

    Mary is six _____ old.
        (quarts-inches-years)

4. 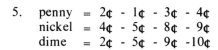 A is called _____.
                    (circle-square-right angle)

5. penny = 2¢ - 1¢ - 3¢ - 4¢
    nickel = 4¢ - 5¢ - 8¢ - 9¢
    dime = 2¢ - 5¢ - 9¢ -10¢

6. Complete this chart.

    | 1 | 2 | 3 | 4 | 5 | 6 | 7 | 8 | 9 |

    | 10 | 11 | 12 | ___ | ___ | ___ | ___ | 17 | 18 | 19 |

    | ___ | ___ | 22 | ___ | 24 | ___ | ___ | ___ | 28 | ___ |

    | 30 | ___ | ___ | ___ | ___ | ___ | ___ | ___ | ___ | ___ |

7. Circle the number that identifies 7 tens in the tens place.
       734   67   371   732

8. How tall do you think you are? _____

9. Circle the item that does not belong in this sentence.
        4 apples and 6 pears and 3 sacks = 10 pieces of fruit.

10. 6 + ___ = 10   10 – 6 = ___

11. 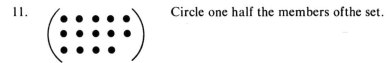 Circle one half the members of the set.

12. Place the symbols in the following problems. $=, \ +, \ -, <, >, \neq$

   4 ☐ 3 = 7   10 ☐ 7

   10 ☐ 2 = 8   7 ☐ 10

   5 + 2 ☐ 7   4 − **3** ☐ 6

13. 20 + 30 = ____   90 − 20 = ____

   80 + 10 = ____   50 − 10 = ____

14. 3 + 3 + 3 = ____   4 + 0 + 5 = ____

                        2 + 1 + 6 = ____

15. 1 2 3 4 5 6 7 8 9 10
    └──┴──┴──┴──┴──┴──┴──┴──┴──┘

   How many 2's in 10? _____

   How many 5's in 10? _____

   How many 3's in 9?   _____

   How many 4's in 8?   _____

   How many 2's in 8?   _____

MATHEMATICS — LEVEL D

Name_____

____ 1. Demonstrates that a set is a group or collection of objects.

____ 2. Demonstrates that a cardinal number tells the number of members in a set.

____ 3. Demonstrates that equivalent sets have the same cardinal number.

____ 4. Demonstrates that an empty set is one which has no members.

____ 5. Demonstrates that the cardinal number of an empty set is zero.

____ 6. Uses the terms greater than and less than.

____ 7. Demonstrates the commutative property of addition. (Two numbers can be added in either order without affecting sum.)

____ 8. Uses number sentences to express subtraction. (7 − 2 = 5)

____ 9. Demonstrates that the sum of any number and zero is that number.

_____ 10. Demonstrates that subtraction is the inverse of addition.

_____ 11. Demonstrates how to count sets of up to 10.

_____ 12. Interprets the concept of place value in two-digit numerals in sequence through 30. (The numeral for ten is "10," meaning 1 ten and 0 ones.)

_____ 13. Demonstrates the order of the counting numbers from 1 through 100.

_____ 14. Counts forward or backward by twos.

_____ 15. Uses number sentences in addition and subtraction to solve simple word problems.

_____ 16. Uses addition and subtraction in problems related to buying.

_____ 17. Interprets decimal place value (relates 2 dimes and 3 pennies to 2 tens and 3 ones).

_____ 18. Demonstrates that cardinal numbers are used to denote "how many."

_____ 19. Reads the ordinal names first through tenth.

DIRECTIONS FOR EVALUATION MATH   D

Instructions for Evaluator

    A.   Have a collection of objects — books, counters, pencils, etc. Have child identify them using the term "set."

        They write on paper what the collection is called.

EVALUATION — MATH D

Teacher _____   Name_____

                                        Date _____

A.

B.   How many members are in each set?

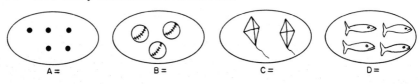

A =   B =   C =   D =

C. Identify the equivalent sets.

    A   B   C   D

D.

                        This set is _____.

E. The number of members in the set in D is: many   few   0   2

F. Use these signs in the following number sentences: $>$ $<$

    10 _____ 7   7 _____ 10

G. $(1 + 2) + 3 = 1 + (3 + 2)$ Draw a line under the statement that is true.

1. $(\square + \triangle) + \bigcirc = \bigcirc + (\triangledown + \triangle)$

2. $(\square + \bigcirc) + \triangle = \bigcirc + (\square + \bigcirc)$

3. $(\square + \bigcirc) + \triangle = \square + (\bigcirc + \triangle)$

4. $(\square + \triangle) + \bigcirc = \triangle + (\bigcirc + \triangle)$

H. $9 - 4 =$ _____

I. $4 + 0 =$ _____ $8 +$ _____ $= 8$

J. If $4 +$ _____ $= 7$ then $7 - 4 =$ _____

K. Identify the numbers of members in each set.

_____   _____   _____   _____

L.   Circle the numeral which tells the number of l's in each number.

22   19   10   28

M. Complete this table from 1 — 100.

1	2	3	4	5	6	7	8	9	10
11				15				19	
21							28		30
									40
									50
									60
				65					70
									80
									90
91									

N.   Count from 12 — 48 by 2's.

     Count back from 68 — 38 by 2's.

O.   Write these stories in number sentences.
     10 fingers; 10 toes.

     How many in all? _____

P.   11 ballons; 3 blew away.

     How many left? _____

Q. If you spent 10 cents for pencils, 5 cents for eraser and 15 cents for paper,

How much did you spend? _____

R. If you had 15 cents and spent 5 cents and then spent 3 cents,

How much would you have left? _____

How much spent? _____

S. .30 + .05 + .03 = _____

How many dimes? _____

How many nickels? _____

How many pennies? _____

T. A. *How many* days in a week? _____

B. *How many* months in a year? _____

C. *How many* fingers have you? _____

D. *How many* toes have you? _____

E. *How many* legs have you? _____

F. *How many* hands have you? _____

U. Arrange in order.

tenth	fifth	_____	_____
second	ninth	_____	_____
first	seventh	_____	_____
eighth	third	_____	_____
fourth	sixth	_____	_____

MATHEMATICS — LEVEL E

Name_____

_____ 1. Associates a two-digit numeral with the number of members in a set.

_____ 2. Interprets price tags in terms of coins to a half dollar.

_____ 3. Interprets the meaning of two-digit numerals (place value).

_____ 4. Uses the pint and the cup as units of measure.

_____ 5. Identifies a line segment.

_____ 6. Identifies a rectangle; square; triangle; and circle.

_____ 7. Chooses from three number sentences the one that is not true.

_____ 8. Finds the sum of two numbers (multiples of ten) (50 and 30).

_____ 9. Demonstrates how many inches make a foot.

_____ 10. Identifies an even number.

_____ 11. Chooses correct operation (addition or subtraction) to solve a problem.

_____ 12. Interprets a calendar date.

_____ 13. Finds the correct amount of change from ten cents.

_____ 14. Demonstrates the value of coins to one dollar.

EVALUATION — MATH E

Teacher _____   Name_____

                                  Date _____

1. • • •   How many members are in this set? _____
    • • •
    • • •
    • • •

2. If you saw a can of soup in the market with this price stamped on it (47¢), what coins would you need to buy it?

_____

3. Circle the correct answer.

   97 means 9 tens and 7 ones   97 means ten tens

          97 means 9 hundred and 7 ones

4. Mary drinks milk from one of the cartons she buys in the cafeteria. Each carton holds a . . . .

   _____ cup   _____ bottle   _____ pint

5. A   B   What name do we give to AB?

   _____ line   _____ line segment   _____ point

6. Match the figures with their proper names.

◯   square

▭   circle

▢   triangle

△   rectangle

7. Circle the one that is *not* true.

    a. $4 + 3 = 3 + 4$ *b.* $10 + 2 - 3 = 7$

                     c. $10 + 2 - 3 = 9$

8. Add the following:

    30         $7 + 10 =$ _____ $40 +$ _____ $= 70$

  $+ 20$ $60 +$ _____ $= 80$ _____ $+ 20 = 40$

9. A foot has how many inches?

    _____ 14   _____ 11   _____ 15   _____ 12

10. What are the following numbers?   2 4 6 8 10 12 14

    _____ odd   _____ even   _____ fractions

11. 12 _____ $3 = 15$ 4 _____ $6 = 10$ 5 _____ $3 = 2$

    9 _____ $2 = 7$ 14 _____ $4 = 18$ 13 _____ $4 = 9$

12   SEPTEMBER 1968

S	M	T	W	T	F	S
1	2	3	4	5	6	7
8	9	10	11	12	13	14
15	16	17	18	19	20	21
22/29	23/30	24	25	26	27	28

This is a calendar for the month of _____ ,
year _____ .
The date today is _____ .
Today is _____ .
(day of week)

13. 10¢ – 5¢ = _____   10¢ – 4¢ = _____

   10¢ – 9¢ = _____   10¢ – 7¢ = _____

14. 10 dimes = _____

   5 nickels = _____

   $1.00 = _____ quarters

   _____ pennies = 1 nickel

   _____ pennies = 1 dime

   _____ pennies = 1 quarter

   _____ pennies = 1 dollar

MATHEMATICS — LEVEL F

Name_____

_____ 1. Uses inches and feet as units of length measure.

_____ 2. Interprets the meaning of numbers represented by three-digit numerals.

_____ 3. Finds the other addend when the sum and one addend are known.

_____ 4. Chooses between addition and subtraction in finding the other number and in finding how many more are needed.

_____ 5. Chooses from four sentences the one that does not belong to a number sentence family.

_____ 6. Compares pints and quarts.

_____ 7. Relates the value of coins to an amount of money.

_____ 8. Uses addition and subtraction language with sums up to 18.

_____ 9. Recognizes a half dozen.

_____10. Interprets a sum of money expressed with the dollar sign and decimal point in terms of the total number of cents.

_____11. Makes comparisons: equality and inequality.

_____12. Relates everyday experiences to telling time. (Ex., chooses clock showing time school begins.)

EVALUATION — LEVEL F

Evaluator:

Each child needs a ruler.

1. Ask child to measure one of the following: evaluator's choice of book, paper, length of room to nearest inch.

EVALUATION — MATH F

Teacher_____   Name_____

Date _____

1.

2. 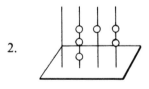 What number is on the abacus? _____

Tell what each number represents . . .   _____ ones

_____ tens

_____ hundreds

3. $15 + \underline{\quad} = 25$

4. $12 \underline{\quad} 3 = 15$ $15 \underline{\quad} 3 = 12$

5. Circle the sentence that does not belong in this sentence family.

    $11 + 3 = 14$ $14 - 3 = 11$ $11 - 14 = 3$
    $3 + 11 = 14$ $14 - 11 = 3$

6. Circle the correct answer.

    a. 2 quarts = 1 pint   *b.* 1 pint = 2 quarts

                    c. 2 pints = 1 quart

7. 4 quarters = _____
                          2 quarters + 5 nickels + 5 pennies = _____
    10 dimes   = _____   4 dimes + 2 nickels + 3 pennies = _____

    5 dimes   = _____

8. $6 + 9$ = _____ $9 +$ _____ $= 18$ $6 +$ _____ $= 13$

    $7 + 8$ = _____ $17 -$ _____ $= 9$ $14 -$ _____ $= 6$

    $15 - 6$ = _____ $13 +$ _____ $= 18$ _____ $- 2 = 16$

9. Give another name for 6.

    ¼ dozen   1 dozen   ½ dozen   2 dozen

10. $1.48 = how many cents? _____

11. Use the sign which makes these sentences true. $> < =$

        6 ? 9 _____
                              $20 + 30 + 9 ? 50 + 9$ _____
        23 ? 35 _____
                              ½ of 40 ? $10 + 10$ _____
        17 ? 17 _____

12. Put correct labels under the clocks.

_____   _____   _____   _____

            lunch time   recess
            school begins   school dismissed

MATHEMATICS — LEVEL G

Name_____

_____ 1. Demonstrates that even numbers are those whole numbers which are multiples of two.

_____ 2. Demonstrates the associative property of addition. $(7+6) + 3 = 16$ or $7 + (6+3) = 16$.

_____ 3. Uses the number line to discover relationships between subtraction facts.

_____ 4. Responds automatically to 95% of the basic addition and subtraction facts.

_____ 5. Reads and writes Roman numerals through XII.

_____ 6. Interprets point, line, and line segment.

_____ 7. Demonstrates how many inches in a foot and a yard and how many feet in a yard.

_____ 8. Tells time to the hour, half-hour, quarter-hour and minute.

_____ 9. Compares quart, pint, and half-pint.

_____ 10. Compares pound and ounces.

_____ 11. Reads a thermometer to nearest 10 degrees above and below zero.

_____ 12. Identifies a thermometer as a vertical number line.

_____ 13. Estimates in addition and subtraction to nearest 10.

_____ 14. Uses addition and subtraction involving zero.

_____ 15. Interprets place value through thousands.

_____ 16. Reads and writes three-place numerals.

_____ 17. Adds and subtracts tens and ones with sums in the hundreds.

_____ 18. Interprets fractional numbers (half, third, fourth).

_____ 19. Measures length to nearest inch, half-inch, and quarter-inch.

_____ 20. Uses addition and subtraction involving renaming ones as tens and ones.

_____ 21. Does column addition where the sum of the ones is in the higher decade.

DIRECTIONS FOR MATH G

Evaluator reads — Children write *answers only.*

4. Addition Facts:

1. 9 + 1	11. 4 + 2	21. 6 + 6	31. 7 + 9
2. 2 + 6	12. 2 + 7	22. 9 + 2	32. 6 + 8
3. 3 + 4	13. 3 + 3	23. 8 + 4	33. 4 + 9
4. 2 + 8	14. 7 + 1	24. 5 + 9	34. 3 + 8
5. 0 + 0	15. 4 + 5	25. 7 + 6	35. 7 + 5
6. 5 + 3	16. 0 + 8	26. 8 + 8	36. 9 + 6
7. 1 + 8	17. 6 + 4	27. 9 + 3	37. 5 + 8
8. 5 + 2	18. 1 + 6	28. 7 + 7	38. 7 + 4
9. 5 + 5	19. 3 + 7	29. 6 + 5	39. 9 + 9
10. 3 + 6	20. 4 + 4	30. 9 + 8	40. 8 + 7

Subtraction Facts:

1. 10 − 1	11. 6 − 2	21. 12 − 6	31. 16 − 7
2. 8 − 6	12. 9 − 7	22. 11 − 2	32. 14 − 6
3. 7 − 4	13. 6 − 3	23. 12 − 8	33. 13 − 4
4. 10 − 8	14. 8 − 1	24. 14 − 5	34. 11 − 3
5. 0 − 0	15. 9 − 5	25. 13 − 7	35. 12 − 7
6. 8 − 3	16. 8 − 8	26. 16 − 8	36. 15 − 9
7. 9 − 8	17. 10 − 4	27. 12 − 9	37. 13 − 5
8. 7 − 8	18. 3 − 0	28. 14 − 7	38. 11 − 7
9. 10 − 5	19. 10 − 7	29. 11 − 6	39. 18 − 9
10. 9 − 6	20. 8 − 4	30. 17 − 9	40. 15 − 8

16. Read to Students

    275,   403,   510

EVALUATION — MATH G

Teacher _____   Name_____

                                  Date _____

1. Circle the even numbers in this list:

    28,   24,   15,   18,   36,   14,   9,   27,   10,   21,   22

An even number can always be divided by what number?_____

2. $(5 + 2) + 3 =$ _____ $+ 2$ $(7 + 3) + 4 =$ _____ $+ 7$

$9 + (2 + 2) = 9 +$ _____

3. Write the number story shown on this number line.

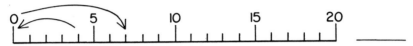

_____

Show this number story on the number line. $8 - 6 = 2$

4. Addition facts

1.	11.	21.	31.
2.	12.	22.	32.
3.	13.	23.	33.
4.	14.	24.	34.
5.	15.	25.	35.
6.	16.	26.	36.
7.	17.	27.	37.
8.	18.	28.	38.
9.	19.	29.	39.
10.	20.	30.	40.

Subtraction facts:

1.	4.	7.	10.
2.	5.	8.	11.
3.	6.	9.	12.

13.	20.	27.	34.
14.	21.	28.	35.
15.	22.	29.	36.
16.	23.	30.	37.
17.	24.	31.	38.
18.	25.	32.	39.
19.	26.	33.	40.

5. Put the numbers 1-12 on the clock face, using Roman numerals.

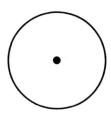

6. Put the names on these illustrations: line   point   line segment

7. Which is the longest?

_____ an inch   _____ a foot   _____ a yard

If a foot is 1/3 of a yard, how many feet are in a yard?

Circle correct answer.   12 inches = yard   foot

36 inches = foot   yard

3 feet   = inch   yard

8. What time is shown on each clock face?

_____   _____   _____   _____

9. Label the drawings as pint, quart, half pint.

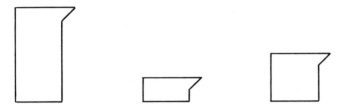

10. A pound contains _____ ounces.   12   15   13   16   8

11. If the temperature was 70° F at 9:00 in the morning and it suddenly
    dropped 10 degrees, what would the temperature be?
    Would it be warmer or colder when the temperature dropped?
    _____

12. Name something you work with often, that if you stood on its end
    would resemble a thermometer.

    _____

    A thermometer looks like a _____ _____ stand-
    ing on its end.

13. Approximate answers to nearest 10.

    a.   c.

    b.   d.

14. *a.* 27 + 30 = _____   *c.* 48 − 30 = _____

    b. 403 + 75 = _____   *d.* 17 − 10 = _____

15. Give the value of each numeral in the following examples:

2705   2_____   8694   8_____

7_____   6_____

0_____   9_____

5_____   4_____

16. Write the numbers I read to you.

_____   _____   _____

Write these numbers in words.

300 _____

275 _____

103 _____

17. $43 + 5 + 30 + 23 = $ _____

$57 + 10 + 25 + 18 = $ _____

$158 - 43 = $ _____

$265 - 65 = $ _____

18. *a.* If you have half an apple, into how many parts has it been divided?_____

b. Three boys each want a part of one candy bar: how much will each receive?_____

c. How much is 1/4 of $1.00?_____

19. Use ruler. How long and how wide is this sheet of paper?

_____ length   _____ width

20.
$$\begin{array}{cccc} 82 & 73 & 94 & 64 \\ +\ 44 & +\ 56 & +\ 31 & +\ 64 \\ \hline \end{array}$$

```
   125          117          123          137
 —  93         —57          —52          —82
 _____       _____       _____       _____


    23           62           16           14
    15           25           27           19
 +  14         + 15         + 10         + 23
 _____       _____       _____       _____
```

MATHEMATICS — LEVEL H

Name_____

_____ 1. Rounds off numbers to the nearest 10.

_____ 2. Estimates sums in addition to nearest hundred.

_____ 3. Estimates answers in subtraction.

_____ 4. Interprets the concept of a plane.

_____ 5. Counts forward and backward by 100's.

_____ 6. Uses the symbols: > (for greater than), < (for less than), and ≠ (for not equal to).

_____ 7. Adds numbers in the hundreds when renaming is necessary.

_____ 8. Adds examples with three addends with renaming of ones as tens and ones; and of tens as hundreds.

_____ 9. Subtracts numbers in the hundreds involving renaming.

_____ 10. Subtracts numbers involving renaming twice.

_____ 11. Demonstrates place value to ten thousands.

_____ 12. Interprets fractional numbers to include fifths and tenths.

_____ 13. Uses the multiplication sign.

_____ 14. Demonstrates the meaning of the words *factor* and *times* in relation to multiplication.

_____ 15. Demonstrates multiplication facts associated with the factor 5.

_____ 16. Finds a factor when the product and other factor are known.

_____ 17. Recognizes that division is the inverse of multiplication.

_____ 18. Demonstrates division facts involving 5.

_____ 19. Identifies problem situation with correct operation. (+, —, ×, ÷)

_____ 20. Divides by 5 when there is a remainder.

DIRECTIONS FOR EVALUATION MATH H

Write answer only.

2. Instructor reads numbers; learners estimate answers to nearest hundred.

    a. 475 + 300 =
    b. 240 + 550 =
    c. 100 + 200 + 360 =

3. Instructor reads . . . .

    a. 500 − 260 =
    b. 150 − 25 =
    c. 800 — 290 =

EVALUATION — MATH H

Teacher_____   Name_____

                                               Date _____

1. Round off these numbers to the nearest 10.

    276_____   62_____   498_____   375_____

2. A.
   B.
   C.

3. A.
   B.
   C.

4. A sheet of paper reminds you of a plane because it:

   _____has edges _____is flat _____is thick

5. What is the pattern?

   A. 1000, 900, _____, _____, _____, _____

      400, _____, _____, 100

   B. 300, 400, _____, _____, _____

6. Use the symbols which make these sentences true. $<$ $>$ $\neq$

      56_____ 62   36 + 42_____ 88

      104_____ 98   103 — 37 _____ 75

7.
$$\begin{array}{r} 258 \\ + 137 \\ \hline \end{array} \qquad \begin{array}{r} 258 \\ + 167 \\ \hline \end{array} \qquad \begin{array}{r} 208 \\ + 187 \\ \hline \end{array}$$

8.
$$\begin{array}{r} 127 \\ 235 \\ + 365 \\ \hline \end{array} \qquad \begin{array}{r} 184 \\ 279 \\ + 326 \\ \hline \end{array} \qquad \begin{array}{r} 129 \\ 108 \\ 215 \\ + 145 \\ \hline \end{array} \qquad \begin{array}{r} 105 \\ 206 \\ 307 \\ + 68 \\ \hline \end{array}$$

9.
$$\begin{array}{r} 682 \\ - 427 \\ \hline \end{array} \qquad \begin{array}{r} 728 \\ - 452 \\ \hline \end{array} \qquad \begin{array}{r} 706 \\ - 524 \\ \hline \end{array}$$

10.
$$\begin{array}{r} 642 \\ - 285 \\ \hline \end{array} \qquad \begin{array}{r} 1354 \\ - 678 \\ \hline \end{array} \qquad \begin{array}{r} 3604 \\ - 538 \\ \hline \end{array}$$

11.   12,345   In this number, 1 represents 1 ten thousand, 2 — 2 thousands. What is another way of saying the value of 12 in this number?

_____

12. $1/2 = 2/4 = 4/8 = 8/16$ etc.

    $1/5 =$ _____ $/10 =$ _____ $/$ _____ $=$ _____ $/$ _____

13. This sign (+) means to add.

    What does this sign tell you to do? ($\times$) _____

14. What is another word for multiply? _____

    What two numbers do we multiply to get 6? _____ _____

    What do you call 2 and 3 in relation to 6? _____

15. Multiply 5 by any uneven number. What do you notice about each answer?

$1 \times 5 =$ _____ $7 \times 5 =$ _____

$3 \times 5 =$ _____ $9 \times 5 =$ _____

$5 \times 5 =$ _____

Now multiply 5 by several even numbers. What do you notice about these answers?

_____

$2 \times 5 =$ _____ $6 \times 5 =$ _____

$4 \times 5 =$ _____ $8 \times 5 =$ _____

16. $4 \times$ _____ $= 8$ _____ $\times 6 = 24$

   $3 \times$ _____ $= 15$ _____ $\times 3 = 24$

17. $6 \times 5 =$ _____ $27 \div 9 =$ _____

   $30 \div 6 =$ _____   _____ $\div 3 = 9$

   $30 \div 5 =$ _____

18. $25 \div 5 =$ _____ $20 \div 4 =$ _____

   $15 \div$ _____ $= 3$ _____ $\div 2 = 5$

19. Put the signs in the following to make them true sentences.

   23 _____ $8 = 15$ 42 _____ $7 = 49$

   35 _____ $7 = 5$ 9 _____ $3 = 27$

20. $27 \div 5 =$ _____ $9 \div 5 =$ _____

   $13 \div 5 =$ _____ $39 \div 5 =$ _____

MATHEMATICS — LEVEL I

Name_____

_____ 1. Interprets the concept of area as the measure of the surface inside a given plane.

_____ 2. Demonstrates multiplication facts involving factor of two.

_____ 3. Uses number line to illustrate understanding of multiplication facts.

_____ 4. Demonstrates division facts with a factor of two.

_____ 5. Divides by two when there is a remainder.

_____ 6. Interprets the role of zero and one in division.

_____ 7. Demonstrates the distributive property of multiplication with respect to addition. $a \times (b+c) = (a \times b) + (a \times c)$.

_____ 8. Multiplies multiples of ten.

_____ 9. Multiplies tens and ones through application of the distributive property.

$$3 \times (20+5) \quad = (3 \times 20) + (3 \times 5)$$
$$= \quad 60 \quad + \quad 15$$
$$= \quad 75$$

_____ 10. Demonstrates the vertical algorism for multiplication.

$$\begin{array}{r} 43 \\ \times\ 2 \\ \hline \end{array} \qquad \begin{array}{r} 43 \\ \times\ 2 \\ \hline \end{array}$$

$2 \times 3 \longrightarrow 6$ OR 86

$2 \times 40 \longrightarrow 80$

$2 \times 43 \longrightarrow 86$

_____ 11. Uses the dollar sign and cents mark in multiplication & division.

_____ 12. Demonstrates multiplication facts with a factor of 3.

_____ 13. Demonstrates division facts with a factor of 3.

_____ 14. Demonstrates that zero divided by any counting number is zero.

_____ 15. Divides multiples of ten.

_____ 16. Demonstrates the conventional algorism for dividing tens and ones.

$$3\ \overline{)\ 69}^{\,23}$$

_____ 17. Multiples with renaming of tens and hundreds.

_____ 18. Demonstrates multiplication facts with a factor of 4.

_____19. Demonstrates division facts with a factor of 4.

_____20. Divides with answers in the tens or hundreds.

_____21. Demonstrates multiplication and division facts with factor of 6.

EVALUATION — MATH I

Teacher_____   Name_____

Date _____

1. The area of a rectangle is 28 inches. Its width is 4 inches.

    How long is it? _____

2. Fill in this table.

X	1	2	3	4	5
1	1	2	3	4	5
2	2	4	6		
3			9		
4				16	
5		10			

3.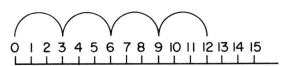

    What multiplication fact is shown on this number line?

    _____

4. $12 \div$ _____ $= 6$ _____ $\div 2 = 5$

    $18 \div 2 =$ _____ $14 \div$ _____ $= 7$

5. $15 \div 2 =$ _____ $13 \div 2 =$ _____

    $9 \div 2 =$ _____ $17 \div 2 =$ _____

6. $15 \div 1 =$ _____ $0 \div 15 =$ _____

$15 \div 0 =$ _____ $\qquad$ $1 \div 15 =$ _____

7. $5 \times (3 + 4) = (5 \times 3) + (5 \times 4)$ Prove that this is true.

_____

8. $40 \times 32 =$ _____ $\qquad$ $30 \times 12 =$ _____

$20 \times 15 =$ _____ $\qquad$ $10 \times 20 =$ _____

9. Is this correct?

$$3 \times 25 = \underline{\qquad}$$
$$3 \times (20 + 5) = \quad (3 \times 20) + (3 \times 5)$$

10.
$$\begin{array}{r} 25 \\ \times\ 3 \\ \hline \end{array} \qquad \begin{array}{r} 37 \\ \times\ 2 \\ \hline \end{array} \qquad \begin{array}{r} 61 \\ \times\ 14 \\ \hline \end{array}$$

11. $2 \times \$1.25 =$ _____ $\qquad$ $\$2.50 \div 5 =$ _____

12. $3 \times 0 =$ _____ $\qquad$ $3 \times 7 =$ _____

13. $18 \div 3 =$ _____ $\qquad$ _____ $\div 3 = 5$

14. $0 \div 4 =$ _____ $\qquad$ $0 \div 2 =$ _____

$0 \div 10 =$ _____ $\qquad$ $0 \div 1 =$ _____

15. $40\overline{)200} \qquad 90\overline{)630} \qquad 70\overline{)280} \qquad 30\overline{)270}$

16. $9\overline{)270} \qquad 6\overline{)420} \qquad 9\overline{)360} \qquad 4\overline{)160}$

17. $6 \times 20 = 6 \times (2 \times 10) \qquad 7 \times 30\ \ = 7 \times$ _____ tens

$= (6 \times 2) \times 10 \qquad\qquad\qquad =$ _____ tens

$=$ _____ $\qquad\qquad\qquad\qquad =$ _____

18. $4 \times$ _____ $= 12$ $4 \times 6 =$ _____ $4 \times$ _____ $= 20$

      _____ $\times 4 = 16$ $4 \times 8 =$ _____ $4 \times$ _____ $= 36$

19. $4 \div$ _____ $= 1$ $8 \div 4 =$ _____ $28 \div$ _____ $= 7$

      _____ $\div 4 = 6$ $16 \div$ _____ $= 4$ _____ $\div 4 = 5$

20. $3 \overline{)147}$ $6 \overline{)126}$ $3 \overline{)279}$

     $4 \overline{)3600}$ $6 \overline{)4806}$ $3 \overline{)1899}$

21.   _____ $\times 3 = 18$ _____ $\div 6 = 7$ _____ $\div 6 = 2$

   $24 \div$ _____ $= 8$ _____ $\times 6 = 36$ $6 \times$ _____ $= 48$

MATHEMATICS — LEVEL J

Name_____

_____ 1. Rounds off numbers to the nearest 10, 100, 1000.

_____ 2. Develops names for fractional numbers greater than 1. $(3/2 = 1\frac{1}{2})$

_____ 3. Measures to the nearest eighth inch.

_____ 4. Demonstrates the commutative and associative properties of multiplication.

      $3 \times 4 = 12$ and $4 \times 3 = 12$. $(3 \times 2) \times 4 = 24$ and $3 \times (2 \times 4) = 24$.

_____ 5. Demonstrates the distributive property of multiplication.

      $3 \times (5+2) = 21$ and $(3 \times 5) + (3 \times 2) = 21$.

_____ 6. Develops algorism for multiplication.

$$
\begin{array}{cc}
123 & 123 \\
\times\ 3 & \times\ 3 \\
\hline
369 \leftarrow (3 \times 3) \longrightarrow 9 & \\
\quad (3 \times 20) \longrightarrow 60 & \\
\quad (3 \times 100) \longrightarrow 300 & \\
\hline
369 &
\end{array}
$$

_____ 7. Writes four related number sentences for multiplication and division for each pair of factors.

_____ 8. Interprets concept of remainder in division.

_____ 9. Divides multiples of ten.

_____ 10. Divides with quotient greater than 10 when divisor is 6.

_____ 11. Interprets the mile as a unit of linear measure.

_____ 12. Relates equivalent measures of time (second, minute, hour, day, week, month, year, decade, century).

_____ 13. Uses time and distance to find speed.

_____ 14. Finds volume in measuring three-dimensional figures (length, width, height).

_____ 15. Uses thermometer to measure temperatures to nearest degree.

_____ 16. Demonstrates multiplication and division facts associated with factor of 7.

EVALUATION — MATH J

Teacher_____   Name_____

Date _____

1. Round or estimate the following to the nearest 10.

   372_____   9_____   46_____   83_____

   To the nearest 100.

   295_____   403_____   720_____   849_____

   To the nearest 1000.

   700_____   1750_____   9200_____   2449_____

2.

$$4/4 + 2/4 = \text{_____}/4 = \text{_____}$$

$$5/5 + 2/5 = \text{_____} = \text{_____}$$

3. Measure book to nearest 1/8 inch. _____

4. _____ × 73 = 73 × 32

    (4 × 7) × 5 = 4 × (7 × _____)

5. 4 × (6 + 2) = (4 × _____) + (4 × 2)

    (9 + 1) × 5 = (5 × _____) + (5 × 1)

6. 432 × 5 = (5 × 400) + (5 × 30) + (5 × 2)

7. Two factors of 20 are 4 and 5.

$$4 \times 5 = \underline{\hspace{1cm}}$$
$$5 \times \underline{\hspace{1cm}} = 20$$
$$20 \div 4 = \underline{\hspace{1cm}}$$
$$\underline{\hspace{1cm}} \div 5 = 4$$

8. 7 $\overline{)25}$ 25 = (_____ × 7) + △

    6 $\overline{)49}$ 53 = (_____ × 6) + △

    5 $\overline{)32}$ 32 = (_____ × 5) + △

9.   30 $\overline{)210}$ 40 $\overline{)2000}$ 30 $\overline{)1800}$ 50 $\overline{)4500}$

10.   6 $\overline{)252}$ 6 $\overline{)174}$ 6 $\overline{)426}$

11. Draw a line under the unit of measure that is the longest.

       yard   mile   inch   foot

12. Match the following:
    a. second   365 days
    b. minute   10 years

c. hour	24 hours
d. day	smallest unit of time
e. week	100 years
f. month	60 seconds
g. year	7 days
h. decade	60 minutes
i. century	30-31 days

13. If it takes 15 minutes to travel 5 miles, how long will it take to travel 60 miles at the same rate of speed?

    hours _____ minutes _____

14. What is the volume of a cube that measures as follows: 5″ long, 3″ high and 4″ wide?

    _____

15. Check temperature in room to nearest degree by thermometer.

    _____

16. $7 \times$ _____ $= 42$ _____ $\times \quad 7 = 35$

    $28 \div$ _____ $= 7$ $49 \div \quad 7 =$ _____

    $14 \div$ _____ $= 2$ $3 \times$ _____ $= 21$

MATHEMATICS — LEVEL K

Name_____

_____ 1. Demonstrates multiplication and division facts associated with factors of 8 and 9.

_____ 2. Finds partial quotients that are multiples of 100.

_____ 3. Relates the properties of a circle to the properties of a sphere.

_____ 4. Identifies radius and diameter.

_____ 5. Identifies a polygon.

_____ 6. Reads and interprets charts.

_____ 7. Demonstrates the operations involved in finding averages.

_____ 8. Uses amount of work and time involved to find rate of work.

_____ 9. Estimates answers in multiplication and division.

_____ 10. Compares fractional numbers (halves, thirds, fourths, sixths, eighths).

_____11. Uses number sentences for addition and subtraction of fractional parts, where the parts are all of the same size.

_____12. Uses division to find number of members in one fractional part of a set.

(¼ of 20 is 5) $4\overline{)20}$ with 5 above

_____13. Interprets place value to millions.

_____14. Multiplies with one factor greater than 100 and product may be greater than 10,000 or in money amounts greater than $100.

_____15. Solves two-step word problems.

_____16. Reads and interprets picture graphs and bar graphs.

_____17. Solves problems where the facts are given and the question must be supplied.

_____18. Finds averages both through use of graphs and through computation.

_____19. Contrasts the centimeter, meter, and kilometer with inch, foot and mile.

_____20. Multiplies with both factors greater than 100.

_____21. Divides by multiples of 10.

Instructions for Evaluator

9. Evaluator read to learners.....

Record your answer, do no pencil figuring.

a. Will 8×23 be closer to 200 or 175?

b. If you divide $5.00 evenly among four people, will each one get *more* or *less than $1.00?*

EVALUATION — MATH K

Teacher _____   Name_____

                                         Date _____

1. *a.* 90 ÷ _____ = 10   *b.* 8 × 6 = _____   *c.* _____ ÷ 7 = 9

d. _____ ÷ 4 = 8   *e.* 40 ÷ _____ = 5   *f.* 9 × 8 = _____

g. 3 × _____ = 27   *h.* 16 ÷ _____ = 2   *i.* 7 × _____ = 56

j. 54 ÷ 9 = _____   *k.* 3 × _____ = 24   *l.* 5 × _____ = 45

2. 102 $\overline{)98750}$ Find a partial quotient.

3. Describe a circle and a sphere.

4. Draw a circle; identify the *radius* and the *diameter*.

5. Identify the polygons by letter. _____

A   B   C   D   E

F   G   H   I   J

6. What does this chart tell you about the sunset?

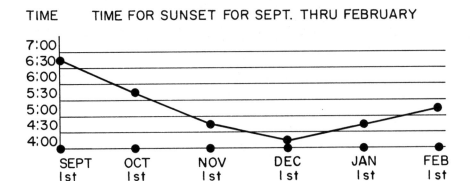

TIME   TIME FOR SUNSET FOR SEPT. THRU FEBRUARY

7. Bowling Scores

Game	Ann	Jane
1	98	103
2	110	111
3	134	110

What is Ann's *average* score? _____

What is Jane's *average* score? _____

8. John could stamp 23 school books with the school name in 20 minutes.

How many books could he stamp in one hour at this rate? _____

9. *a.*

b.

10. *a.* $1/2 = $ _____ $/4 = $ _____ $/8$ *b.* $1/3 = $ _____ $/6$

11. *a.* $1/2 + 1/2 = $ ____   *c.* $3/6 - 2/6 = $ ____   *e.* $1/5 + 1/5 = $ ____

b. $2/4 - 1/4 = $ ____   *d.* $4/8 - 3/8 = $ ____   *f.* $1/3 + 1/3 = $ ____

12. There are 20 chairs in the classroom: $1/4$ of them will be sent to another classroom.

How many chairs will be sent? _____

13. Complete this place value chart, giving the value of each number here.

14. *a.*   269   *b.*   584   *c.* $6.39
        × 75   × 39   × 65

15. There are 12 members of a scout troup selling tickets to a play. If each member sold 15 tickets and each ticket cost $.35 ....

How much was collected for the tickets? _____

16.   ATTENDANCE AT BALL GAMES FOR ONE WEEK

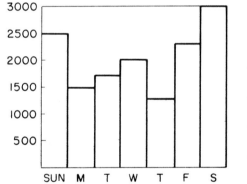

What does the graph show you?

_____

_____

_____

_____

17. The drug store at the Prospect Shopping Center has an average of 537 customers a day. It was open last year 365 days.

How many customers did they have for the year? _____

18. Attendance for ball games in ₌ 16 was:

Sun. — 2600   Wed. — 2000   Sat. — 2998
Mon. — 1505   Thurs.— 1323
Tues. — 1943   Fri. — 2501

What was the average attendance? _____

19. *a.* Approximately how many centimeters are on a foot ruler?

        _____ 30   _____ 20   _____ 12   _____ 15

     b. How many meters in a yard? _____

     c. Is a kilometer more or less than a mile? _____

20.   *a.*   384   *b.*   507   *c.*   813   *d.*   686
            × 536   × 709   × 678   × 427

21. *a.* 60 $\overline{)1288}$ *b.* 30 $\overline{)3728}$ *c.* 50 $\overline{)4168}$

MATHEMATICS — LEVEL L

                               Name _____

_____ 1. Interprets place value through billions.

_____ 2. Interprets Roman numeration system (C = 100; XXX = 30; M = 1000; D = 500; L = 50).

_____ 3. Demonstrates that the sum of two even numbers or two odd numbers is always even.

_____ 4. Demonstrates that the sum of one even number and onè odd number is always odd.

_____ 5. Demonstrates that the product of two even numbers or one odd number and one even number is always even.

_____ 6. Demonstrates that the product of two odd numbers is always an odd number.

_____ 7. Renames numbers to thousands in addition and subtraction.

_____ 8. Approximates numbers to nearest thousand.

_____ 9. Interprets open sentences and solution sets.

_____ 10. Uses dollar sign and cents point in adding numbers representing amounts of money up to hundreds of dollars.

_____ 11. Uses the number line to illustrate addition and subtraction.

_____ 12. Identifies relevant information in word problems.

_____ 13. Uses the distributive property of multiplication to find product up to 999,999.

_____14. Multiplies with two-place numerals as both factors.

_____15. Multiplies with three-place numerals as both factors.

_____16. Uses terms: divisor, dividend and quotient.

_____17. Renames measures in multiplying (ounce, pound, etc.).

_____18. Uses geometric terms: path, point, line, line segment, closed path, ray, angle.

_____19. Interprets perpendicular and parallel lines.

_____20. Divides with non-zero remainders.

_____21. Demonstrates the distributive property of division and the conventional division algorism.

_____22. Divides measures (feet, inches, etc.).

_____23. Compares fractional numbers — recognizes that the fractional number with smallest denominator is the greater number.

EVALUATION — MATH L

Teacher_____   Name_____

Date _____

1. Identify the place value.

2. Write Roman numerals for the following:

1000	=
50	=
100	=
500	=
30	=
40	=
1968	=

3. Determine whether the answer is odd or even; mark O or E.

   a. 15 + 5 =   *f.* 25 + 3   =

   b. 10 + 2 =   *g.* 31 + 1   =

   c. 3 + 1 =   *h.* 16 + 14 =

   d. 2 + 2 =   *i.* 40 + 40 =

   e. 6 + 4 =   *j.* 13 + 3   =

   Fill in the blanks in these statements:

   When two odd numbers are added, they make an _____ number.

   When two even numbers are added, they make an _____ number.

4. Fill in this table . . .   O = odd   E = even

+	E	O
E		
O		

5. Fill in this table . . .   O = odd   E = even

X	E	O
E		
O		

6. Demonstrate this rule with a problem:

   Odd number × odd number = _____ number.

7.   *a.*   3,291   *b.*   42,187   *c.*   7,006   *d.*   8,650
               6,477   77,318   – 5,718   – 8,429
               8,202   479
            + 9,953   + 69,532

8. Approximate numbers to nearest 1,000 (round off to nearest
   1,000) . . . . .

   a. 7,519 _____   *b.* 3,331 _____

   c. 8,712 _____   *d.* 1,720 _____

9. m = 5, n = 14.   Complete the following.

   a. m + n = _____

   b. m is > or < n_____

   c. n − m = _____

10. *a.* $6.78 + $3.45 + $5.89 = _____

    b. $32.79 + $9.24 + $78.47 = _____

11. Write the problems shown on the number lines.

    a.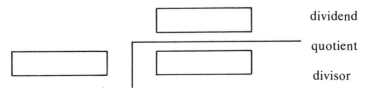

    b.

12. 23 boys and 21 girls decided to have a party Friday at 2:00 p.m. Each child brought 20¢ for refreshments. If the ice cream cost $5.00, how much did they have to spend for the other things they needed for the party?

    _____

13. *a.* 4 × (42 + 8) = 4 × _____

    b. 435 × 571 = _____

    (400 + 30 + 5) × 571 = N

14. 35 × 73   = _____

15. 203 × 162 = _____

16. Label in the correct positions.

    dividend

    quotient

    divisor

17. 8 (8 oz.) packages = _____ pounds

18. *Label*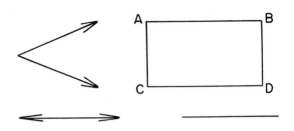

     path
     point
     line
     line segment
     closed path
     ray
     angle

19. *Label*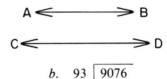

     perpendicular
     parallel

20. *a.* 73 | 1936   *b.* 93 | 9076

21. $365 \div 5 =$ _____

     Circle correct sign. $(300 \div 5) + (60 \div 5) + (5 \div 5) = \neq 73$

22. 15 feet of board divided into 4 sections of equal length . . . . . .

     _____ feet   _____ inches

23. Use correctly. > <

     a. 1/2 _____ 1/3   *c.* 1/4 _____ 1/3

     b. 1/6 _____ 1/8   *d.* 1/5 _____ 1/7

MATHEMATICS — LEVEL M

Name_____

_____ 1. Finds perimeters of all geometric shapes.
_____ 2. Uses units of measure to find area.
_____ 3. Graphs numbered pairs.
_____ 4. Uses bar graphs to compare information.
_____ 5. Uses the terms common factor and greatest common denominator.
_____ 6. Expresses fractional numbers in lowest terms.

_____ 7. Adds and subtracts fractions with like denominators.

_____ 8. Finds the least common denominator.

_____ 9. Adds and subtracts with unlike denominators.

_____10. Divides to find quotients greater than 100, including situations where one of the partial quotients is 0.

_____11. Identifies the characteristics of rectangular prisms, cubes, triangular prisms, pyramids, cylinders, cones and spheres.

_____12. Identifies the characteristics of a place value numeration system having a base other than ten. (Base 6)

_____13. Uses decimal notation to symbolize tenths, hundredths, thousandths.

_____14. Adds and subtracts mixed numbers with like and unlike denominators.

_____15. Adds and subtracts decimals.

_____16. Uses ratio to compare large numbers.

_____17. Multiplies and divides fractional numbers with like and unlike denominators.

EVALUATION — MATH M

Teacher_____   Name_____

Date _____

1. Find the perimeter of the following polygons:

2. Find the areas for figures with the following dimensions:

    a. $7' \times 6''$ _____   c. $20' \times 17'$ _____

    b. $15'' \times 2''$ _____   d. $13'' \times 13''$ _____

3. Identify the numbered parts in the following illustrations.

4. Draw a bar graph to show the following information:

Classroom attendance for week

Mon.	—	33
Tues.	—	30
Wed.	—	31
Thurs.	—	30
Fri.	—	32

5. Identify the factors of 18 and 24. _____

   What numbers are common factors? _____

   What is the greatest common factor? _____

6. Express these fractions in their lowest terms.

   6/12 _____   7/14 _____   2/8 _____ _

   9/12 _____   15/18 _____

7. *a.* $1/6 + 3/6 =$ _____   *c.* $5/10 + 1/10 + 7/10 =$ _____

   b. $2/5 + 4/5 =$ _____   *d.* $7/12 + 9/12 + 1/12 =$ _____

8. *a.* $4/9 - 1/9 =$ _____   *c.* $7/8 - 3/4 =$ _____

   b. $12/17 - 3/17 =$ _____   *d.* $9/16 \div 5/16 =$ _____

9. *a.* $3/4 + 2/3 + 1/3 =$ _____   *c.* $3/4 - 1/3 =$ _____

   b. $1/3 + 1/2 + 3/10 =$ _____   *d.* $3/4 - 3/5 =$ _____

10. *a.* $6 \overline{)2438}$ *b.* $3 \overline{)5307}$ *c.* $8 \overline{)7534}$

11. What is the major difference between plane figures and space figures? Identify these figures.

12. Write the number given below in base 6.

    a. . . . .

    . . . .

    b. Write 30 in base 6.

13. State the value of the numbers to right of decimal point.

    a. 3.4   value of 4 = _____

    b. 6.32   value of 32 = _____

    c. 4.736   value of 736 = _____

14.   *a.* 8 3/7   *b.* 3/4   *c.* 11 3/4   *d.* 7 3/5
              1/4   + 3/4   − 5 1/4   − 5 7/15
          + 9 1/2
          _____   _____   _____   _____

15. *a.* 8.27 + 6.49 + 3.07 + 5.80 = _____

    b. 7.314 − 6.965 = _____

16. For a picnic the buyers allowed 50 pounds of hamburger to 100 people. They figured on 2 hamburgers per person; how much hamburger would be in each burger?

    _____

17. *a.*   1/2 × 1/2 = _____   *c.* 9/5 × 1/2 = _____

    b. 1 7/10 ÷ 3/7 = _____   *d.* 7/8 × _____ = 7

MATHEMATICS — LEVEL N

Name_____

_____ 1. Identifies numeration system in bases other than ten.

_____ 2. Demonstrates multiplying by 10, 100, etc. (moving digits to left).

_____ 3. Uses Roman numerals up to 1000 (M).

_____ 4. Interprets the concept of the union of sets.

_____ 5. Interprets the concept of the intersection of two sets.

_____ 6. Adds columns including up to 5-digit numbers.

_____ 7. Subtracts numbers up to 6-digit numbers.

_____ 8. Uses the terms average, mean, median.

_____ 9. Adds and subtracts fractions and mixed forms.

_____10. Adds and subtracts decimals and whole numbers.

_____11. Uses formulas for finding area and perimeter.

_____12. Uses maps and floor plans to determine rate, distance, time, and related measures.

_____13. Uses bar graphs, broken-line graphs, and pictographs in relation to everyday life.

_____14. Uses the algorism involving whole numbers (long division).

EVALUATION — MATH N

Teacher_____   Name_____

Date _____

EVALUATION — MATH N

Directions for Evaluator:

2.   Read — students record answers without *pencil* figuring.

     a. $10 \times 50 =$ *d.* $100 \times 63 =$

     b. $10 \times 85 =$ *e.* $100 \times 400 =$

     c. $10 \times 92 =$ *f.* $100 \times 5 =$

1. Write the following numbers in base ten.

    a. 100   *b.* 100   *c.* 100
          five   nine   eight

2. Listen to tester.

    a.   *d.*

    b.   *e.*

    c.   *f.*

3. Fill in this Roman numeral table.

	hundreds	*tens*	*ones*
1	C		I
2			
3			
4			
5	D		
6		LX	
7			
8			
9	M		

4. A $(2, 4, 6) \cap$ B $(1, 2, 3, 4)$ =

5.

               6 5 2
               4 3 1
               A   B

Identify the intersection of the two sets.

n A = (6, 4, 5, 3)
n B = (5, 3, 2, 1)

A $\cap$ B = _____

6. *a.* 6,083   *b.* 6,634
       + 1,696   + 5,288

7. *a.* 9,504   *b.* 8,544
       − 7,595   − 1,847

8. These were the test scores in one classroom in math:

15	19	13	10	15
13	18	16	7	
20	18	15	11	
17	21	15	12	

a. What is the average score? _____

b. What is the mean? _____

c. What is the median? _____

9.   a. 3 4/9   b. 2 7/12   c. 5 4/11
               4   2 3/4   1 1/2
      + 7 5/6   + 2 1/5   + 3 5/22

          d. 8 3/11   e. 7 3/5
          − 6 1/3   − 5 7/15

10. a. $4.7 + 6.3 + 9.8 + 0.5 =$ _____

b. $8.27 + 6.49 + 3.07 + 58 =$ _____

c.   85.8   d.   8.375
    − 16.9   − 2.796

11. Complete the tables.

AREA

	Length	Width	Area	
A	4'	5'		Sq. ft.
B		6'	30'	" "
C	10'		40'	" "
D	16'	15'		" "

PERIMETER

	Length	Width	Perimeter
E	10'	12'	
F	15'		70'
G	5'	4'	
H		11'	38'

12. Ruler needed.

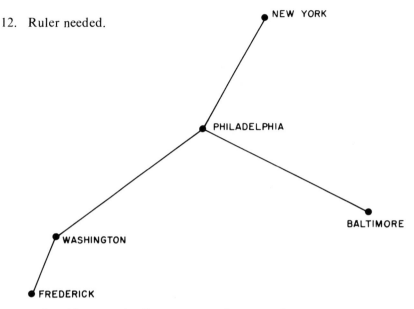

On this map the line segments between the towns represent roads. The map has been drawn to scale. Each segment on the map represents a certain distance on the ground. Measure the segments to the nearest inch to find the answers.

a. The distance from Frederick to Washington is 40 miles. On the map that distance is _____ inches. One inch on the map means _____ miles on the ground.

b. How far is it from New York to Baltimore? _____

c. How far is it from Baltimore to Frederick by way of Philadelphia?

_____

d. If 1 inch on the map means 100 miles on the ground, how far is it from Philadelphia to Frederick? _____

e. If 1 inch on the map means 25 miles on the ground, how far is it from Frederick to New York? _____

f. If the scale is 1 inch to 20 miles, which distance is greater, from Philadelphia to New York, or from Philadelphia to Frederick?

_____

g. If the scale is 1 inch to 40 miles, about how far would it be for a crow to fly from Baltimore to Frederick? _____

13.   TIME SPENT MAKING MODEL

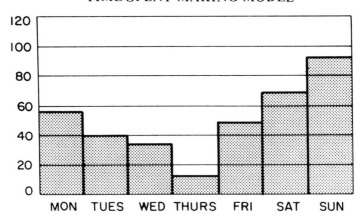

A. This record is for_____days.
B. Average number of minutes per day. _____
C. List days more than average time._____
D. List days less than average time._____

14. Tell what you do to divide this problem. Give the steps.

6 $\overline{\smash{)}\,4356}$

MATHEMATICS — LEVEL O

Name_____

_____ 1. Uses reciprocals in division.
_____ 2. Multiplies fractions and mixed forms.
_____ 3. Divides fractions and mixed forms.
_____ 4. Multiplies and divides decimals.
_____ 5. Applies ratio and proportion in comparing.
_____ 6. Uses terms radius, diameter, and circumference.
_____ 7. Identifies percent as a numeral equivalent to the fraction that shows a denominator of 100.
_____ 8. Finds percent of a number.
_____ 9. Renames percents as fractions.

_____ 10. Uses circle graphs.

_____ 11. Applies percent to practical problems involving commission.

_____ 12. Finds a number when a percent of it is known.

_____ 13. Uses the term rational number as another name for fractional number.

_____ 14. Identifies the properties of a rational number.

_____ 15. Identifies the symbol of the square root $\sqrt{}$

_____ 16. Interprets the meaning of a square root.

_____ 17. Compares positive and negative numbers. (Thermometer and number line).

_____ 18. Adds and subtracts positive and negative numbers.

EVALUATION — MATH O

Teacher_____   Name_____

                                          Date _____

1. Work the problems and circle the reciprocal.

   a. $3/5 \div 2/3 = n$ *b.* $9/16 \div 3/8 = n$

2. *a.* $1/6 \times 1/4 = n$_____   *b.* $7 \times 5/7 = n$_____
3. *a.* $7\ 1/3 \div 2 = n$_____   *b.* $3\ 1/5 \div 2\ 3/4 = n$_____

4. *a.*   What is the ratio of the number of circles
                                      to the number of triangles?

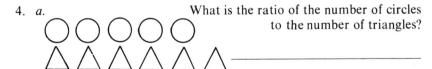

   b. Complete this ratio table.

1	2	3	4	?	?
7	?	21	?	35	42

5. *a.* 45 $\overline{\smash{\big)}\ \$\,21.60}$ *b.* 61 × .93 = N _____

6. Draw a figure and label radius, diameter, circumference.

7. *a.* What is another way of writing 90:100? _____

    b. Is 57% more or less than one half? _____

    c. What percent would one third be? _____

8. 85 children went to the picnic. 15% could not go because they were away on vacation. How many children would have been there if all had been home at the time? _____

9. Complete this table.

fraction	¼	?	?	¾
%	25%	50%	33⅓%	?

10. Draw a circle graph to show the time you spend in school each day.

11. *a.* The school sells cokes for 10¢. They make 10% profit on each coke. How much will they make on 6 dozen cokes? _____

     b. Do you think this is enough commission when they have to furnish ice with the cokes?

     _____   _____
       yes   no

12. The class collected $42.00 for their trip. 25% was used to hire a bus.

   How much money did they have left for food? _____

13. Another name for fraction is:

   whole number   reciprocal   rational   interger

14. *a.* Name all the rational numbers between 1/8 and 1/4.

   _____

   b. 1/2, 2/4, 5/10 are called _____ fractions.

   c. 1/4 + 2/4 + 3/4 = 3/4 + _____ + 2/4

   d. 7/13 − 5/13 = _____

   e. 2/5 × 3/4 = 3/4 × _____

   f. 9/10 − 1/6 = _____

15. If $\sqrt{64}$ = 8, what is $\sqrt{100}$? _____

16. ⌐‾ is the inverse of what operation with which numbers?

   Give example.

17. *a.*

   $$-5\ -4\ -3\ -2\ -1\quad 0\quad 1\quad 2\quad 3\quad 4\quad 5\quad 6\quad 7\quad 8$$

   1 − −3 =   −2 + 4 =

   b. What instrument do we use and hear quoted daily, that uses positive and negative numbers? _____

18. *a.* 6 + 5 = N (   )   *d.* 3 − 5 = N (   )

   b. 5 + 4 = N (   )   *e.* 1 − 4 = N (   )

   c. 5 + 8 = N (   )   *f.* −9 + 8 = N (   )

SUMMARY

The basic objectives of the mathematics program should be to help each child develop skill in logical reasoning and computation; to develop an understanding of the place of Mathematics in our society; to develop desirable work habits and attitudes from Mathematics; and to develop procedures for solving problems with the use of mathematical knowledge.

In addition to the need for understanding spoken and written expressions which involve mathematical concepts and number relationships, children must also acquire facility in dealing with numbers, the decimal system, fundamental processes, measurement, and techniques of problem solving.

Teachers must plan instruction to include real life situations, actual objects, manipulative and pictorial materials to aid children in developing skill in dealing with the abstractions of number relations. Continuous appraisal of each child's progress enables the teacher to ascertain strengths and weaknesses, provide appropriate learning activities, and select the most effective instructional materials. This appraisal of each child's ability and achievement is necessary to provide for individual differences.

6

TEACHING IN THE
SOCIAL STUDIES
NONGRADED LEARNING CENTER

The objective of the activities of the Social Studies Learning Center should be to help children become socialized. The social understandings, skills, and attitudes which the child learns enable him to make a satisfactory transition from the society of the home to that of the school. In the problem-solving activities of the elementary school he learns more about the geography, history, economic conditions, and social problems which concern people in his school and community as well as in other countries. This should help him to understand himself in relation to others and to understand others, to become more skillful in getting along well with people, and to make useful contributions to his home, school and community.

Instructional materials, community resources, activities (individual, committee, and class) and evaluation procedures should be selected and organized so that children may become self-governing and socially conscious members of our democratic society.

PHILOSOPHY OF SOCIAL STUDIES

Well-planned programs should include content, activities, and materials pertaining to human relationships in the home, school, community and other places. Experiences should be provided to help children become effective as individuals and as group members. The here and now should be given first emphasis. In other words — real life situations.

Attention should be given to the major areas of living — that is, transportation, communication, industry, conservation, aesthetic and religious expression. In this way children develop deeper insights into the ways in which man meets the basic needs for food, shelter, clothing and security. Art, literature and music should be brought in as needed to enrich the social learnings.

A main purpose of instruction in social studies is to help children become socialized. Every subject in the curriculum should lead pupils to find themselves as an integral part of a continuous sphere of humanity. We should be as familiar as possible with our neighbors of the world in order to prepare children for the land of tomorrow. We must concentrate on human values and social sciences — the curriculum must be internationally minded.

Teachers must spend more time in helping students understand the political and social problems of the world. Students should be made aware that man is still evolving and that they have a share in making the great expectations of the human race come true.

MAJOR OBJECTIVES OF SOCIAL STUDIES

1. *Develop knowledge and understanding* — Generalizations should be allowed to grow out of a study — not used as a starting point.
2. *Develop attitudes and behavior that make for good citizenship* — Basic factors in developing these attitudes and behavior patterns:
   a. The teacher must exhibit desirable attitudes.
   b. Many opportunities must be provided for children to become active citizens in the school community (class meetings, student council, etc.).
   c. There must be an informational base to attitude and behavior so that the child can respect his own feelings and conduct intellectually.
   d. The child must have a well-adjusted personality. The teacher can contribute to the child's emotional adjustment through her warmth, friendliness, and acceptance.

3. *Develop skill in applying scientific thinking to social problems*
 — Allow children to think and work out problems for themselves.
4. *Develop skill in handling tools of Social Studies —*
 a. Study skills — reading and interpreting books, maps, charts,
 etc.
 b. Judgment skills — critically analyzing news reports, films,
 etc. Distinguishing fact from fiction.
 c. Creative skills — preparing and giving reports, sketching
 maps and diagrams from firsthand experience, interviewing,
 etc.

DEMOCRATIC VALUES IN SOCIAL STUDIES

In order for democratic values to be really learned by children,
they must be lived in all phases of the school program. Following is
a list of some basic democratic values which have implications for
the Social Studies program:

- Government *of* a group is effective only if there is government
 by the group.
- Human well-being, happiness and good will toward others are
 fundamental.
- There is faith in the ability of men to govern themselves wisely.
- Consent of the governed is a basic element in democratic
 procedure.
- Self-direction and self-discipline in accordance with group
 welfare are significant aspects of democratic living.
- Freedom of inquiry with the free play of intelligence upon all
 problems is essential.
- Majority decision with minority protection determines policy.
- Each individual is respected and accorded equal justice and
 equal opportunity.
- Individual responsibility and freedom go hand in hand.

TEACHING FOR CONCEPT DEVELOPMENT

The activities of the Social Studies Learning Center should be
organized around major concepts rather than around isolated facts.

It is these concepts of "big ideas" which are the important content outcomes. A concept is not taught directly, but developed gradually as children add knowledge to these major ideas continuously.

In a first-rate report which would be difficult to augment or improve, Roy A. Price and his associates have presented *Major Concepts for the Social Studies.* The study was done at the Social Studies Curriculum Center, the Maxwell Graduate School of Citizenship and Public Affairs in cooperation with the School of Education, Syracuse University.

Copies of this report may be obtained by writing the Social Studies Curriculum Center, 409 Maxwell Hall, Syracuse University, Syracuse, New York 13210.

ACTIVITIES IN SOCIAL STUDIES

Opportunities should be provided for the development of problem-solving skills, democratic behavior, group action skills, significant concepts and understandings, insight into social functions and processes, skill in the use of materials, and the acquisition of functional information.

Experiences should be within the range of ability of the group, be designed to meet individual differences, and provide opportunity to satisfy social and personal needs of children. Social Studies should provide opportunities for:

- Social interaction and improvement of democratic group processes.
- Creative experiences.
- Developing basic skills (reading, spelling, etc.).

A sound program for Social Studies should have the following characteristics:

- It should be based on the child's background experiences.
- It should provide for creative experiences.
- It should provide activities for individual abilities, needs and interests of children.
- Planning should be for a longer period than a day.
- Experiences should be related to life situations, based on purposes real and important to children.

- It should contribute to the total development of children (tolerance, attitudes, appreciations, etc.).
- Data gathered should be authentic.
- It should place the responsibility of learning on the child.
- It should provide for social interaction.

TEACHING TECHNIQUES FOR SOCIAL STUDIES

How is an activity selected?

According to:
- Children's interest
- Maturity level of the pupils
- Previous studies
- Community needs and resources
- Availability of materials
- Social needs and problems
- Nature of the learning process
- The needs of society
- The needs of children, such as their need to achieve, to manipulate, to construct, to create, to communicate, etc.

How does a teacher build a rich background of experience?

- Investigates community resources.
- Makes a collection of materials pertinent to the activity.
- Does some realistic thinking about objectives.
- Reviews and evaluates materials.
- Outlines the study and activities.
- Compiles annotated bibliography.

How are purposes stated?

- Must be specific according to study.
- Must be consistent with goals of social studies.
- Must lead to improvement of behavior.
- Must be stated according to contribution they can make to the child.

What are some techniques for initiating an activity?

- An arranged environment — display of objects, pictures, and related materials

- Group discussions
- Continuing experience derived from previous study
- Important current events and incidents
- Films, film strips, excursions, field trips, books, etc.
- Resource visitors
- Materials brought in by children

What are the criteria for a good initiation?

- Arouses group interest in central theme or problem.
- Raises questions and issues demanding research.
- Stimulates interest in many kinds of activities.
- Provides common experiences from which to plan.
- Allows for pupil participation.
- Leads to group planning on ways to solve problems.
- Aids pupils in selecting and defining significant problems.
- Employs a variety of materials.

What are the criteria for determining major problems and needs?

- Maturity levels of pupils
- Stimulation of interest of pupils
- Provision for individual differences
- Stimulation of problem solving
- Contribution to purpose of the activity
- Consideration of psychological factors

What are the criteria for selecting culminating activities?

- Will a culminating activity contribute to social learning?
- Is it worth the time, effort and expense?
- Do the children see sense in it?
- Will it be childlike?
- Is it a natural outgrowth of preceding activities?
- Does it suggest a new area of study?
- Will it help to organize the children's thinking?
- Does it provide opportunities to apply key learning?
- Does it stimulate democratic sharing?
- Will each child have an opportunity to participate?
- Will it help to evaluate the achievement of purpose?

What are some types of culminating activities?

- Dramatizations, puppet shows
- Exhibits, demonstrations, murals, etc.
- Excursions
- Discussions and presentations
- Programs: quiz, musical
- Reports
- Art work

How may an activity be evaluated?

- Teacher may observe and record pupil behavior and growth.
- Recordings may be made.
- Charts, graphs, and records may be kept by each child.
- Questionnaires, checklists, inventories may be used.
- Pupils may keep scrapbooks and diaries.
- Case studies and case conferences may be used by teachers.
- Oral discussions may be carried on.
- Anecdotal records may be kept by the teacher.
- Teacher and pupils may plan and utilize tests.

MATERIALS FOR THE SOCIAL STUDIES LEARNING CENTER

There are four types of instructional resources in a balanced Social Studies program:

1. *Community resources* — field trips, resource visitors, persons to interview, field studies, service projects and surveys.
2. *Audio-visual materials* — models, specimens, objects, pictures, maps, globes, charts, graphs, diagrams, films, recordings, etc.
3. *Construction, dramatics and creative expression* through art, music and literature.
4. *Reading materials* — textbooks, trade books, references, magazines, encyclopedias, pamphlets, and newspapers.

BASIC GUIDELINES IN SELECTING MATERIALS

- Materials of instruction should be used to achieve specific purposes.

- The varying levels of concreteness of experience with materials should be recognized. (Consider maturity of pupils.)
- The learning center should be viewed as a laboratory — a planned environment — to stimulate learning.
- The use of materials should be viewed as an integral part of the sequence of experiences in the study.
- Children must be ready for the use of selected instructional materials if maximum learning is to be achieved.
- Maximum learning can be secured only if plans are carefully made for the use of materials.
- New experiences with materials must be related to the child's background of experience in such a way that continuity of learning is assured.
- Equipment and materials used in the program should not draw attention away from significant social learnings.
- Follow-up activities should flow naturally and reasonably out of each experience.
- Arbitrary rules of procedure cannot be followed dogmatically in the utilization of materials. (Don't follow a manual word for word — use it as a guide or for some suggestions. Be creative.)
- Materials should be organized and arranged in a systematic manner if maximum utilization is to be secured.
- A wide variety of materials is needed to promote social learning.
- Materials of instruction should be evaluated before, during and after utilization.

EVALUATING MATERIALS

1. *Purpose* — How is it related to the study and how will it help the pupils? Motivation or culmination?
2. *Variety* — Use different materials for different purposes. (Ex.: Use a model to show how something works.)
3. *Appropriateness to maturity of children* — Children must readily understand material.
4. *Content* — It should be significant to children and authentic.
5. *Physical qualities* — It should possess attractiveness, clearness of presentation.

6. *Time, effort, expense* — Is it valuable enough to the children to merit its selection?

COMMUNITY RESOURCES

The good elementary school is a community school. The community is the setting in which the child lives and learns, in which he develops meanings and concepts essential to an understanding of group living. In this setting he experiences life in a democracy. Experiences in church, stores, theatres, home, neighborhood and school become his background of meanings for study, thought, and expression. The community is the child's laboratory for learning about man's way of living.

The community provides first-hand experiences in the social functions of group living. Some of the richest instructional resources for the Social Studies are found in the local community: field trips, resource visitors, local radio, interviews, etc. Children can cooperate in local projects and become participants in community activities. The child's own daily experiences in the community are a resource which can enrich learnings in the Social Studies.

SAMPLE FIELD TRIP PLAN

Field Trip —

Baltimore Museum of Art
31st & Charles Streets
Baltimore, Maryland

Purpose —

As a culminating activity to bring together the learnings of the group for a definite period — the study of other civilizations and the beginnings of life in America — Egypt, Renaissance, 18th century and Colonial life.

Also to get acquainted with the interior of the museum, what it offers and where to find it.

Preliminary — (prior to trip)
1. Some discussion of well-known artists and other types of creative art in which the culture of the countries may be seen.
2. Bring pencils — wear comfortable shoes, coats.
3. Basic safety rules — also courtesy measures.
4. A brief discussion of what will take place.
5. Make buddy assignments.

Procedure —
1. Arrive at museum
2. Introduce ourselves to receptionist
3. Guide will be assigned — will show us the whole museum with emphasis on the cultures mentioned above.
4. When finished give out guide sheets (see Figure 6-1) and ask children when finished to return to reception desk. If not finished, give specific time to return. Clocks are found throughout museum. (Guide should be given a list of things on guide sheets so he'll be sure to mention all of them.)
5. Groups may go to lecture room for recapitulation if there are any questions. If children have no trouble locating articles and have paid attention to guide, asking questions as they went along, there may be no real need for this activity. (Don't have it if it isn't needed.)

Evaluation —
Evaluate the trip with the children after returning to school and lead into the follow-up activities.

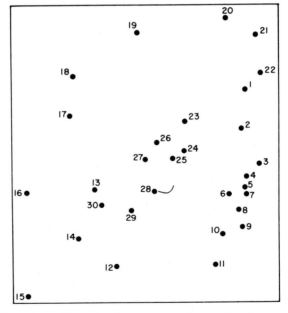

If you can find these things in the museum draw a line between the correct numbers. Follow the dots and see who can finish first!

1-2   an old clock
2-3   Eltonhead Manor
3-4   home of Thomas Stone
4-5   a painting of Mt. Vernon

5-6   two horse paintings
6-7   a pair of silver shoe buckles
7-8   an 18th century piano
8-9   vases from Cyprus
9-10   an illuminated picture
10-11 a warrior's silver helmet
11-12 Renaissance Room
12-13 mosaic of lion & cow
13-14 statue of lion & serpent
14-15 collection of daggers
15-16 Egyptian papyrus
16-17 Egyptian bracelet & ring
17-18 a mummy in the case
18-19 Chinese vases
19-20 a watch & pearls
20-21 a picture of woman & piano
21-22 fans
22-23 painting by Reynolds
23-24 Belgian hippopotamus
24-25 ukelele shaped watch case
25-26 "The Thinker" by Rodin
26-27 Painting by Sir Thomas Lawrence
27-28 Painting by Picasso
28-29 "Titus" by Rembrandt
29-30 Roman sculpture

MAPS AND GLOBES

Globes and maps are used to solve many problems and answer questions that arise in Social Studies. Simple maps are used to show key places in the community and neighborhood. Others are used to show places in the state, nation and world.

Some specific uses of maps and globes are:

- determining distance between various places
- locating historical places
- comparing selected regions, or countries with reference to area, resources, population, surface features, etc.
- identifying and determining relative location of countries, oceans, rivers, continents, etc.
- mapping field trips taken by group
- studying pictorial maps to find out about food, shelter, etc.
- using maps from newspapers to study current events
- using maps in scrapbooks and reports to summarize data

- studying maps to discover relationships and to make inferences
- making outline and relief maps to illustrate significant relationships

Globes and maps should be used as an integral part of the problem-solving process. They can be used to give an overview of places being studied, to stimulate questions about ways of living, products, etc., and to secure information. They also may be used in giving reports and sharing information.

CONSTRUCTION AND PROCESSING MATERIALS

The value of construction lies in its contribution to social learning, not in the products made. Children are eager to make things, to use tools and materials, and to create objects they can use in their activities. Therefore, the child may be motivated to read for details of construction.

Construction for group needs provides opportunities for cooperative planning and evaluation, sharing materials and tools, and accepting responsibility. Construction provides opportunities to improve problem-solving ability. The concreteness of construction gives a realistic approach to solving problems which are meaningful to children.

Children produce and use objects which represent those being studied. Meanings may be clarified, enriched, and deepened. Activities of this type provide opportunities and motivation for the development of language and number skills.

Processing materials in Social Studies is the changing of raw products or semi-processed materials (i.e. yarn) into products that can be used. Some examples are making cottage cheese, processing wool and flax, dyeing fabrics, weaving, making soap, etc.

This kind of activity is valuable because opportunities are provided for engaging in processes related to various studies. Experiences should be realistic, authentic, and involve maximum participation on the part of children.

CREATIVE EXPERIENCES

Dramatic play is informal and creative portrayal of experience without a set pattern or memorization of parts. Play is a natural means of expression for children; it is a fundamental activity of childhood. Through play, children express themselves with wholeheartedness, sincerity, interest, and concentration. It is satisfying to them, and serves both as an outlet for expression and as a means for gaining new experiences.

In dramatic play in the Social Studies individuals identify themselves with persons and objects they have studied in various ways. Children act out what they have experienced.

Play outside of school differs from dramatic play in school. Outside play is without supervision, while at school they are guided to evaluate their play and plan ways of making it more educative. Dramatic play creates new interests, problems and needs. It contributes to the development of democratic group-action skills. In dramatic representation as a group, children must be helpful, cooperative, courteous, sensitive to the needs of others, responsible, and tolerant of each other.

Dramatic play affords opportunities for evaluation of learning. Teachers observe children to gain insight into many aspects of child development and social learning. As children become absorbed in a given situation, they release tensions, feelings, and attitudes toward themselves and others. Language growth and concept development are stimulated. Growth in dramatic play is a steady progression from individual play to large-group play.

Rhythmic expression in the Social Studies is the child's interpretation through bodily movement of impressions secured through his own experiences. It differs from dramatic play in that the emphasis is upon rhythmic bodily movements with musical accompaniment. It is different from creative dance in that the child is interpreting something learned in the Social Studies.

Growth in rhythmic bodily expression progresses from simple interpretation of single episodes to more complete patterns of expression centered in a unifying theme.

EVALUATION IN THE SOCIAL STUDIES

Evaluation is the process of making value judgments. It has no meaning except in relation to goals and purposes. Evaluation in

Social Studies should bring about desirable behavior changes.

Recognizing Democratic Behavior in Children

1. *Responsibility* — Children set up worthy purposes and help to plan ways to achieve them. Group tasks are accepted as willingly as individual jobs. A *we* feeling is exhibited in all group work.

2. *Concern for Others* — Children are sensitive to the needs, problems, and interests of others at home, in school, and in the community.

3. *Open-Mindedness* — Children consider, explore, and use ideas of others as well as their own.

4. *Creativeness* — Children search for and use new ideas to solve problems and to express thoughts growing out of their experiences. They enjoy creative thinking and sharing ideas with others. They evaluate their own work.

5. *Cooperation* — Children share ideas, materials, and pleasures with others. They are eager to work with others and to contribute to group projects.

The appraisal of outcomes of learning experiences in the Social Studies leads to evaluation of the program. Criteria must be adapted and changed to meet specific needs. Evaluation of the Social Studies program should be done continuously.

SUMMARY

In Social Studies instruction teachers should not be so much concerned with which countries are studied or what units have been covered; they should be more concerned about the development of major concepts and desirable patterns of behavior.

The main purpose of the Social Studies is to help children become socialized. Activities and experiences in Social Studies should lead to the development of a positive self-concept in each child.

Children need to become skillful in human relations, economically efficient and accepting of certain civic responsibilities. In order for these values to be really learned by children they must be lived in the Social Studies Center as well as in all phases of the school program.

7

TEACHING IN THE SCIENCE
NONGRADED LEARNING CENTER

The objectives of the activities of the Science Learning Center should be to help children learn some generalizations and science principles which they can use in solving problems of their everyday living. Through these experiences children should develop a scientific attitude and grow in ability to solve problems which are real to them.

Science activities should create in children an interest in and an appreciation for their world. The main purpose of instruction in Science should be to help the child learn the science concepts and principles which he will need in understanding his surroundings.

PHILOSOPHY OF SCIENCE TEACHING

Science is man's action toward understanding, interpreting, changing, and controlling his physical environment. It is basic to the adjustment of the individual. In a sense, Science is an aspect of man himself, a part of living. The Science program:

- is an organized part of the curriculum and is consistent with the philosophy and purposes of the total school program.
- fosters the preservation and advancement of our democracy, which depends to a great extent on the behavior patterns developed in children and youth.
- uses the large patterns of the universe (space, time, energy, change, adaptation, interrelationships, variety, and balance) as

guidelines for instruction in the total Science program.

- includes all pupils and recognizes and nurtures the interests of students possessing aptitudes needed for scientific vocations and avocations.
- adds meaning and effectiveness to every experience and conditions emotional responses.
- develops individuals who are able to reach conclusions based on the use of scientific methods in the study of problems.
- relates to the available natural, cultural, and human resources by using them as content and/or interpreters of content.

GOALS OF SCIENCE TEACHING

The goals of the Science program are:

1. developing and maintaining interest in Science.
2. using methods of Science in solving problems.
3. learning to think scientifically.
4. helping children adjust to change.
5. acquiring a basic knowledge of scientific principles.
6. developing social and moral responsibility for scientific progress.

The achievement of these goals will enable children to:

1. develop an appreciation of our scientific heritage.
2. develop an appreciation of Science in other fields.
3. understand the part technological changes play in changing standards of living.
4. develop an awareness of the varieties of plant and animal life and their relationships to each other through an understanding of the cycles of nature.
5. develop a feeling of appreciation for the things around them.
6. develop awareness of the qualifications required for our future in a scientific world.
7. interpret natural phenomena.
8. identify problems.
9. realize the value of experimentation in solving problems.
10. think logically, plan effectively, and draw valid conclusions

- to question and yet respect authority.
- to suspend judgment until they have adequate information.
- to differentiate between fact and opinion.
- to realize that our concepts of truth change.
- to recognize that nothing can happen without cause and effect.

11. utilize the skills in such areas as reading, outlining, reporting, and arithmetic in organizing and using material effectively.
12. develop basic behavior patterns of responsibleness, resourcefulness, critical-mindedness, open-mindedness.

TEACHING FOR CONCEPT DEVELOPMENT

The activities of the Science Learning Center should be organized around major concepts in each of three areas: Living Things; the Earth and the Universe; Materials, Energy and Change. It is these concepts or "big ideas" which are the important content outcomes. A concept is not taught directly, but develops gradually as children add knowledge to these major ideas continuously.

Pupils should be guided in their exploration of the world of *Living Things* with emphasis on a different aspect of the topic at each level of understanding. Students become aware of the different kinds of living things in their environment and discover the conditions necessary to keep them alive. Characteristics of various plants and animals then become the center of discovery and interest. The concepts of continuous growth and change and adaptation to environment are developed. This is followed by a more thorough study of the life processes and the interrelationships which exist among living things and their environment. The development of these concepts should enable each child to interpret intelligently what he sees going on in the world of living things about him.

Concepts in the Area of Living Things

1. Plants and animals are living things.
2. All living things have certain characteristics in common.
3. Certain conditions are necessary for life.

4. Plants and animals differ in observable characteristics.
5. Plants and animals reproduce their own kind.
6. Plants and animals are constantly changing.
7. Conditions in habitats vary.
8. Living things are adapted to their environment.
9. Living things are interdependent.
10. Cells are the basic units of living matter.
11. There is an interchange of matter and energy between living things and their environment.
12. There is balance in nature.

Pupils explore and observe to become familiar with the earth and sky in their study of *the Earth and the Universe.* Emphasis is placed on the variety of land and water forms and on objects in the day and night sky. Important effects of air, water, and sun on our earth are explored. Pupils continue their studies to become better acquainted with the characteristics of the earth on which they live and with the characteristics of the solar system. They learn about the interrelationships which exist among bodies in our solar system. An appreciation and understanding of man's never-ending attempt to learn about his universe and what lies beyond it in space is of vital importance to today's children.

Concepts in the Area of the Earth and the Universe

1. Land and water forms vary.
2. Weather changes.
3. The day sky and the night sky change.
4. There are regular, predictable movements of the earth.
5. The sun is a source of light and heat.
6. A cycle of evaporation and condensation keeps the water of the earth in constant circulation.
7. The earth's surface is constantly changing.
8. The sun is the center of a huge system of heavenly bodies that revolve around it.
9. The universe is very large.
10. Everything in the universe is in motion.
11. The universe is constantly changing.
12. Universal gravitation and inertial motion govern the relations of all celestial bodies.
13. Changes in the earth's atmosphere affect the weather.

In their study of *Materials, Energy and Change* children have many opportunities to experiment. They learn to identify the properties of materials with which they have come in contact. Pupils engage in activities which will help them understand something of the composition of matter, the forms in which it exists, and how matter changes. Through their work with the various kinds of energy (sound, magnetism, electricity, heat, etc.), pupils begin to develop some ideas of what energy is and how it can be controlled and used.

Concepts in the Area of Materials, Energy and Change

1. Materials have properties by which they can be identified.
2. Materials exist as solids, liquids, and gases.
3. Matter can be changed by energy.
4. Matter is composed of small particles.
5. Energy is required to set an object in motion.
6. Objects in motion continue to move until some force stops them.
7. Things can be made to move more easily.
8. Magnets produce forces.
9. Simple machines make work easier by transferring a force.
10. Energy manifests itself in different ways (forms).
11. Under ordinary conditions matter and energy can be changed, but can neither be created nor destroyed.
12. With extraordinary (uncommon) methods, matter can be destroyed to release energy.
13. The sum total of matter-energy is conserved.

The learner is encouraged to look upon Science as methods of investigating and as knowledge of our environment gained by using these methods. Attitudes favorable to continuous learning are fostered, and the techniques for acquiring new knowledge are developed. These attitudes and skills should enable children to function effectively in a changing world.

SUGGESTED PROBLEMS FOR STUDY

Following is a list of suggested problems which could be used to develop the concepts listed in the three major areas previously described:

Living Things

1. What living things are in our environment?
2. What do living things need to stay alive?
3. How do plants differ?
4. How do animals differ?
5. How do living things change?
6. How are plants and animals adapted to live in their environment?
7. How do life processes relate living things to their environment?
8. What can we learn about ourselves?

The Earth and the Universe

1. What do we see on the earth and in the sky around us?
2. How does the sun affect the earth?
3. How does water get into and out of the air?
4. What are the characteristics of the shape and surface of the earth?
5. What is our Solar System like?
6. How does the earth's surface change?
7. What makes the different kinds of weather?
8. How is weather forecast?
9. What do we know about space and how do we learn about it?

Materials, Energy and Change

1. What kinds of materials are around us?
2. How do forces move things?
3. What are magnets and how are they used?
4. What can we learn about sound?
5. How do we use simple machines?
6. What is the composition of matter and how is it changed?
7. How can energy be controlled and used?

TEACHING TECHNIQUES FOR SCIENCE

The wide variation of pupils' abilities, interests and needs makes it impossible to plan a course of study or units which can be used for all. However, the following guidelines of sample units of study should provide ideas from which teachers can tailor activities to meet the needs of a particular child or group of children.

In examining the format of these samples one should note that the scope gives a concise picture of the breadth and limitations of the unit. The suggested "sub-problems" are in "teacher language." In planning with pupils, teachers will need to determine how much pupils already know, and provide sufficient background so that they can participate in raising their own questions.

With each sample are listed the major content understandings, which are necessary to a solution of the problem. These, too, are in teacher language. Children should arrive at these or similar understandings through the many activities in which they engage.

The format for activities includes two major divisions: The *Notes for the Teacher* section contains some suitable, or representative, ideas that may be used as model or sample activities. No attempt was made to provide all the desirable activities which could be used in solving a given problem. Pupils and teachers are urged to add others. Notes are also included for the teacher explaining procedures and giving background content information.

Encouraging Learning Through Discovery includes ways of helping students learn through the discovery approach by using the processes of Science. The most important thing to remember in teaching Science is to have children doing things. Don't do things for them; guide them to do the experiments and activities for themselves. Keep the children active.

LIVING THINGS — How can we find out what animals need
to live and grow?

Understandings
> Animals need certain things in order to stay alive.
>> Food, water and air are factors affecting animal growth.
>> Some need parental care for a period of time.
> When animals are kept in the classroom, homes and care must be provided.
>> The home should be like the natural place where the animal lives.
>> Regular provisions should be made for supplying its common needs.
>> Animals that are useful to man should be returned to their natural habitat after they have been studied.

Notes for the Teacher

In helping pupils learn through observation, it is important for them to observe a variety of animals before arriving at a conclusion — pets, birds, fish, turtles, grasshoppers, worms, caterpillars, etc.

When animals are brought into the classroom, it is important that pupils plan carefully to take care of all their needs.

Help pupils learn in a variety of ways — visit a zoo, visit a pet shop, visit a farm, look at films, and read books.

Encouraging Learning Through Discovery

Discuss some things that we can do to learn what animals need to grow.

Make a bird feeder and bird bath and watch the birds use these.

What other things can we do to help us discover what animals need?

LIVING THINGS — How are human beings like other living things? How are human beings unique?

Understandings

Human beings are living organisms, having the same needs and performing the same processes as other living things.

The human body, like all living things, is made of structural units called cells.

Human beings, like other living things, can move, take in and use food and oxygen, give off waste materials, grow, reproduce, and react to their surroundings.

All living things need food, oxygen, and water to stay alive.

Living things require energy to carry on the life processes.

Human beings are unique in some ways.

The human brain is larger in proportion to body size than that of any other mammal.

Man possesses a brain with which he is able to reason and to remember.

Man's nature includes strong feelings (emotions).

Man's opposable thumb enables him to be a tool-using animal.

Man's nerve cells are more highly developed than those in other animals.

Man has a more erect form of locomotion.

Man has an erect posture.

Notes for the Teacher

An interesting way to develop an appreciation of the human body would be to have pupils discuss the statement, "The body is a wonderful machine," and compare the human body to a machine.

To develop an appreciation of the many things the human body can do, have pupils keep a record of all the things their bodies have done during the period of a day. Pupils should have a better understanding of how the body does these things when the study is completed.

A chart comparing things which humans can do with what other living things (plants and animals) can do could stimulate good discussion.

It would be interesting to note which of the functions the human body performs automatically (without conscious effort of the individual) and which ones require thought.

Help pupils further their understanding of the concept that all living things are divided into two groups, plants and animals, and that human beings have many of the same characteristics and needs as other living things.

Help pupils direct their thinking towards the unique characteristics of humans.

Have pupils tape their thumbs to the first finger of their hands and then try to pick up a pencil. What other things couldn't we do if we didn't have an opposable thumb?

Plan a class discussion to arouse interest in and heighten awareness of the uniqueness of humans in the area of feelings and attitudes. From consideration of their own feelings in specific situations, pupils may come to understand that:

Our feelings are always with us.

They affect our actions and the way our body functions.

They continue to develop as we mature.

We can learn to recognize our feelings and handle them.

Encouraging Learning Through Discovery

How are our bodies like machines?

How are they different from non-living machines?

What are some of the things our bodies have done today? Can other living things do these same things?

Are there things that we, human beings, can do that other living things cannot do?

What significance does this have?
What responsibilities does this place on us?

THE EARTH AND THE UNIVERSE — What conditions of the atmosphere affect the weather?

Understandings
> We live at the bottom of a vast ocean of air (atmosphere) which completely envelopes the earth.
> Weather is the condition of the air.
> The temperature and movement of the air cause changes in the weather.
>> (A change in one usually produces a change in the other.)
> The condition of moisture in the air affects the weather.
>> (Clouds, fog, sleet, snow, rain, and hail are formed from water vapor in the air.)
> Pressure of the air affects the weather.
>> (Air is densest near the earth's surface because of the earth's gravity and the resulting weight of more air above it.)

Notes for the Teacher
> Have a class discussion centered around readily observable and other familiar weather phenomena — clouds, fog, rain, hail, variable temperatures, etc.
> How are all these weather conditions concerned with air?
> As a result of this discussion, pupils' interest and curiosity should be aroused enough to warrant an investigation of cloud formation and causes of precipitation.
> Encourage investigation into less familiar conditions of the atmosphere, such as temperature and pressure.
>> (Thermometers should be used to measure air temperature. A simple barometer can be used to help develop an understanding that air exerts pressure.)

Encouraging Learning Through Discovery
> What do we know about weather from our own observations?
> How can we find out and what can we learn about the conditions of the atmosphere that affect the weather?
> How can we summarize our learnings?

THE EARTH AND THE UNIVERSE — Why does man want to explore and travel in space?

Understandings

Man considers the unknowns of outer space a challenge.

Man's desire for greater understanding of his environment causes him to explore space continuously.

Exploration of space requires the involvement of many areas of Science.

Notes for the Teacher

The pupil's own ideas as to why man is eager to explore space can be a starting point for this investigation. Have pupils present their ideas. List the ideas on the chalkboard. Discuss them. Evaluate them. Which ideas seem most likely? Which ones least likely?

Guide pupils to see that different areas of man's knowledge could benefit from his space explorations.

This is a good opportunity to help pupils discover in space exploration as in all science investigation that seeking answers raises more questions to be answered and presents new opportunities for research and investigation.

The space exploration program requires background and insight into many areas of Science as well as application of the fundamental processes of Science.

Help pupils identify and investigate some of the many areas of concern such as mathematics, electronics, chemistry, biology, and astronomy.

Encouraging Learning Through Discovery

What reasons can be found for man's desire to travel in space?

How is space exploration comparable to other explorations made by man throughout history? How is it different?

What other major science explorations can be identified as current interests to man?

What areas of Science and technology are involved in an exploration of space?

MATERIALS, ENERGY AND CHANGE — How are materials grouped?

Understandings

Materials exist as solids, liquids, and gases.

Notes for the Teacher

Help children discover some characteristics of the three forms of matter. Select a group of solids that differ in appearance. Put them together on a table. Ask pupils what these things have in common. Do the same thing with a variety of liquids, again asking how they are alike. Blow up a balloon and put it next to an "empty" glass. What do these two things have in common? Help pupils summarize, from their own observations, the characteristics of each of the three forms of matter.

Pupils should be guided to see that each thing in the first group has its own particular shape which it retains. These materials are called *solids*.

The thing that is alike about the materials in the second group is that a container is needed to hold each of them. They are called *liquids*. They take the shape of the container but do not necessarily fill it.

Air in the balloon and in the glass takes the shape of its container and also fills it completely. Air is a *gas*.

Encouraging Learning Through Discovery

What can we learn about each form of matter?

Can we organize other materials in these three classifications?

What can we learn about water?

MATERIALS FOR THE SCIENCE LEARNING CENTER

This center should house all of the basal textbooks of many science series as well as paper backs, magazines, and other periodicals. There should be a variety of materials and equipment: tape recorders, record players, microscopes, micro-projectors, binoculars, gauges of various sizes, aquariums, celestial globes, animal cages, weather instruments, filmstrips, film loops, projectors, SRA Labs, etc.

The following is a suggested list of materials which could be included in the Science Center. This list is in no way considered complete; there is a limitless amount of different science materials available and nothing should be excluded.

I would suggest that at least five textbooks of each level from each of the following series be used:

Allyn & Bacon, *Exploring Science*
American Book Company, *ABC Science Series*
Ginn & Company, *Science Today and Tomorrow*
Harcourt, Brace and World, *Concepts in Science*
Harper and Row, *Today's Basic Science*
D. C. Heath and Company, *Heath Science Series*
J. P. Lippincott Company, *Science For Modern Living*
Lyons and Carnahan, *The Developmental Science Series*
Macmillan Company, *The Macmillan Science Series*
Rand McNally Company, *Junior Scientist Series*
Scott-Foresman Company, *Basic Science Program*
L. W. Singer Company, *Singer Science Series*
Winston, *Understanding Science Series*

I would suggest the following material as being desirable for the Science Center:

Benefit Press — 1900 N. Narragansett Ave., Chicago, Ill.
   "What Is It?" — Science Shelves (No. 1, Cat. No. 396001)
Coronet Instructional Films
   2 each: Heart, Cells, Solar System books
Nelson F. Deal — 140 N. Artizan St., Williamsport, Md. 21795
   3-D Plastic Study Charts: 8 1/2" x 12" are suggested for use
      by students; a larger one is available for teacher use.
   Human Body In . . .
      Skeleton, Circulatory System, Digestive System,
      Olfactory
   General Botany
      Root and Stem, Flowers, Fruits and Seeds, Leaves
   Lunar Map
   Vertebrates
      Mammals, Reptiles, Amphibians, Birds, Fish
   Invertebrates
      Insects
   3-D Earth Map
      Surface Earth, North America, Europe, South
      America
   3-D Study Charts
      General Zoology (Vertebrates)
      General Zoology (Invertebrates)
      Human Body
      General Botany
Ginn & Company — 72 Fifth Avenue, New York, N.Y. 10011
   "Finding Out Classroom Library"
Graflex, Inc., Programmed Learning Dept. 10924, Box 101,
   Rochester, N.Y.

"Life Cycle of Insects," No. 67008
"An Introduction to Entomology," No. 67002
"Using Cloud Appearance to Predict the Weather," No. 67012

Harcourt, Brace & World, 757 Third Avenue, New York, N.Y.
"100 Invitations to Investigate"
1 each level — Classroom Laboratory

Learning Materials, Inc. — 425 N. Michigan Avenue, Chicago, Ill.
"The Green Plant"

Macalester Scientific Company, 186 Third Avenue, Waltham, Mass. 02154
AAAS — "A Process Approach"

Charles E. Merrill Books, Inc. — 1300 Alum Creek Drive, Columbus, Ohio 43216
1 set Science Skill Cards, No. 1500

National Audubon Society — 1130 Fifth Avenue, New York, N.Y. 10028
Ecology Chart
Wildflower Chart
Leaves of Common Trees — Simple
Leaves of Common Trees — Compound
Evergreen Leaves
Forest Food Chain
Miniature Chart Food Chain
Set of 70 Nature Bulletins

Science Materials Center — 59 Fourth Avenue, New York, N.Y.
Maximum-minimum thermometer
Wall barometer
Hygrometer
Demonstration barometer
Large 9" barometer
Large 9" hygrometer
Large 9" thermometer
Rain gauge
Weather vane
Magnets
Hand lenses
Tape measures
Bar magnets
Celestial globes
1 Elementary Planetarium
Hot plate
Convection box

Prisms
100 Petri dishes
Flasks (250 Ml, 500 Ml, 1000Ml)
Funnels
Test tubes
6 Aquariums (10 gal.)
Aquarium starter sets
Butterfly nets
Terrariums
Animal cages
Record (songs of insects)
1 Solar system
1 Climaterius

Science Research Associates, Inc., 259 East Erie Street, Chicago, Ill. 60611
Earth's Atmosphere Lab, No. 3-7001
Weather & Climate Lab, No. 3-7021
Solar System Lab, No. 3-7100
SRA Inquiry Development: Physical Science 26 film loops, teacher's experiment kit, student experiment kit and idea book.
Graph & Picture Study Skills Kit, No. 3-4000

Webster Division, McGraw-Hill Book Co., Manchester Road, Manchester, Mo. 63011
ESS "Small Things" (Study of Cells)
"Kitchen Physics" — ESS (Study of properties of liquids)
ESS "Gases and Airs" (Air: expansion, displacement, etc.)
ESS "Bones" (Familiarity with several animal skeletons)
ESS "Batteries and Bulbs" (Properties of electricity and magnetism)

World Book — Harcourt, Brace & World
30 World Book "Space" reprints
Gyroscopes
Radiometers
Map of solar system, planets and outer space
Gasoline and diesel engine models
Jet engine model
Steam turbine model
Steam engine model
Atomic electric power plant kit
Relief globes (hydrographic & physiographic)
30″ Contoured relief globe

OTHER RESOURCES

There are many other resources, in addition to those suggested, which are available to the teacher and which will contribute to a good Science program.

The Earth and Space Science Laboratory: For example, in Frederick County, Maryland, the elementary Science program includes instruction in the Earth and Space Science Laboratory, located at the South Frederick Elementary School. The main teaching instrument in the laboratory is a Spitz A_3P projector. This modern instrument is capable of projecting points of light on the 24-foot overhead dome, thereby reproducing visible objects of the night sky. In addition to showing the apparent motion of the sun and visible planets and satellites, moving objects often obscured in our night sky may be stopped for study. Star color, moon phases, and arrangements of stars in constellations may be clearly presented in the planetarium. Many auxiliary devices such as a sound system, slide projectors, and instruments useful in studying distances or special relationships are included in the planetarium chamber.

Besides the planetarium, the Earth and Space Science Laboratory contains a classroom, exhibit area, ambulatory (a walkway flanked by murals of sky phenomena at the entrance to the planetarium chamber), and two science workrooms equipped for experimentation in astronomy and geology.

The units of study in the area of the Earth and the Universe will be enhanced by the use of the Earth and Space Science Laboratory. This kind of facility is available to many school systems. The use of these facilities makes it possible for classes to have common experiences of seeing phenomena of earth and space relations which cannot be duplicated in the regular classroom or learning center.

The Frederick County Outdoor School: Some objectives of the curriculum can be achieved more effectively outside the formal classroom in an outdoor situation. As a part of the outdoor education program of Frederick County, each sixth year group and a teacher spend one week at the Outdoor School, Camp Greentop, located in Catoctin Mountain Park. The program of the Outdoor School is closely correlated with regular classroom instruction. During the week that pupils spend at the Outdoor School, classroom learnings become more meaningful through the application of knowledge to practical outdoor situations. What precedes and follows the outdoor experience takes on new meaning.

The following activities are representative of the type of science experiences which are possible at the Outdoor School:

Weather — Predicting weather by considering air temperature, humidity, wind speed and direction, sky cover, precipitation, and barometric pressure which are recorded daily; making comparisons by temperature studies in open fields, dense woods, stream areas; making comparisons of morning and evening temperature changes and temperature variations due to altitude.

Rocks and Minerals — Observing and testing hardness, color, cleavage of rocks; studying geological formations; observing the effect of weathering, plant growth, and water on the earth's surface.

Plant Life — Studying plant succession, lichens, mosses, weed plants, and trees; climax stand of timber; learning classification and use of plants; noting relationships of plants to animals and animals to plants; observing adaptation of plants to their surroundings; recognizing need for planting trees.

Animal Life — Exploring the natural habitat of squirrel, rabbit, muskrat; learning about the homes, habits, and foods of local reptiles (poisonous and non-poisonous snakes, turtles), deer, fish, and insects; collecting insects; studying animal tracks.

Astronomy — Viewing planet(s) and moon through a telescope; observing fall or spring constellations and the ecliptic (sun and star time).

Mathematics — Using a compass and topographic maps, estimating heights and distances.

There are many opportunities for outdoor education. Teachers and children at all levels find the school grounds, park, farm, wood lot, and lakes valuable resources for enhancing science instruction.

Resource People: The planned Science program involves many areas of science, presenting opportunities for using resource people from the community who can make some specific contribution. They can enrich and broaden the Science program with their specific knowledges. There are times when resource people could make a contribution in the classroom and other times when it might be best for the children to visit them.

EVALUATION IN SCIENCE

Evaluation in Science, as in every other area, should be done continuously. The suggestions for evaluating pupil growth are not meant to be used as the only means of evaluation. If we hope to develop in children a scientific attitude, we must also develop ways of evaluating for this objective. Much of the school's evaluation is in terms of factual information learned. This evaluation is necessary, but it is also necessary that evaluation be made of the pupil's progress toward behavioral goals. This is a much more difficult task. Some desired behavioral outcomes are described and some ways of evaluating in terms of these objectives are suggested. Pupils should be involved in setting up behavioral as well as content goals and in evaluating their progress toward them. The evaluation suggestions which follow may serve as examples for teachers to use in constructing other methods for measuring growth and development of skills and attitudes.

EVALUATION
What living things are in our environment?
What do living things need to stay alive?

Desired Behavioral Outcomes	Ways of Evaluating
Do pupils show evidence of an understanding of the characteristics of living things?	Have pupils test their learnings by classifying a collection of things not previously discussed as living or non-living.
Do pupils show evidence of developing and maintaining an interest in living things? What instances give evidence that the pupils' attitudes and behavior towards living things are changing?	Keep anecdotal records of resourcefulness and initiative displayed by individuals, such as: What pupils report. What you see pupils do. What they tell about the things they bring in. (Ex.: How they care for and play with a pet.) What pupils do to care for living things in the classroom and elsewhere.
Do pupils use a variety of resources in order to find solutions to a problem? Are pupils becoming more aware of the cause and effect relationships between living things and their environment?	Observe resources used by pupils as they work toward solution of problems.
Do pupils show an increased continued interest in what living things need to stay alive?	Keep an anecdotal record of materials contributed voluntarily by pupils.
Are pupils acquiring a science vocabulary?	Note the use made of Science-related words with precise meanings as reports are given and discussions held.

EVALUATION What makes the different kinds of weather and how is it forecast?	
Desired Behavioral Outcomes	Ways of Evaluating
Do pupils show a greater ability to observe conditions which will help them forecast the weather?	Note whether pupils observe and talk about changing weather conditions. Do they make proper use of cloud charts, weather maps, and other similar information?
Do pupils have a greater understanding and appreciation of the work of the weather bureau and how it affects the lives of people?	Ask pupils to imagine themselves in a situation where no weather reports were available for a one-week period. Their lives would have to go on as usual during that week. Have them write a brief description of the effects which a lack of weather reports might have on their lives.
Have pupils gained in their ability to do independent research? Do they suggest additional problems and seek solutions for them?	Keep records of individual methods which pupils use to gather information, such as resource persons, references, films, field trips, etc. The teacher should consider: Does the pupil identify new problems of interest? Are the problems clearly stated and defined? Does he propose hypotheses? Does he seek factual evidence? Is he willing to change his opinions when facts do not support them?

Does pupils' interest extend beyond actual classroom activities?	Allow time for pupils to bring in and share any new knowledge, experiences, and interests which they have on the subject of weather. Make note of any special interest area you may hear in extemporaneous discussions outside of class time and use these ideas for enrichment activities.
Are pupils able to discern differences between fact and superstition in weather sayings?	Discuss various sayings and folklore about the weather. Are any of these sayings supported by scientific facts?

SUMMARY

In the Science instruction field teachers should not be so much concerned about which units are studied or what material is covered; they should be more concerned about the development of major concepts and desirable patterns of behavior.

Children come to school eager to learn about themselves, other living things and their various surroundings and how all of these affect their way of life. Children need to be active; the Science Center should buzz with activity; children should be "doing" things.

If teachers will recognize children's interests, encourage and help them to find answers for themselves, not only will their present interests continue but in addition, new ones will spring up. Teachers in the Science Learning Center must continuously strive to provide activities which will help children become more interested in and appreciative of their world. By so doing teachers will better meet the needs of individuals.

8

UTILIZING THE
INSTRUCTIONAL MATERIALS CENTER

The Instructional Materials Center with all its available resources, human and material, should exist to further the objectives of the school. A nongraded school should have an Instructional Materials Center that operates as a teaching service. All persons in the school team, adults and children, should find it easy and satisfying to use the center. The center should be directed, organized, staffed, and housed so that the needs of the school and the neighborhood that it serves will be met effectively.

PHILOSOPHY OF THE INSTRUCTIONAL
MATERIALS CENTER

Where the real purpose of the Instructional Materials Center is understood by everyone in the school, the center becomes an essential element in operating a good instructional program in every learning center, in extra-curricular activities and in the homes of the community.

The school library is incorporated as an integral part of the IMC. The basic function of the IMC is not just the selection, management and circulation of books, but rather it is one of assistance in helping the teaching team to perform the instructional process most effectively through making all kinds of books and materials and equipment available.

The IMC is the heart of the instructional program, as most

school activities become associated with the library. A good center includes not only reading but many other activities as well. It is the main instructional aids center including audio-visual materials and equipment.

The services of the Instructional Materials Center should:

- teach children to use basic library procedures and skills.
- suggest teaching aids appropriate for the instructional program.
- provide leadership in selecting, organizing, housing, and using library materials.
- help children in assigned and recreational reading.
- provide reading materials for individual children.
- prepare and distribute book lists, filmstrip guides, etc.
- provide information concerning library materials available from other sources.
- make arrangements to borrow materials from other sources.

A good elementary school must have an IMC that operates as a center of teaching services and instructional materials. It must be the heart of the instructional program. Everyone in the school (teachers, students, parents and the community) should find it easy and satisfying to use the services provided.

PERSONNEL FOR THE INSTRUCTIONAL MATERIALS CENTER

IMC personnel must be completely involved in cooperative working relationships with all other members of the instructional staff in planning how the center is to be used. The coordinator of the center should have at least one full-time assistant. The center staff must be well acquainted with the nature and purposes of modern education and must share in all professional in-service activities. As accepted members of the teaching staff, they need to be involved in curriculum planning to be able to participate intelligently in classroom activities and to be able to conduct their service so that it is an integral part of the school environment for learning.

Materials implement, enrich and support our educational programs. A wide range of materials on all levels of difficulty, presenting many points of view and varied understandings and backgrounds, is necessary to meet the needs of individual students.

The selection of appropriate instructional materials to be used by pupils is a major responsibility of the coordinator of the IMC.

SELECTION OF MATERIALS

In selecting materials the following guidelines should be kept in mind:

- Materials should be accurate and interesting in content.
- The concepts treated must be within the understanding of students who will use the materials.
- The content must be significant.
- Materials should enrich the life of the individual by widening boundaries of thought, presenting an honest picture of life, developing an understanding of people, and fostering positive values.
- Reference, social studies, and science materials must be kept up-to-date.
- The treatment of social studies materials must emphasize desirable social attitudes and ideas and loyalty to the principles of American democracy.
- The reading level of books, including vocabulary, sentence structure and paragraph structure, must be suitable for pupils who will use the materials.
- Books must be written in a style that is appealing, readable, clear and dynamic.
- Factual books should have an appropriate number and variety of illustrative materials, including pictures, maps, charts, graphs and diagrams, which contribute to the understanding of the basic relationships and which clarify and enrich the content.
- Factual books should include appropriate tables of contents, indexes and appendixes.
- The authors of books should have had training and experience in the fields about which they write.
- The format of books should be of a high standard. Type should be clear, legible, and large enough to be read without eyestrain; paper of durable weight; illustrations clear and well spaced. The books should be appropriately bound.
- Reputable, unbiased, professionally prepared selection tools should be used.
- Gifts must conform to the criteria for materials selection if they are to be accepted.

SERVICES PROVIDED BY THE IMC PERSONNEL

To Pupils:

1. Help establish a climate of learning by attitude and personality.

2. Cooperate with the teachers in teaching basic skills required to use any library with ease and assurance, preferably in relation to work going on in other centers in the school, as needs arise.

3. Assume responsibility for library orientation of new students to the school library.

4. Make the library an inviting and stimulating source of learning and enjoyment.

5. Make a special effort to provide materials for both the superior and the below-average student, giving attention to their reading level and conceptual development.

6. Promote democratic practices through:
   a. sharing the responsibility for a fair distribution of materials and their prompt return.
   b. appealing to students' consideration for others to maintain a reasonably quiet atmosphere.
   c. inviting students to submit requests for books to be ordered.

7. Take an active and personal interest in reading needs and habits and encourage reading on a progressive scale of maturity, but avoid denying the student his own final choice.

8. Help to locate material for individual reference problems after the student has made a reasonable effort.

9. Provide informal reading guidance and the opportunity to share and enjoy books.

10. Impress upon teachers the need of encouraging children to use the IMC.

To Teachers:

1. Become acquainted with the curriculum and the way each teacher interprets it.

2. Meet with new teachers to introduce them to the resources and services.

3. Provide service generously with creative imagination and understanding, knowledge, approachability and adaptability.

4. Share responsibility for book selection policy and its implementation.

5. Seek cooperation in the purchase of library materials.

6. Seek cooperation in discarding materials.

7. Personally acquaint teachers individually with books, pamphlets, magazine articles, filmstrips and records which they would enjoy or appreciate knowing about.

8. Share with teachers the indexes and published bibliographies of instructional materials and assist teachers in selecting printed and audio-visual materials for classroom planning.

9. Inform teachers of new equipment and materials that have been acquired.

10. Cooperate with teachers in providing materials for bulletin boards and other displays.

11. Advertise materials through the use of displays, exhibits, bulletin boards, talks.

12. Provide for housing and circulating appropriate professional materials.

13. Encourage teachers to discuss curriculum materials needed.

14. Assist in planning for effective use of instructional materials and equipment.

15. Provide bibliographies related to curriculum areas.

16. Provide a well-balanced collection of various types of materials, printed and non-printed, selected in terms of the curriculum and the needs of the pupils.

17. Organize materials in such a way that the result will be a smoothly running, efficient and functional IMC that contributes to the achievement of the objectives of the school.

18. Plan with the teacher for a circulation of materials for which there might be a great demand. Provide reserve collections if needed.

19. Encourage the teaching of specific library skills at different levels, based on needs.

20. Inform teachers systematically of student interests and needs as observed in the use of instructional materials.

21. Work closely with the school administrator to provide the program best suited to the purposes of the school and keep the administrator informed about accomplishments and needs of the program.

The newer methods of teaching make greater demands on the IMC than have ever been made before. The trend toward using more and varied materials is unmistakable. The various plans of supervised study and the long-range assignments demand increased reading materials. Schools using the newer curriculum approaches find it necessary to make increased demands upon the IMC. They further need to have much library material on hand in the classrooms and learning centers where the activities are taking place. Provision must be made to check out many books and much material for long periods of time. Some of the material could remain in the learning centers as a permanent collection. Other materials should be transferred from the IMC for the period needed and replaced at the close of the study.

In addition to the plan of lending materials to the learning centers for the duration of a particular study or activity, other methods of making material available are: have children leave the learning centers and come to the IMC individually during class time; have classes come to the IMC during class time; place books on reserve shelves. The most satisfactory methods appear to be those of developing libraries in each learning center and of sending pertinent materials as needed. This type of service demands a coordinator who keeps in touch with the work of the centers. He must be familiar with modern methods of teaching and should not be unduly concerned if a few books disappear when they are freely available in the learning centers and in the open stacks in the library.

An Instructional Materials Center cannot be wholly successful unless the teachers are aware of its resources, see the possibilities of its use as an instructional aid, and encourage its use through the procedures they employ in their teaching. The use of the IMC by the teachers themselves is one of the best ways of encouraging children to use it.

PHYSICAL ARRANGEMENTS

The facility for the Instructional Materials Center should be as large as possible and preferably in the center of the building to provide easy access from all other areas. There needs to be adequate shelving for a large collection of library books, small seminar rooms, a "living room" corner to encourage recreational reading, places for individuals and small groups to use audio-visuals, filing space for pictures and other instructional materials, typing and duplicating facilities, work space for groups and individuals, display areas for creative work and racks for displaying paper backs. See Figure 8-1 for an example of a "living room" corner.

Figure 8-1

In Figure 8-2 you can see several students using filmstrips and viewers. In Figure 8-3 the coordinator of the Instructional Materials Center is helping several students learn to use the card catalog to locate books in which they are interested.

Figure 8-2

Figure 8-3

Pictured in Figure 8-4 is a small group of students in a seminar room discussing several readings which they have done on a particular subject. In Figure 8-5 the assistant in the IMC is helping a child in finding some specific information in a reference book.

Figure 8-4

Figure 8-5

MATERIALS AND EQUIPMENT

The following is a suggested list of materials and equipment which could be included in the Instructional Materials Center:
- Large collection of library books
- Large collection of paper backs
- Work space for showing a film or examining a map as well as reading a periodical or book
- Conference space for groups to meet
- Files of textbooks, manuals, workbooks and teaching guides
- Typing and mimeographing facilities
- Filmstrips
- Recordings (tape and disc)
- Slides and transparencies
- Maps, charts, globes, graphs
- Single concept films (film loops)
- Slide projector
- Single concept projector
- 8mm Sound projector
- 8mm Super 8 movie camera
- Polaroid camera
- Tape recorders
- Filmstrip previewers
- Opaque projector
- Headphone sets
- Filmstrip projectors
- 16mm Movie sound projectors
- Overhead projectors
- Record players

SCHEDULING

Because of the complexity of the Instructional Materials Center, the variety of materials housed there, and the constant need for children and adults to visit, I would suggest that there be no regularly scheduled time for class groups. Rather, I'd suggest that anyone and everyone be afforded the opportunity to visit the IMC whenever and as often and for as long as there is a need.

SUMMARY

As one recognizes unique needs in a nongraded program, he should plan ways to meet them. The Instructional Materials Center is not just a reading room or a place to sign out books. It is the heart of the instructional program.

The main function of the IMC is not just the selection, management and circulation of books, but rather it is to help the teaching teams perform the educational process most effectively through making all kinds of books and instructional materials and equipment available.

It was emphasized in this chapter that the personnel of the IMC must be completely involved in cooperative working relationships with all other members of the teaching staff in planning how to use this center most effectively, and what materials are necessary to meet the needs of the children, teachers, and members of the community.

9

SPECIAL TEACHERS, TEACHER AIDES, VOLUNTEERS, STUDENT AIDES IN THE NONGRADED SCHOOL

UTILIZING AUXILIARY PERSONNEL

In a nongraded program, where each child is being instructed on his own achievement level, the auxiliary personnel (teacher aides and volunteers) help teachers individualize instruction and help fulfill the goals established for the program.

I'd like to point out that neither aides nor volunteers are prerequisites to nongrading. A nongraded program can be successful without these assistants, but they put the "icing on the cake." The more adults sharing the work load, the more success you can have in meeting the unique needs of individuals.

By using these additional auxiliary personnel we are able to free the teachers of many time-consuming tasks and clerical jobs, and thus provide them more opportunities for individualizing instruction.

Although aides are paid and volunteers are not, both may perform the same tasks. However, since the volunteer is not paid, she is not required to accept the obligations and discipline that are required of aides or teachers. She is seldom on the job every day; several half-days is the usual schedule.

Some of the duties of aides and volunteers include taking attendance and keeping routine records; collecting funds for various purposes and keeping accounts; correcting objective tests and making up lists and charts for the teachers; supervising playground activities; supervising the lunchroom; helping younger children with their clothing; supervising lavatory periods; checking out library books; caring for and operating audio-visual equipment; typing and duplicating; answering the telephone; running errands to the office; filing work in children's folders; making arrangements for field trips; assisting children in construction of bulletin boards, etc.; supervising quiet activities and rest periods; listening to and sharing thoughts as they are dictated by children; and supervising a classroom while a teacher is attending an in-service meeting.

Although many of these tasks are closely related to the teaching function, aides and volunteers are not replacing the teacher. A teacher has the responsibility of analyzing the instructional needs of her students, or prescribing the course of study that will best meet those needs, and of utilizing the resources of an aide or volunteer in helping to carry out her plans.

In summary, the philosophy on the use of an aide or volunteer should be that her activities be restricted only by her own personal limitations in any duty that the regular classroom teachers assign to her.

Teachers are grateful for that part of the aide program which frees them from playground duty, lunchroom duty, staying with children for the late afternoon buses, supervising bathroom periods, and the like. All of these jobs are necessary, but should not have to be done by professional teachers. By freeing teachers from such work, we enable our professional staff to use that time to plan and prepare their classroom work and coach individual children. The teachers feel better about their profession; their status is raised in the eyes of parents and pupils; and they have an opportunity for an occasional break. Therefore, their attitudes and morale are better and they have more energy for classroom work.

In a nongraded program, where each child is being instructed on his own achievement level, the clerical aides help teachers individualize instruction by preparing all kinds of drill and practice exercises on different levels of difficulty. These are given to individual children according to their achievement levels. This enables pupils to work independently while the teacher circulates throughout the room giving individual help, or calling together small groups for further instruction. Thus, while most of the students are working independently, the teacher has time to confer with individuals who are having difficulty as well as those working on special projects and depth studies.

The presence of other adults in the classroom encourages teachers to examine their own attitudes, personality traits, and classroom standards and procedures. We have found that many teachers are now making more detailed and better lesson plans because they have help in providing and carrying out more worthwhile learning activities for individual children.

The opportunity to employ teacher aides encouraged us to consider whether or not aides could be trained to be more than just clerks. After much debate we concluded that a properly trained aide or volunteer should be able to perform limited instructional tasks under the general guidance and supervision of a classroom teacher. Since we believe that the primary purpose of teacher aides is to increase the effectiveness of the teacher in the classroom, it therefore seems logical that aides should help carry out teacher-made plans for large- and small-group instruction.

Certainly a teacher aide can read a story to a group of children, or repeat teacher directions, or help a child locate information in the school materials center, or listen to a child read orally, or even help several children in drill exercises.

Some educators feel that if teacher aides spend part of their time in assisting with the teaching function, they are infringing upon the prerogatives of the regular teaching staff. A matter of great concern here is that aides can be employed for less money and could eventually replace the teacher.

My answer to this concern is that if a teacher does not have the ability to analyze the instructional needs of her students, prescribe the course of study that will best meet their needs, and utilize the resources of an aide in helping to carry out her plans, then maybe the teacher should be replaced.

Because of the uniqueness of each nongraded, team-teaching program, I feel that on-the-job training by the staff is the best method of getting the most help from aides. We conducted an orientation program in which teachers learned what the aides could do, and how (with the use of aides) they could improve instruction. We explored the various abilities and skills of the aides; taught them how to use the office machines, files, and audio-visual equipment and materials; assigned them to suitable work; supervised and evaluated their work.

In a graded school, many children who are achieving below grade level in the skill subjects receive little or no help because teachers are too busy with others and may regard those who can't read as hopeless cases. However, in a nongraded program aides were trained to work with these individuals, using flash cards, writing experience stories with small groups, and continuing phonics drills on a one-to-one basis. One-to-one mathematics drills can be successfully conducted by some aides.

Pictured in Figure 9-1 is an aide as she uses flash cards with several students. This warm-up exercise is done each day before regular reading class with the teacher. These are review words; this activity helps the children recall difficult words and sets the stage for a directed reading lesson with the teacher. Meanwhile, the teacher is working with another group while this group is getting warmed up.

Figure 9-1

In Figure 9-2 the aide is typing an original experience story for a child as it is dictated. The child will take her own typed story back to her desk and paste it into her own book of stories.

Figure 9-2

An aide in the classroom gives opportunity for two groups to have adult leadership. (See Figure 9-3.)

Figure 9-3

Figure 9-4 illustrates the one-to-one relationship; one adult to one student.

Figure 9-4

In Figure 9-5 the aide is supervising a group of children in the hall as they are sharing library stories. Each child is trying to summarize his book in one sentence.

Figure 9-5

The aide in Figure 9-6 is working with a small group on a mathematics drill exercise which has previously been taught by the teacher.

Figure 9-6

In Figure 9-7 the aide is signing out library books to children before school.

Figure 9-7

The aide in Figure 9-8 is duplicating classroom work to help the teacher provide independent study activities.

Figure 9-8

Using plans made by classroom teachers, aides help children who have been absent with back assignments. Also, they can see that preassigned work is carried out and assist individuals who are having difficulty when the classroom teacher has been excused for in-service meetings.

SCHEDULING AUXILIARY PERSONNEL

In our nongraded program, the use of teacher aides and volunteers is closely tied to individualization of instruction. We gave these auxiliary people on-the-job training for each task they were asked to assume.

Because of the variety of talent and ability, we felt we could best utilize our aides by pooling their time rather than by assigning them to a specific teacher all day.

Teachers were asked to request an aide for a particular time for a particular job. From these requests a weekly schedule was set up. If an aide was requested to type experience stories from 9:00 a.m. to 10:00 a.m., then Mrs. E was assigned. If an aide was needed to help get the children washed up for lunch, then Mrs. G could do the job.

Some aide time was unscheduled to provide flexibility so that a teacher could request additional help for an extra task not included on the schedule. This might be a one-time-only task. At the beginning of each term each teacher submitted her request for aide time on a weekly basis. For example, see Figure 9-9.

REQUEST FOR AIDE TIME

TEACHER: ___Mrs. X_____ R O O M
                                                         _21___

MONDAY   9:00 — 10:15   Type Experience Stories
TUESDAY
WEDNESDAY   9:00 — 10:15   Type Experience Stories
THURSDAY
FRIDAY   9:00 — 10:15   Type Experience Stories

COMMENTS: __I would like someone to help__
__get the children ready for lunch at 11:00 a.m.__
__everyday__

Figure 9-9

After all these requests were summarized in the office, a weekly schedule was made for aides. In order to honor the requests made by Mrs. X above, each Monday, Wednesday and Friday, an aide who types, Mrs. E, was assigned to Room 21 from 9:00 a.m. to 10:15 a.m. Another aide, Mrs. G, who does not type, was assigned to Room 21 every day at 11:00 a.m. to help the children wash up for lunch. The sample schedule in Figure 9-10 shows how the aides were scheduled for every Friday. Similar schedules were made for each day of the week.

Every Friday Aide E spends from 9:00 a.m. to 10:15 a.m. in Room 21 typing experience stories as they are dictated by individual children. At 10:15 a.m. she goes outside for playground duty during the morning recess. After a short break she goes to Room 4 where she assists the teacher by checking arithmetic papers and helping children with assigned individual work. At 11:45 a.m. she goes to the cafeteria for lunchroom duty. Since she is unscheduled for the afternoon, she goes to the office to type and duplicate classroom work for teachers. Occasionally she is assigned to a class for a special project or as extra help for a teacher not scheduled to have aide assistance at that time.

| **FRIDAY** | | | | | | | | |
AIDE	9:00	10:00	11:00	12:00	1:00	2:00	3:00	3:30
A	R18		P R16	NHD	R10	NHD R15		
B	SPG	R6	LD		P UN	SHD R6		
C	R17		P R18	LD	SHD R18	R5		
D	UN		R22	LD SHD	R3	P R13		
E	R21		P R4	LD UN				
F	R2		P	LD NHD	UN			
G	R1		NHD R21	LD P	UN			
H	R3		R16	LD UN R8		P R8		
I	Attendance		UN	LD	Attendance	UN		
J	UN		LD	P NHD UN	R7	R12 R7		
K	SPG	UN R8		P	R4	R12		
L	R14		SHD R11	LD	UN			

KEY TO AIDE SCHEDULES

NHD — North Hall Duty
SHD — South Hall Duty
LD — Lunchroom Duty
P   — Playground Duty
UN — Unscheduled Time to Provide the Flexibility
SPG — Special Group Instruction
R18 — Assigned to Room 18

Figure 9-10

Through this type of scheduling the teachers know which aide they will have on which day, at what time, and for what task. They also know that they can get additional help by requesting it through the office. By pooling aide time in this manner we feel we are getting the most help from our teacher aides and volunteers.

AUXILIARY PERSONNEL IN LEARNING CENTERS

In the Learning Center approach, which is a consistent variation of the basic nongraded philosophic tenets, a center is an actual geographic location or section of the school which houses all the materials, books and equipment for a particular discipline.

Since each center is planned for, organized, and operated by a disciplinary teaching team, I would suggest that teacher aides and volunteers be assigned to a particular center. They, too, could become better acquainted with the materials of one discipline, and thus be more able to assist children in the activities of the center. The duties and responsibilities of the aides and volunteers in each center would be defined and coordinated by the teaching team of each center.

EVALUATION OF AUXILIARY PERSONNEL

The primary reason for employing aides and using volunteers in a nongraded program is to give additional help to teachers so that they will do more individualized teaching. This also provides more opportunities for individuals to have success with learning.

Teacher aides have provided much opportunity for teachers to work with smaller groups, knowing that the other part of the class is being supervised and directed properly.

The aides have allowed teachers to become more closely related by taking over bus duties and lunchroom duties which in turn has permitted teachers time to sit down together in an informal situation.

Children enjoy opportunities for more association with adults. They see aides and volunteers as friendly people who want to help. One of our aides takes pride in telling about the worst discipline problem in the school and how this ten-year-old boy comes to see her during her free time. The improvement in his attitude and behavior seems to stem from the realization that this aide really cares about what happens to him.

Aides helping in the classroom have made a great difference in the learning situation for each child. We have noticed the following changes in our pupils:

- a more positive self-concept.
- a feeling of being successful in some way.
- an improved attitude toward authority figures.
- improved social behavior in work and play.
- more respect for the care of property.
- greater group acceptance.
- increased school attendance.
- a greater sense of responsibility and pride.
- a more relaxed attitude toward adult visitors in the school.

THE ROLE OF SPECIAL TEACHERS

Fulfillment of the goals of a nongraded program depends greatly upon the effective utilization of special teachers. Through cooperative planning, specialists not only give instruction in their area of major interest but also enrich the overall program.

Each child is naturally creative. Through creating he expresses himself and finds release from inner tensions. The special subjects provide much opportunity for developing this creativity. In addition to individual attention to specific needs, these areas involve group activities where the individual alone is inadequate. Although each player plays and each singer sings, it is not a band or chorus until it is the group acting as one. A mural is painted by many and each must work individually, but all must work in harmony toward a common goal under a common leadership.

THE ART CENTER

Art is a vital part of any nongraded program of education because we are trying to provide for the needs of children. An art program should be designed to fit each student's needs and provide for independent thinking. Art is for everyone, not for just a select few, and each child has the opportunity to develop to the extent of his interests and abilities.

From our knowledge of individual differences has come the conviction that each child's art should reflect his uniqueness. Children learn about art in relation to their needs and interests. The learning rate, the material mastered and the nature of the work vary greatly within any group of children. We must provide variation in every art experience as children experiment with new materials.

Each child is creative but in different degrees and in different ways. This creativity needs to be encouraged and developed. We must provide creative opportunity for each child so that he can become more independent and resourceful in his thinking as he uses a variety of art materials to express himself.

Because of the wide range of abilities within any group it is impossible to set a rigid standard for any given "grade." Art is naturally a nongraded subject. The art program must be built on individual, independent growth with the only possible standard being one which fits the individual.

In making plans for art education in a nongraded program one should consider the following purposes.

Art activities must:

- provide for individual differences.
- develop imagination and resourcefulness.
- build self-confidence.
- recognize each child's creativity.
- organize emotional expression.
- develop aesthetic values.
- develop each child's appreciation of others.

Art is expressive and the child's development is expressed in symbols which he creates. He communicates his ideas through the use of his symbols. Art, like reading, must be geared to and based on experience. The child draws and manipulates to express his inner feelings and ideas about himself and his environment.

The art program should be concerned with helping the child have rich experiences, stimulating him to express these experiences with art materials, making these materials available to him, and encouraging him to create. Because of the belief that each child has his own rate of learning, no time limits should be set. When a child is ready to begin, he begins; when he has progressed to the next level, he moves into it.

The art teacher should have a regularly scheduled lesson every week with each heterogeneous, multi-age, homeroom group. During these lessons, the children have an opportunity to explore the possibilities of various art media. The children learn some techniques of handling these different materials and have a chance to try them for themselves. Some children complete a project in a single class period; others just get started and come back later to complete it. (See Figure 9-11.)

In addition to regularly scheduled lessons the art teacher, several times during the week, assists individuals and small groups on special projects, classroom groups on bulletin boards or other class projects, and large groups on big projects such as a schoolwide art exhibit.

Figure 9-11

The art teacher sets the tone and creates an atmosphere for creativity through her enthusiasm for art activities. She knows which children need to be inspired, which need a little guidance, and which need only praise and encouragement. She knows how to motivate and teach children without infringing on each child's right to determine his own organization, shapes, and colors. She conducts art activities on a personal and individual basis with much flexibility. The Art Center should be a beehive of activity.

THE MUSIC CENTER

Music is not something for the exceptional few of uncommon talent. On the contrary, music is a creative, expressive impulse that is born in every normal child. That is what music education is for — to help children use their musical powers to create not only more life but also a better life.

There is something in music for every individual child. Music is *in* people, it comes *from* people, and it is *about* people *for* people. Because it is creative self-expression it would be unrealistic to set up goals for every child to achieve at a certain grade level. Individuals vary in their ability to learn and in the time needed, and so musical skills are developed sequentially. This, then, follows the development of the nongraded school. Again the ability to read would probably coincide with an aptitude for music reading but would have nothing to do with innate talent for rhythmic coordination and vocal achievement. These needs are met through culminating activities, such as programs utilizing the best talent and cooperation of each child. While some children sing, others dramatize, dance, and play instruments.

Consequently, the total music program provides experience in singing, rhythms, playing instruments, creative activities, guided listening, harmonic experiences, and advanced guidance and cooperation in glee club and band. This enables each child to find some area of musical expression that will continue into adult life. It is hoped that music will speak to the ears, tongues, fingers, toes, nerves, hearts, and minds of *all* the children — the slow and faltering as well as the nimble and sensitive.

To develop any degree of musical literacy it should be done sequentially; thus starting where the child is and meeting his immediate needs. Only in this way can music be SELF-expression instead of a superficial exposure to certain grade level goals. True to the nongraded ideal are teachers, both music specialists and classroom, who evaluate the children to determine their proper level of experience in all concept areas. The teacher is then better able to develop sequentially in the class basic musical attitudes, understandings, and skills. Once developed, this musical literacy will enable each child to gain maximum enjoyment and satisfaction from an art form which has been his heritage from time immemorial.

Music not only develops self-expression but also self-direction. If music is taught to be enjoyed as a relaxation, a release from tensions and routines, an enrichment of one's tastes and values, it will become an outlet for development of the personal qualities of emotional sensitivity, concentration, coordination, imagination, and perhaps discipline and accuracy in the mastery of an instrument. It would seem, therefore, to provide a good use of increased leisure time that would help lesson the insecurities of the world.

Each heterogeneous, multi-age homeroom group should be scheduled to visit the Music Center at least once a week. In addition to the regularly scheduled visits, individuals and small groups should be able to visit the center to pursue special interests. (See Figure 9-12).

Figure 9-12

Instrumental music is a part of the total curriculum. Instrumental music classes are scheduled for those students who wish to take advantage of the opportunity to perform on any legitimate string, wind, or percussion instrument.

The instrumental teacher cooperates fully with the faculty and administration and takes part in many activities, both curricular and extra-curricular. He meets frequently with parents and takes an active part in community affairs because he realizes the contribution music can make to the social, mental, and spiritual development of the child.

THE PHYSICAL EDUCATION CENTER

A nongraded program with its child-centered curriculum should provide for many kinds of educational activities. Physical education experiences should be included because those experiences are important to the child's complete development and because they can do things for a child that other areas of the curriculum cannot do. All of a child's responses, whether they be intellectual, emotional, social, or physical, are interrelated.

Physical education is one way to meet the needs of children. .
Although the major function of physical education is to help
children keep well and grow strong through participation in
physical activities, it also has other purposes that are related to
social and personal development.

The program has as its purpose the development of the whole
personality of each child — physical, social, and emotional. The
areas of social development that are especially benefited concern
desirable attitudes and an understanding of the role of a member of
a group. Physical education prepares boys and girls to participate in
wholesome physical recreation and helps them develop concepts
and habits of healthful living.

In planning the physical education program it is necessary to
have teachers who understand children and who recognize the
contributions physical education can make to growth and development; facilities, equipment, materials, and supplies adequate
in kind, quality, and number to serve all children; time in the daily
schedule adequate to meet the need for activity; and a program
based on the needs and interests of boys and girls. In setting up
objectives to meet these needs a physical education program should
provide opportunities for each child to develop the following
qualities:

- physical power, endurance, stamina, agility, coordination, and
  sense of balance.
- an understanding of why it is important to observe rules which
  make for better and safer participation.
- ability to assume and carry out responsibilities.
- ability to accept success and defeat in a sportsmanlike manner.
- physical and social skills which enable him to participate in
  recreational activities at any age.
- consideration for the rights of others.
- skills that lead to safe living, such as using equipment safely.
- ability to enjoy group activities.

Each heterogeneous, multi-age homeroom group should be
scheduled for physical education at least once per week. In addition
to the regularly scheduled visits, individuals and small groups
should be able to visit the center to pursue special interests.

UTILIZING PEER TEACHERS

The behavior of a child at any age is strongly influenced by the opinions of his peers. Under the guidance of the teacher, children can enter constructively into the instructional phase of school life.

Peer teaching can be done successfully in several ways. Perhaps the easiest way is on a one-to-one basis. This works well in drill work where both need to practice the same thing — maybe some division facts. They could take turns in checking each other orally. (See Figure 9-13.)

Figure 9-13

One-to-one situations are limitless. Another example might be one child listening to another give his campaign speech which he has prepared for the student body in seeking the office of president of student council.

A teacher could divide his room into many small groups (2 to 3 children) and have peer teachers from other rooms come in to give specific instruction. The teacher could plan all the details with the peer teachers or he could simply give them the task and leave the selection of materials and methods to the students. This is a highly successful technique; children speak each other's language and they can often explain something to peers much more easily than adults can. In Figure 9-14 the teacher is explaining to several student aides the task for a particular group.

Figure 9-14

Figure 9-15 shows a student aide instructing a group of peers.

Figure 9-15

In another situation a child who is very good at oral reading might spend a few minutes reading orally to a peer group of less mature readers.

Experience has proven that many times the peer teacher is learning as much as if not more than those being taught. It should be pointed out also that a peer teacher is continuing to develop a positive self-concept as he participates in this leadership role.

SUMMARY

Special teachers have a very important part in a nongraded program. With some flexibility in the scheduling and some extra time allotted, the specialists work with individuals and large and small groups on special projects and programs in addition to their regular classroom visits.

Specialists should work with real children rather than with so-called average "grade" groups. With imagination, courage, and a willingness to learn what the needs of children are, special teachers are very important members of the teaching team. The method by which they are scheduled gives them opportunities to meet these needs when, together with other members of the staff, they have determined general and specific curricular needs.

The success of a nongraded program depends greatly on activities and experiences provided by specialists working closely with the total staff on the total school program, which is geared to meet individual needs.

Through the hiring of teacher aides and the utilization of volunteers, the effectiveness of the teacher in the classroom can be increased, and this increased effectiveness is to the child's advantage. The success of a nongraded program is due largely to the utilization of the many and varied talents of auxiliary personnel. Those parents who have become so involved have also become a reservoir of goodwill and support for innovations in education.

Peer teaching is a real example of the nongraded philosophy. In these experiences children are learning as they live and work together and become more and more concerned for the "human" characteristic of their school life.

10

EXTENSIONS OF THE
NONGRADED PHILOSOPHY

Nongrading is a way of life. A nongraded school should not be a place where you go to suffer through five hours a day and then go somewhere else to have your pleasure. School should be a continuation of one's style of living.

Through the activities in a nongraded program, children learn to understand personal differences in others and to prize these differences. Children learn to accept as reality in our society differences in race, socio-economic status, speech patterns, etc. Each person sees himself as a worthwhile human being with a contribution to make to the society in which he lives.

The most important characteristic of a nongraded school is the "human" element. Each person is "human" and should be treated as such. I'd like to describe two projects which were developed at South Frederick Elementary School. Because of the concern for people, I consider these projects as extensions of the nongraded philosophy.

THE "LIVING ROOM" APPROACH

The children in this project were assigned to these rooms prior to the conception of the "living room." Those assigned to these rooms were the older (5th and 6th year) children who had made the least achievement in their previous years in school.

It was felt that these children had potential and yet for some reason they had not been motivated to use it. Many of these children did not like school; some had poor attendance records; many were finding it difficult to conform to the rules and regulations and, therefore, were the discipline problems.

OBJECTIVES OF THE EXPERIMENT

The basic objective of this experiment is to provide an environment which is more conducive to learning than is the typical schoolroom setting. If children develop about 50 percent of their general intelligence and basic knowledge before entering school, then perhaps the home atmosphere should be continued at school.

The "living room" concept is designed to provide a more natural and relaxed atmosphere which should help children to find their places in their society; this "living room" is a place where children can learn to live and work with others — a place where each can find success and self-realization. (See Figure 10-1.)

Figure 10-1

The specific objectives of this experiment are to help each child feel that:

He Belongs — is accepted, will be missed if he is not present, will be welcomed back after each absence, and has equal opportunity in the group.

He Is at Ease with the Group — recognizes that he will make mistakes but knows that they will be accepted as authentic manifestations of himself, and hence are learning experiences.

He Is Successful — is accomplishing, knows and feels where he is going, is putting forth his best effort to reach his goals, and feels confident.

He Has a Responsibility to the Group — can help others, and can make a positive contribution to the success of the group.

DESCRIPTION OF THE EXPERIMENT

Every child has the potential for many types of growth. Some lie dormant throughout life. Others are developed in part. The determination of which possibilities are realized, and the degree to which any is fulfilled, is a function of the environment.

If children are to develop their intellectual potential, society must provide an environment that is intellectually stimulating and in which achievement of an intellectual nature is respected and nurtured.

The emotional climate of a learning situation determines how well the pupil will obtain functional behavioral changes. Unless the emotional content of the situation is conducive to the acceptance of new information, that information will appear irrelevant and will be rejected. In every situation, boys and girls are striving to feel right about themselves, to feel that they have worth, to feel that they are accepted.

Each child is uniquely different. Meeting individual differences is not a technique; it is a way of living — a style of life. It includes accepting others, respecting their contributions, working for the kind of group operation in which each individual knows he has a part, and encouraging each child to give his best in each situation.

The determination of group direction and policy is based upon the individual decisions of group members. If the society is to improve, or even sustain itself, its individual members must be able to make wise decisions. Each must be able to decide for himself what he values, what he wants, and what is the best method of obtaining it. Thus, in our democratic society, the school must place a major emphasis on helping the individual become self-directing.

For this experiment all of the school desks and chairs have been taken from two classrooms and replaced with living room furnishings — sofas, rockers, recliners, rugs, floor lamps, televisions, etc. (See Figure 10-2.)

Figure 10-2

The activities of this experiment are designed to help children develop a positive self-concept. A team of two teachers, two aides, two volunteers, and student tutors work with 55 children assigned to this project. The program is markedly different from the regular school program. Included as an integral part of the school experience are field trips, sociodrama, psychodrama, informal role playing, dramatizations, art, music, physical education, library, home economics, industrial arts, outdoor education and experiences in worthwhile leisure time activities. (See Figure 10-3.) Many small group, quiet games are used as seen in Figure 10-4. This experiment is not a textbook oriented program.

Figure 10-3

Figure 10-4

There are many opportunities for one-to-one relationships (one child to one adult). This is possible due to the team effort. These opportunities provide not only assistance on individual projects, but also discussions of personal problems and guidance toward solution. (See Figure 10-5).

Figure 10-5

Provisions are made for small group and individual sessions to satisfy individual special needs in coordination, to provide opportunity for creative activity, to provide recreational activities to relieve nervous tension, to provide social situations that will result in more functional behavior patterns, to provide opportunity for development of leadership, and to provide opportunity to develop sufficient skills for satisfaction in accomplishment.

At this point, it might be asserted that the program is not solely and exclusively designed to produce behavior that in societal terms is totally functional. Accompanying a healthy self-awareness will be desires and attempts by the child to conform his environment to him. Out of this will thrust his creative urges. In short, the child should realize himself to be a maker of culture as well as a bearer.

Field trips to places of interest and historical significance in the immediate and surrounding areas, to places of business, and to recreational areas serve as a basis for extensive development of children's oral and written vocabulary through discussion, writing of experience stories, and dramatizations. The social benefits derived help these children to function in a social situation comfortably, less compulsively, and more intelligently. Knowledge of the community and the surrounding area should develop pride in the children as they begin to find their place in the society in which they live.

EVALUATION OF THE EXPERIMENT

The effectiveness of this experiment covers an appraisal of change in the children's attitudes and progress throughout school and to some extent outside of school. Growth in grasping the concepts necessary for everyday living are evaluated.

The attitudes to be developed are indicated in behavior that shows that the child likes school, the teachers, other adults, most of his peers, and wants to participate in group activities and to secure the approval of his peers and teachers. Our evaluation is based on the child as a growing individual rather than on a comparison with other children.

Teachers keep anecdotal records and sociometric diagrams.

Standardized achievement tests were given during the last week of September and again during the first two weeks of April to give some statistical data of growth. A summary of these test results is found in Figure 10-6. The period of time between tests was about seven months. Since the children had been in the "living room" experiment for seven months the average growth according to this standardized test should have been seven months (.7).

You can see from the scores that everyone made more than the normal expectation. More significant than this is the fact that the group median score was raised a year (1.0) or more in each area tested.

WORD MEANING				ARITHMETIC COMPUTATION		
	Low	Median	High		Low	Median	High
Pre-test	2.1	3.2	5.4	Pre-test	−2.0	3.4	4.1
Post-test	3.4	4.3	7.0	Post-test	3.3	4.5	5.3
Growth	1.3	1.1	1.6	Growth	1.3	1.1	1.2

PARAGRAPH MEANING				ARITHMETIC CONCEPTS		
	Low	Median	High		Low	Median	High
Pre-test	2.0	2.8	3.4	Pre-test	2.1	2.4	6.8
Post-test	3.4	4.0	6.0	Post-test	3.3	3.9	7.6
Growth	1.4	1.2	2.6	Growth	1.2	1.5	.8

SPELLING				ARITHMETIC APPLICATION		
	Low	Median	High		Low	Median	High
Pre-test	−2.0	2.9	5.3	Pre-test	2.3	3.2	4.1
Post-test	3.1	4.0	6.4	Post-test	3.6	4.2	5.8
Growth	1.1	1.1	1.1	Growth	1.3	1.0	1.7

WORD STUDY SKILLS				SOCIAL STUDIES		
	Low	Median	High		Low	Median	High
Pre-test	−2.0	2.1	3.1	Pre-test	2.8	3.4	5.2
Post-test	2.9	3.7	5.2	Post-test	4.0	4.5	6.3
Growth	.9	1.6	2.1	Growth	1.2	1.1	1.1

LANGUAGE				SCIENCE		
	Low	Median	High		Low	Median	High
Pre-test	−2.0	2.4	3.3	Pre-test	2.6	3.3	4.3
Post-test	3.0	3.9	5.0	Post-test	3.8	4.5	5.4
Growth	1.0	1.5	1.7	Growth	1.2	1.2	1.1

Figure 10-6

Reporting to parents is done through conferences, home visits and narrative reports rather than by a report card. In Figure 10-7 (below) are the guidelines for evaluation of each child in the living room project.

Teachers will appraise each child to see if he:
- participates as an acceptable member of the class in such activities as playing simple games, singing songs, engaging in rhythmic activities, listening to stories and presenting ideas orally.
- participates as a member of a smaller group in the class activities, involving dramatic play, block building, use of playground equipment and other materials.
- assumes responsibility for following school rules.
- understands personal differences in others and prizes these differences for their value to the group.
- accepts differences in race, socio-economic status, etc.
- assumes responsibility for working harmoniously and effectively with both older and younger children as well as adults.

In evaluating each child teachers will use the following guideposts:
- How well is the child balancing his own assets and liabilities?
- How is the child using the opportunities and outlets for expressing and satisfying his feelings, his problems?
- What evidence is there that the child is growing away from forms of more infantile behavior?
- What regressions are in evidence? How frequent and how serious are these regressions?
- What evidence in the child's verbal responses such as belligerence, profanity, or stuttering are indicative of the present state of his mental health?
- What evidences can be gathered of the child's present self-evaluation?
- Does he listen attentively to the teacher's instructions to the group and follow them?
- Is he developing skill in such activities as using art materials, singing a tune, contributing ideas orally, climbing, running, skipping, etc.?
- Does he talk about his home and the things he does to help at home?
- Does he participate in community activities (i.e., Scouts)?
- Does he know that he should await his turn?
- Does he avoid arguments over decisions in games?

- Does he know that he should be modest in winning?
- Has he improved in leadership and followship ability?
- Is he interested in a variety of activities?
- Is he interested in the welfare of others?
- Has he learned to be cheerful, generous, and tolerant?
- Is he honest in his play relationships?
- Has he learned to be courteous and to cooperate for the common good?
- Has he developed loyalty to the team?
- Has he learned to control inferiority, disappointment, fear, irritation, hate, resentment, worry, frustration and anger?
- Can he make adjustments to time, space, distance and direction?
- Does he have the respect of his playmates?
- Can he adjust to the interests of the group?

Figure 10-7

SUMMARY OF "LIVING ROOM" EXPERIMENT

Unless each child can believe in himself, that he has worth and is able to contribute to the group, his potential for aggression or withdrawal is strong and his attention cannot focus on new information and experience. Learning must be relevant and in context — a reflection of the flow and direction of *his* life.

This experiment was designed to promote the development of self-concepts and, thereby, help each child to progress from dependence on adults for direction and control to self-direction and self-discipline, and to establish orderly working conditions so that learning activities will proceed smoothly and joyfully.

Through the activities of this project children have learned to understand personal differences in others and to prize the differences for their value to the various activities of the group. Children have learned to accept as reality in our society differences in race, socio-economic status, speech patterns, etc. They have learned how to welcome and orient new children into the group. They have learned that courtesy and good manners are not something artificially "put on" for company, but are the spontaneous natural outgrowths of concern for human relationships. Each child has begun to see himself as a worthwhile human being with a contribution to make to the society in which he lives. They now like school and see school as a place where they learn as they live.

COMMUNITY SCHOOL PROJECT

A school should be a place where the learning process is a continually evolving process. School should be more than just a place where children come for five or six hours a day, and are then released to shift for themselves to find fun and entertainment.

A school should be a focal point of the community. All parents look at education, the best education, as the key to the dreams and aspirations they hold for their children.

But all too many times education is thwarted in youth because children feel a certain alienation from the institution. Often the school does not have the warmth and security of the home. The transition for the child is too harsh and difficult to accept, and it is then that the future high school dropout is made.

The only way to combat this is to make the school a living, breathing part of the everyday experience of each member of the community, by bringing the parents into the school, making them a part of it, and giving them an investment in it both intellectually and emotionally.

The Community School project is another extension of the nongraded philosophy because here too the major concern is for people. In the South Frederick community there was a real need for a recreational center. People needed a place to meet.

The staff at the school had for quite some time felt that school and the school building should be something more than a place of books, pencils, and paper, into which children march every morning, stay a few hours, and in many cases flee to something more fun and interesting elsewhere.

If the school building squats unused and deserted the rest of the day and if we believe that the school building belongs to the people of the community, then it *really* should belong to them.

PHILOSOPHY OF THE COMMUNITY
SCHOOL PROJECT

The South Frederick Elementary Recreation Project (PREFS) is an attempt to infuse an authentic community life into a building that heretofore was, during after-school hours, the neighborhood's prime target for burglary and vandalism. The rocks that went through the dozens of windows were a product of a certain rage. Here were hundreds of square feet of usable space under a roof that squatted empty and unused during the most delightful periods of the day. There was equipment in that building that was great to use, but it was locked up. The simplest empathies come hard for "professionals." The very term seems to preclude and encourage a suspicion.

There have been other projects of a similar nature in similar neighborhoods. They have had varying degrees of life in them. It seems that most of them sprang up from a very utilitarian necessity — the need to stop the dollar drain resulting from damage to the school.

We were aware of the desirability of not only stopping the damage to the building, but also of stopping the insidious destruction of the character or life of the school. If a school's style is to be destroyed, then whatever happens to the building is irrelevant.

When we speak of style we speak of a consistent mode of life. If a school is a totalitarian state during school hours and attempts through some magical transformation to become a place of fun and freedom in the evening programs, the inconsistency is certain to weaken the program.

The PREFS Program was intended specifically to be a natural extension of the school day. A nongraded school is a place where one has opportunity to continue his own style of living. A revolution of sorts is to be found in the "living room" concept's experiential approach to learning. The idea would be only a clinical half-measure if there was not a supplementary program in which a child and his people could experience school as a style of life. This is the purpose of the PREFS Project. It is a natural extension of the nongraded philosophy.

PLANNING THE ACTIVITIES

What makes this project genuinely unique is something more than the fact that we were asking people to make the school a viable, pulsating part of their community lives. We were asking that it be an active element in the family structure. There have been many theoretical pronouncements of this sort without an accompanying style. The composite programs, highly organized and structured, have had every virtue in them except life.

Rather than plan a program for the members of the community and say to them, "These are the activities we have planned for you; come and take advantage of them," I chose to involve them and have them plan their own activities. Since we were interested in meeting the needs of the people, we invited several parents to organize a committee of parents to be the "board of directors." A group of 15 volunteers agreed to plan and supervise the activities.

The plans included numerous activities for *everyone* in the family. The building was to be open two evenings and Saturdays each week. The planning committee had organized themselves to provide supervision for each activity. Figure 10-8 is the announcement sent to all homes in the community.

The PREFS Program

South Frederick Elementary Recreation
Program

The staff of the South Frederick Elementary School has for quite some time felt that school and the school building should be something more than a place of books, pencils, and paper, into which your children march every morning, are here for a few hours, and then in many cases flee to something more fun and interesting elsewhere.

The building squats unused and deserted the rest of the day.

We have felt that if this building belongs to the people of the South Frederick Community, it should *really* belong.

Other things besides academic matters should happen here.

There are, we feel, other equally important and meaningful things in our lives.

This is an invitation to join with us in making the school a live, breathing part of the community.

Beginning Thursday, October 10, and every Saturday, Tuesday, and Thursday evening thereafter the school will be open to South Frederick District families. On Tuesday and Thursday evening the school will be open from 6:45 to 9:45 p.m. On Saturday we will open at 10:00 a.m. and close 4:00 p.m.

There will be numerous activities that will be organized for EVERYONE in the family, from baby to grandparents. There will be:

Athletics of all types	Home Improvement
Ping Pong, Basketball, etc.	Horseshoes
Sewing Classes	Wood Working (W/power
Dancing Classes	tools)
Library Study Rooms	Roller Skating
Card Games	Pop Dancing
Chess, Checkers, etc.	Places for small bands
Cooking	to practice, etc.

These are just a few of the activities we will start with, and with your suggestions, many more will be added as you desire them.

Again we would like to emphasize *this is for the whole family.* There will be baby sitting provided for mothers with small children.

This coming Sunday, October 6, there will be a film shown in the gym (free of charge). The film concerns another community that has tried the same things and is an entertaining and beautiful presentation. The film will be shown at 2:00, 3:00, 4:00 and 5:00 p.m. Discussions and answers following each showing.

We hope that you will take serious note of this program and join with us in making the South Frederick District an even better place to live with each other.

Yours sincerely,

Lee L. Smith, Principal

Figure 10-8

THE NATURE OF THE ACTIVITIES

Since the board of volunteers wanted PREFS to be more than simply an evening school with applicable rules and regulations, the program was not highly organized and structured. They felt that the interest centers should be open, and should contain interesting activities, but that a person should not have to enroll or register, but should be free to come and go as he desired. Above all they felt that a formal structure and discipline would do the project in with a vengeance. If this project was to be for the community, then it must be responsive to the community's experience.

Over 500 residents of the community turned out for the opening night, and the average attendance remained between 400 and 500. As a group requested a new activity, necessary arrangements were made. The activities changed from time to time. The needs of the community were being satisfied.

One such happening took place during the second week of the project. A teen-age boy came in and said to one of the adult supervisors, "Hey man, where's the art junk?" In reply the adult said, "Would you like to teach an art class?" The shocked teen-ager replied, "Who, me? Man, I've been away for 30 days; I'm a drop-out and a trouble maker!" When assured that this didn't matter he readily agreed and rapidly formed the basis for his art class.

He gathered about 50 interested children and started them on a rigorous program of sketching various still-life subjects. It was apparent that the children knew and understood their new instructor and they had a tremendously good time. We viewed the forming of this art class as justification for our belief that whatever happens at PREFS in the line of activities should not be a matter of legislation, but rather a spontaneous manifestation of real interest.

EVALUATING THE PROJECT

Since the program is highly unstructured and informal there is no formal evaluation. However, in the case of our teen-age art teacher, I'd like to relate future happenings. He appeared during the regular school day and asked if he could be a volunteer aide in one of the "living rooms." After serving in this capacity for several weeks he decided that he'd have to leave. As he left he said, "If school had been like this I never would have dropped out!"

We later found out that he has returned to his own school and has resumed his studies. He told the counselor that his associations at South Frederick had helped him realize that school could be a place where one could continue living. We now refer to him as our "drop-in."

Another measure of the success of the project can be simply stated by the fact that burglary and vandalism is on the decline. As a result of applying the nongraded philosophy both during the regular school day and after school hours, we feel strongly that the school is a live, breathing part of the community and that the community is a much better place in which to live.

11

TEACHING FOR CONTINUOUS EVALUATION
IN THE NONGRADED SCHOOL

The evaluation of the work of children in a nongraded program must be unique for each individual. In the nongraded school, learning becomes a developmental process; each child proceeds irregularly at his own rate. Based on the philosophy of continuous progress for each child, the program requires continuous evaluation.

CHARACTERISTICS OF EVALUATION

The first step in planning for evaluation is to study the characteristics of good evaluation. The following are suggested guidelines for a good program of evaluation:

1. Evaluation is related to the objectives of instruction; a good program of evaluation should be consistent with the accepted objectives of the local school and the entire school system.
2. Evaluation should be concerned not only with how much was learned, but also with the present and future value to the child; the teacher should be concerned with the less tangible outcomes of the learning experiences and the means whereby she can help the children evaluate their growth in this area.
3. Evaluation should use a variety of techniques and instruments such as standardized tests of achievement, case studies, anecdotal records, sociometric tests, questionnaires, check lists, observations, home visits, conferences, etc.

4. Evaluation should include a system of reporting pupil progress to parents; the system should report progress in all areas of growth — that is, physically, mentally, socially and emotionally.

5. Evaluation should be basic to curriculum improvement; growth in grasping the concepts necessary for everyday living should be evaluated as well as the progress in the fundamental skills, and the curriculum should be revised to include activities which provide for growth in all these areas.

6. Evaluation should be continuous throughout the child's years in school; appraisal of development is cumulative from day to day, week to week, and year to year.

7. Evaluation should be based on the comprehension of the abilities and needs of each child as a growing individual instead of on a comparison of one child to another.

8. Evaluation should provide for participation by all concerned; the child being evaluated should have a share in determining the objectives, selecting techniques of appraisal and interpreting the results.

9. Evaluation should be descriptive in terms of desired behavior; the actions of children which represent their achievement of objectives should be clearly identified. Everyone concerned should be clear as to his goals. Descriptions of behavior should be simple, clear, and as complete as possible.

10. Evaluation should be good for the child whose behavior is being appraised; evaluative procedures should never be unfair, negative, or destructive in their total effect. The child should be permitted to keep his self-respect and help in the planning for his own appraisal.

STEPS INVOLVED IN EVALUATION

It is important for each teacher to understand the close relationship between purposes, procedures, and techniques in a good evaluation program. The following steps in planning for evaluation should increase the effectiveness of instruction:

1. *State the objectives.* The purpose or goal should be stated to include progress toward the objective as well as final achievement of it.

2. *Define the objective in terms of behavior.* The objectives should be translated into operational terms — the way people act when they have achieved the objectives.
3. *Identify situations in which the behavior may occur.* The times, places, and circumstances where children may display the defined behavior should be determined.
4. *Collect evidence of the behavior.* Appropriate instruments and techniques should be selected and applied, the data collected and reported, and all information organized and analyzed concerning the outward signs of actions and responses.
5. *Interpret the evidence in terms of the objective.* The extent to which the child has reached the objective should be determined.
6. *Modify practices on the basis of the appraisal.* The behavior samples collected should reveal needs for changing the educational environment to modify further the behavior toward the desired goals. Teaching practices should be altered for improved progress toward the objective.

MEETING INDIVIDUAL NEEDS

The nongraded system of grouping does not create harmony among the learner, his developmental pattern, and the subject matter. Therefore, a change in curriculum content organization is necessary. In the skill areas of Mathematics and Language Arts, skills are listed by levels in a developmental pattern. These levels are much smaller segments than grade standards and each child may proceed through the levels at his own rate.

The needs, interests, and working levels of the pupils, not the arbitrary designation of grade expectancy and time allotments, determine the learning experiences selected by the teachers. This flexibility and permissiveness enables teachers to adjust their programs in quantity, rate, scope, and emphasis to meet the range of individual differences which exists within any group of children.

THE LEVELS APPROACH

If a nongraded school program is based on the concept of continuous growth and not on a specified time to be promoted or retained, a different method of evaluation and reporting pupils' progress is necessary. Evaluation must be continuous.

I'd like to illustrate evaluation procedures in a nongraded program using the levels approach by describing the South Frederick plan. In grouping the children into classrooms we assigned from one to nine levels to each homeroom on a multi-age basis. We disregarded grade and chronological age and considered achievement levels. The teams of teachers regroup the children for instruction in the skill areas of Language Arts and Mathematics. This plan narrows the range of achievement within each instructional group. No time limits are set on the progression of a student from one level to another and students are advanced to the next level whenever they are ready.

The teacher in the classroom has daily opportunity to observe and evaluate the performance of the children. When she feels that a child or a group of children is ready to move on to the next level, she makes this recommendation to the office. The form used for this request for evaluation is shown in Figure 11-1.

```
        REQUEST FOR EVALUATION    (Prepare in Duplicate)

Name of Pupil _____ Date _____

Present Level _____ Circle one - Language Arts  -  Math

Specific reasons for request: _____

_____

_____

_____

_____

_____|‾|_____
                                Home Room│Teacher

                                Principal or Vice Principal

 *  *  *  *  *  *  *  *  *  *  *  *  *  *  *  *  *  *  *  *  *  *  *

                    REPORT OF EVALUATION
```

Figure 11-1

As suggested in Chapter 4, we have one person who does all the evaluations in Language Arts. She also does all the record keeping and prepares all the progress reports to parents.

When a child or an instructional group has completed the skills for a particular level and all the items on the skill sheet (Figure 11-2) have been checked, the evaluation is conducted by our Developmental Reading teacher.

LANGUAGE ARTS — LEVEL G

Name_____

Comprehension Skills

_____ 1. Finds factual information

_____ 2. Groups and classifies facts

_____ 3. Expands and illustrates concepts

_____ 4. Identifies characters by pantomime, role-playing, and dramatization

_____ 5. Notes details to main events (sub-sentences)

_____ 6. Has increased in ability to draw and make inferences

_____ 7. Makes comparisons

_____ 8. Has increased in ability to find sources of information

_____ 9. Notes clues

_____10. Is able to interpret author's purpose

_____11. Recognizes plot structure (problem)

_____12. Extends social attitudes

_____13. Main ideas

_____ (a) Selects titles

_____ (b) Selects sentences which express main ideas

_____ (c) States main ideas in own words

_____14. Can read simple charts, maps, graphs, tables, and diagrams

_____15. Participates in the reading of good literature

_____16. Is improving in ability to answer questions that are:

_____ (a) concrete

_____ (b) creative

_____ (c) abstract

_____17. Uses evaluative criteria in self-selection of reading materials

Word Attack Skills

_____ 1. Has increased skill in using vowel digraphs

_____ 2. Understands and knows meaning of prefixes *un* and *re*

_____ 3. Has developed auditory discrimination of polysyllabic words and accent

_____ 4. Understands _er_ as agent

_____ 5. Understands _er_ as comparative

_____ 6. Understands use of suffix _ly_

_____ 7. Can attack words by:

_____ *(a)* Using pictures for clues

_____ *(b)* Reading to the end of the sentence and making a guess

_____ *(c)* Checking that guess by phonetic clues

_____ *(d)* Using structural clues

_____ *(e)* Checking himself by asking the teacher

Language Skills

_____ 1. Uses capital letters to begin:

_____ *(a)* Names of days of the week

_____ *(b)* Names of holidays

_____ *(c)* Names of streets and roads

_____ *(d)* Names of special places and special groups of people

_____ *(e)* First letter of first word and first letter of all important words in a title

_____ 2. Capital for letter _I_

_____ 3. Recognition of groups of words that are sentences

_____ 4. Uses _did, done, ran, run,_ correctly

_____ 5. Has acceptable slant in cursive writing

_____ 6. Letters used in cursive writing are of acceptable size

_____ 7. Can write samples of comprehension skills

Spelling Skills

_____ 1. Connects specific consonant sounds with the letters which spell them

_____ *(a)* Knows that the sound of _s_ is often spelled with _c_

_____ *(b)* Knows the _ks_ sound is often spelled with _x_

_____ *(c)* Knows the sound of _f_ in the final position is sometimes spelled with _gh_

_____ 2. Recognizes combinations to look for in spelling vowel sounds

_____ *(a)* Knows that _er_ ending is usually spelled _er_ but sometimes it is spelled _or_

_____ *(b)* Knows that in words spelled with _ar_, the sound of _a_ when followed by _r_ is different from the _a_ of _hat_ or _rain_

_____ 3. Understands and uses the following structural generalizations:

_____ *(a)* Forms plural or past tense of many words which end with _y_ by changing _y_ to _i_ before adding _es_ or _ed_

_____ *(b)* Makes new words by adding _ing_

_____ *(c)* Doubles the final consonant of many words before adding *ing*

_____ *(d)* Forms the past tense of some verbs by changing the spelling

_____ *(e)* Makes new words of many words by adding *r, er, st,* or *est*

_____ *(f)* Counts the syllables in a word by counting the vowel sounds

_____ *(g)* When words have two consonants between vowels, tries first to divide the word between consonants

_____ *(h)* When words have one consonant between vowels, first tries to divide the word before the consonant

_____ *(i)* For long words which are made up of two short words, spells the words first and writes them together

_____ 4. Uses an apostrophe to show that letters have been omitted in contractions

Figure 11-2

She is pictured in Figure 11-3 as she evaluates a child on her understanding of the skills for a particular level. The instruments used in these evaluations have been developed by our staff to check the skills on each level. A complete description of all of the language arts skills and evaluations is given in Chapter 4.

Figure 11-3

The procedure for evaluation in mathematics is very similar. When a request for evaluation is made for a child or an instructional group the testing is done by one of the vice principals. Since our school is housed in two buildings we have a vice principal in each. Each carries out the function of evaluation in the area of mathematics within his building. In Figure 11-4 the vice principal is conducting a math evaluation. A complete description of all of the mathematics skills and evaluations is given in Chapter 5.

Figure 11-4

If the results of the evaluation are in accord with the teacher's recommendation (and generally they are) then a progress report (see Figure 11-5) is prepared for the child to take home immediately so that the parents will know that he has made progress.

Figure 11-5

SOUTH FREDERICK ELEMENTARY SCHOOL

FREDERICK, MARYLAND

21701

NONGRADED PROGRAM ** PROGRESS REPORT

DATE _____

As of this date, _____ has

progressed as indicated below:

Language - From level _____ to level _____.

Language Arts Teacher _____

Mathematics - From level _____ to level _____.

Mathematics Teacher _____

He / she will be assigned to homeroom _____

LEE L. SMITH
Principal

Sometimes, as a result of a prolonged illness, a discipline problem, a personality clash, poor attendance, or similar reasons, we feel it necessary to make an adjustment by transferring a child to another room or team to help meet his particular needs and to make a better teaching-learning situation for all. When this happens we usually schedule a conference or at least make a phone call to explain the move. A letter follows the verbal explanation. (See sample in Figure 11-6).

SOUTH FREDERICK ELEMENTARY SCHOOL

Frederick, Maryland

21701

DATE _____

Dear Mr. and Mrs. _____

    In our work with children we often feel the need to make

adjustments in their class assignment to provide a better placement

within the school program. Accordingly, we have reassigned

_____ to Room _____.

His/her new teacher will be _____.

    Please call the school office if you wish further information.

Sincerely,

LEE L. SMITH
Principal

Figure 11-6

When an entire instructional group (5-15) moves to the next level, the same teacher usually keeps these students and then begins the group in a new level. If only one or two children are progressed and the teacher has their new level already in operation in her classroom, she simply puts these students in that group. If the new level is not already in operation within this classroom or team, these two children would be transferred to another team where their new level did exist.

When the evaluation indicates a deficiency in the understanding of several skills, suggestions of materials and methods are given to the teacher to help her in guiding the child to overcome these deficiencies.

We keep many records of pupil progress. The information on these forms is used when relating progress to parents as well as in planning his future learning activities. For example, the secretary (Figure 11-7) keeps a record of the children who leave school during the day because of illness or other similar reasons.

Figure 11-7

Whenever a child is reassigned to a different room or group or whenever it seems desirable to discuss a child's progress with his parents, the secretary (Figure 11-8) uses the phone to schedule a conference for the principal or teacher or both.

Figure 11-8

REPORTING TO PARENTS

Ideally, all evaluations and reporting of the progress of each child should be done in conference with the child and his parents or guardian. However, since we have not yet been able to make arrangements for this many conferences, we developed a report card to be sent home in addition to the promotion letters and letters of reassignment. (A sample report card is shown in Figure 11-9.)

BOARD OF EDUCATION OF FREDERICK COUNTY
SOUTH FREDERICK ELEMENTARY SCHOOL
FREDERICK, MARYLAND

PROGRESS REPORT   **NONGRADED SCHOOL**

PUPIL _____

SCHOOL YEAR_____

TO THE PARENTS._____

The educational welfare of children and youth is best served when there is complete understanding and cooperation between the home and the school. To promote such understanding we prepare this report on the progress of your child.

This report is designed to measure the progress of your child in terms of his own maturity and ability. Comparison with other children or groups of children is not encouraged.

Reporting periods close at the end of November, February, April and the school year. A space is provided for the teacher to request a conference. Please contact the teacher and arrange a conference if indicated. You are invited, however, to ask for a conference any time.

                LEE L. SMITH
                Principal

Reporting pupil progress to parents is a very important function of the school. The staff of the South Frederick Elementary School has been granted approval to institute the nongraded concept of organization. This is in line with our belief in the need of varying patterns of educational practice. We feel sure that this plan will provide desirable experiences for children.

                C EDWARD HAMILTON
                Assistant Superintendent

Figure 11-9

This report is designed to relate the progress of your child. Our program is organized in a series of levels (A through O) in the skill areas of Language Arts and Mathematics. In each level there are specific skills to be mastered. Levels circled indicate mastery by your child. The skills for the level on which your child is operating are listed on the insert. Those **not** checked show the need for further instruction.

LANGUAGE ARTS	MATHEMATICS
Level A	Level A
Level B	Level B
Level C	Level C
Level D	Level D
Level E	Level E
Level F	Level F
Level G	Level G
Level H	Level H
Level I	Level I
Level J	Level J
Level K	Level K
Level M	Level M
Level N	Level N
Level O	Level O

The basic aim of our curriculum is not merely the acquisition of facts and skills, but also the development of basic concepts which will cause the child to adjust his thinking, change is ideas, and alter his values and behavior.

Through educational experience in Social Studies, Science, Art, Music, and Physical Education as well as Language Arts and Mathematics, each child will develop the understandings and concepts which are basic to successful living.

Check marks indicate that your child is making satisfactory progress in the following areas:

Figure 11-9

	NOV	FEB	APR	JUNE
SOCIAL STUDIES				
Demonstrates an understanding of the world and its people.				
Demonstrates concern for others.				
Demonstrates self-control.				
SCIENCE				
Applies scientific facts and methods.				
ART				
Demonstrates interest in art experiences				
Applies ideas and materials creatively				
MUSIC				
Participates in music activities.				
Applies music skills.				
PHYSICAL EDUCATION				
Participates in group and individual activities.				
Applies fundamental skills.				
WORK AND STUDY HABITS				
Follows directions.				
Studies independently				
Participates in group work.				
Applies library skills				
Uses reference materials.				

Figure 11-9

TEACHER REQUESTS CONFERENCE

☐	☐	☐
TERM 1	**TERM 2**	**TERM 3**

* *

ATTENDANCE - DAYS ABSENT TO DATE

NOV._____ FEB._____ APR._____ JUNE _____

* *

PARENT'S SIGNATURE

TERM 1
TERM 2
TERM 3

COMMENTS:

ASSIGNMENT FOR NEXT YEAR.................................... **ROOM** ....

Figure 11-9

Each teacher uses a list of skills for Language Arts and Mathematics for each child with whom she is working. These lists are used daily in planning instruction and keeping records for each child. As a child masters a particular skill it is checked on his skill sheet. When all the skills for a particular level are mastered, the child is progressed to the next level. At the time report cards are sent home these skill lists are included so that the parents can see specifically which skills need to be mastered.

For example, if Susie Smart takes her report home with Levels A and B circled in Language Arts and Levels A, B, C, D, E, and F circled in Mathematics, she would have included with her report the list of skills for Level C in Language Arts and the list of skills for Level G in Mathematics. The skills checked on these lists would indicate mastery. Thus, the parent would know exactly which skills would require further instruction.

In Social Studies, Science, and other areas listed, check marks would indicate satisfactory progress. For example, if all items in this section are checked except the last two (applies library skills; uses reference materials), then the teacher would request a conference with the parent (back of card) to discuss with the librarian and parents specific ways in which the parents could help the child overcome his deficiencies. This type of card could be termed a "written conference."

One of the desired outcomes of our nongraded program is to help pupils develop behavior that reflects democratic living. Three main categories of democratic behavior are responsibility, cooperation, and personality. In Social Studies, as well as in other phases of school work, the teacher provides experiences which enable pupils to gain independence.

In order to know if she is doing this, the teacher needs some method of evaluation. One method is anecdotal records. A much quicker method is a checklist of desirable behavior traits, such as that shown in Figure 11-10, which is used by some of our teachers. This is very easily duplicated — one for each pupil. Across the top is placed the date at which the child was checked so as to show progress in becoming a democratic personality.

Name _____

Cooperation

shares ideas and materials							
eager to work with others							
abides by majority decision							
follows directions							
listens attentively							
cleans up properly							
works quietly							
takes turns willingly							
accepts his share of work							
plays cooperatively							
helps others							
acknowledges mistakes							
cooperates in making and observing rules							

Personality

plays well with classmates							
shows interest in others							
accepts newcomers							
listens to ideas of others							
willing to make changes							
accepts help and suggestions							
encourages others							
corrects own mistakes							
participates in variety of activities							
shares possessions							
is courteous							
is trustworthy							
is truthful							
is friendly							
is pleasant							

Responsibility

helps in planning							
willing worker							
completes a job							
tries to be accurate at all times							
works on own problems							
works on problems with others							
follows group plans and decisions							
uses tools and materials carefully							
helps others							
seeks help when it is needed							
works well without supervision							
respects property of others							
respects rights of minorities							
works well with others							
accepts responsibilities							
respects his own property							

Figure 11-10

Through the use of this plan the program is no longer geared to the basal textbook approach. Teachers use a variety of materials including trade books, paperbacks, tapes, records, films, filmstrips, experience stories, concrete materials and programmed materials as well as basal texts in teaching the skills and concepts listed.

The teacher selects the material which will best satisfy each instructional need. The materials vary from day to day. A child or an instructional group does not use the same basal reader day after day and page after page. Instead he uses only that section on a certain day to meet a particular need.

As previously indicated, the *best* report card is *no* report card at all. The child himself is the best means of taking information home. If the child is happy at school and understands his program of education, then he will continually tell his parents about the things that are happening at school.

An open-door policy in a school organization encourages parents to visit any time to see the program in action. With such a policy in operation, and with parents visiting frequently for observations and conferences, perhaps in several years the written report card will cease to exist.

In order to have time during the week for conferences, as well as time for staff planning, a school could choose to extend the school day by 30 minutes on Monday, Tuesday, Thursday, and Friday. This would be a gain of two hours per week. Children could then be dismissed at noon on Wednesdays to provide time for the important tasks of planning and reporting to parents through conferences.

Since many children ride buses or have working mothers, I would further suggest that dance studios, scout leaders and so forth be encouraged to schedule their programs for Wednesday afternoons and to utilize the school building. Volunteer parents could also plan and supervise club activities. This plan would provide children more time to pursue special interests such as a creative art project.

I would like to emphasize that our program, which is based on the philosophy of continuous progress for each individual, has shown that careful observation and shifting from group to group and class to class and team to team makes it possible for each child to be placed where he can develop best. Evaluation must be a continuous process.

SUMMARY

In summary, the organizational patterns of nongrading and team teaching, which promote the philosophy of continuous progress for each individual at his own rate, can be evaluated in terms of the development of skills and concepts, but the real evaluation of our nongraded program lies within the development of the inner self. Nongrading is a way of life.

Every child has the potential for many types of growth. Some lie dormant throughout life; others are developed in part. The determination of which possibilities are realized, and the degree to which any is fulfilled, is a function of the environment.

If children are to develop their intellectual potential, the school must provide an environment that is intellectually stimulating and in which achievement of an intellectual nature is respected and nurtured.

The emotional climate of a learning situation determines how well the pupil will obtain functional behavioral changes. Unless the emotional content of the situation is conducive to the acceptance of new information, that information will appear irrelevant and will be rejected. In every situation, boys and girls are striving to feel right about themselves, to feel that they have worth, to feel that they are accepted.

Each child is uniquely different. Meeting individual differences is not a technique; it is a way of living — a style of life. It includes accepting others, respecting their contributions, working for the kind of group operation in which each individual knows he has a part, and encouraging each child to give his best in each situation.

Although it is quite important to learn to live with other people, it is imperative that each child learn to live with himself. Each must learn to understand his assets and use them constructively. He must discover his shortcomings and, if possible, improve on them. He must develop a sense of responsibility to others and a balancing sense of self-protection sufficient to keep him functioning at an efficient level.

Complete understanding of oneself is continuous and on-going. Successful living is not a thing but a process, a continuous movement toward ever changing value goals. The primary function of the nongraded school program should be to provide an environment which would enhance the development of values and attitudes.

The curriculum should not be a formal one emphasizing mastery of subject matter as an end in itself, but rather it should emphasize the development of the child and take into consideration his interests, abilities, and experiences. The subject matter should be presented in such a way as to help him grasp its functional value in relation to the problems of everyday living with which he is confronted.

All learning should deal with aspects of the society in which the child lives and ways in which these aspects are important to him. The child's experience should be related directly to his environment, and thus enable him to acquire the tools he will need as he continues to grow.

The goals and purposes of a nongraded program could best be served by open-space learning centers and the use of disciplinary teaching teams. By placing students and teachers in one area where they could work together easily, give suggestions to each other, hear each other and help each other, all would benefit.

I view the "learning center" approach as a consistent variation of the basic nongraded philosophic tenets, in that a center is an actual geographic location where a child can work independently with a series of related activities which are designed to promote independent understanding of certain concepts. The teachers would assist students where needed in the selection of appropriate centers and activities. Ultimately, the child would develop the ability to schedule himself and discipline himself to carry out his own scheduled activities.

This would include self-directed movement throughout the building to appropriate learning areas according to schedules that have been formed by each child the previous day. A period of time at the beginning of each day should be used for planning and a period of time at the end of each day should be used for evaluation.

In the nongraded school, teachers must provide many opportunities for a growing, responsible independence, with each child gradually accepting more responsibility for his own learning and assuming greater self-direction. Emphasis should be placed on the personal development of the individual and on self-understanding.

A child's development of a positive self-concept, of attitudes and values, and of standards of behavior is influenced by the atmosphere and the environment in which he lives and learns. A well-developed human being is one who has self-respect, because this is a basic need of all humans. A major task of the teacher is to help each child develop and maintain self-respect.

The activities of a child are directed toward satisfying his needs. His growth pattern affects his behavior and he has problems when he cannot satisfy his needs. All of his behavior is caused. In order to help each child find satisfaction in learning and to develop self-confidence, the nongraded school should plan a program to help children live a better and richer life in school.

The teacher needs to have faith in the child. Assume that he will utilize his time wisely and give him the freedom to plan his schedule. If and when you find that he needs guidance, help him to make a well-rounded schedule. Don't do it for him. Don't tell him what to do and when. Help him to see the value of the wise use of his time.

The teacher is the most important single factor in the development of a school environment which will promote the philosophy of nongradedness. Children look to the teacher as an example. They see how she lives more than they hear what she tells them to do. Nongrading must be the teacher's "style of living."

Children look to teachers for guidance in the solution of their everyday problems; they expect teachers to be able to understand and help solve the problems of group living. That's what school is all about.

Children look to the teacher as the expert in human relations. The teacher should guide children in making decisions which will result in higher qualities of living and provide experiences which will lead to higher levels of thinking.

This "expert" should see her role as a resource person; she should provide guidance in group activities of planning, fulfilling and evaluating the total program; she should help children interpret the values and attitudes which are developed through "living" together at school.

Through the activities outlined in this book, children should learn to understand personal differences in others and to prize these differences. They should learn to accept as reality in our society differences in race, socio-economic status, speech patterns, and other similar variations. Each child should begin to see himself as a worthwhile human being with a contribution to make to the society in which he lives.

A teacher who witnesses this kind of growth and understanding in children realizes that living and teaching in a nongraded school can be a most rewarding experience.

INDEX

A

Abstraction, 150
Accuracy in mathematics, 150
Achievement tests, standardized, 280
Aesthetic values, 39-40, 266
Aides, teacher, 254-264 (*see also* Auxiliary personnel)
Anecdotal records, 215, 280, 301
Art, 265-267 (*see also* Special teachers)
Audio-visual materials, 215, 248, 250
Authoritarian role, 42
Auxiliary personnel:
  abilities and skills, 256
  aides are paid, 254
  back assignments, 261
  clerical aides, 255
  duties, 254-255
  evaluation, 264
  free teachers, 254
  in learning centers, 263-264
  increase effectiveness of teacher, 256
  influence on teacher, 256
  limited instructional tasks, 256
  not prerequisites to nongrading, 254

Auxiliary personnel: *(Cont.)*
  not replacing teacher, 255
  on-the-job training, 256
  orientation program, 256
  philosophy on use, 255
  scheduling, 261-263
    one-time-only tasks, 262
    pooling time, 261
    teachers' requests, 261
    unscheduled time for flexibility, 262
    weekly schedule, 261
  teachers grateful, 255
  time on job, 254
  volunteers not paid, 254
  work with poor achievers, 257

B

"Back-to-back" plan, 68
Basal textbook approach, 303
Bibliographies, 248
"Board of directors," 286
Building, 31

C

Case conferences, 215
Case studies, 215

311

Classroom environment, 35
Clerical aides, 255
Community resources, 215
Community School project:
    evaluating, 289
        burglary and vandalism decline,
            289
        not formal, 289
    nature of activities, 288
        average attendance, 288
        manifestations of interest, 288
        new activities requested, 288
        not enroll or register, 288
        not highly organized and struc-
            tured, 288
        open interest centers, 288
        responsive to community's ex-
            perience, 288
    philosophy, 284-285
        community life, 284
        consistent mode of life, 285
        natural extension of school day,
            285
    planning, 285-287
        activities for *everyone*, 286
        announcement, 286-287
        each activity supervised, 286
        members of community, 286
        parents as "board of directors,"
            286
Computation, 149, 150
Creative skills, 211
Critical thinking, 40
Curriculum:
    broad and flexible program, 23
    develop thought process, 23
    guidelines, 23-24
    not a formal one, 23
    organized series of experiences, 24
    purpose of learning activities, 24
    self-acceptance, 23
    self-discovery, 23
    sequence of instructional skills, 23

D

Democratic values in social studies,
    211
Diaries, 215
Direction, self-, 34-58 (*see also* Teach-
    ing)

Discipline, self-, 34-58 (*see also*
    Teaching)
Discussion experiences, 36, 215
Display areas, 250
Duplicating facilities, 250

E

Emotional needs, 35
Estimation, mathematical, 149-150
Evaluation, continuous:
    characteristics, 290-291
    levels approach, 292-299
        achievement levels, 293
        continuous growth, 292
        deficiencies, 298-299
        homeroom assignments, 293
        instruments used, 296
        Language Arts, 294-296
        many records of progress, 299
        mathematics, 296
        no time limits on progression,
            293
        progress report, 297
        record keeping, 294
        request for evaluation, 293
        testing by vice principal, 296-297
        transferring a child, 298, 299
    meeting individual needs, 292
    reporting to parents, 300-303
        anecdotal records, 301
        checklist, 301
        conferences for staff planning,
            303
        democratic personality, 301
        extending school day, 303
        Language Arts and Mathema-
            tics, 301
        observation and shifting, 303
        open-door policy, 303
        promotion letters, 300
        reassignment letters, 300
        report cards, 300
        Social Studies and Science, 301
        variety of materials, 303
        "written conference," 301
    steps involved, 291-292
    summary, 304-307
Evaluation experiences, 37, 43

Experiences, variety, 37-41 (*see also* Teaching)
Experiential background, 39

F

Field trips, 277, 279
Filing space, 250
Filmstrips, 248, 250

G

Generalization in mathematics, 149
Globes and maps, 215, 219-220
Goals and objectives:
  purposes, 31-32
  specific, 32
Government, student, 45-57
Group plans, 35
Group process, 44

I

Independent work experiences, 36
Instructional Materials Center:
  materials and equipment, 252
  personnel, 245-246
  philosophy, 244-245
    assisting teaching team, 244
    audio-visual materials, 245
    heart of instructional program, 244
    main instructional aids center, 245
    reading and other activities, 245
    school library, 244
  physical arrangements, 249-251
    adequate shelving, 249
    display area, 250
    filing space, 250
    in center of building, 249
    large as possible, 249
    "living room" corner, 249
    places to use audio-visuals, 250
    racks for paper backs, 250
    small seminar rooms, 249
    typing and duplicating, 250
    work space, 250
  scheduling, 252
  selection of materials, 246

Instructional Materials Center *(Cont.)*
  services by personnel, 247-249
    coordinator, 249
    lending materials, 249
    long-range assignments, 249
    more and varied materials, 249
    newer curriculum approaches, 249
    permanent collections, 249
    plan of supervised study, 249
    to pupils, 247
    to teachers, 247-248
  summary, 253
Instrumental music, 269
Intellectual environment, 35

J

Judgement skills, 211

L

Language arts:
  activities in center, 82-83
  goals and objectives, 77-78
    enjoy reading, 77
    improve communication of ideas, 77
    read more efficiently, 77
    sequential program of reading, 77
    written communication, 78
  guidelines for teaching, 76-77
  materials, 79-82
  skills and evaluations, 83-147
    alphabet, 87, 89, 124
    base words, 139
    classifying words, 91
    compound words, 90
    comprehension skills, 93, 95, 100, 102, 108-109, 110-111, 117-118, 120-121, 131-132, 134, 136
    consonants, 98
    contractions, 90
    dictionary page, 128-129
    extension of reading experiences, 144-145
    final endings, 98, 104, 105, 140

Language arts *(Cont.)*
  following directions, 86, 89-90, 129, 142-143
  graph, 126-127
  language skills, 94, 96, 101, 103, 109, 111-112, 118-119, 121-122, 132-133, 135, 138
  letters, 124, 143-144
  listening, 84, 92, 107, 108, 112-113
  looking, 84
  multiple meanings, 97
  opposites, 87
  oral reading, 88
  parts of speech, 124-125, 139, 140
  phonetics, 123, 141
  plurals, 123
  prefixes, 104, 140-141
  pronoun referents, 88, 92-93
  rhyming words, 86, 98-99
  root words, 97
  seeing relationships, 116-117
  sight vocabulary, 85
  speaking, 84
  spelling skills, 94-95, 96, 101, 103-104, 109-110, 112, 119-120, 122, 133, 135, 138-139, 145-146
  stories, 86, 105-107, 114-116, 127-128, 130-131, 143
  study of table of contents, 129-130
  syllables, 141
  tables, 142
  visualizing-illustrating, 99
  vocabulary, 123
  vowels, 97, 98
  word attack skills, 94, 96, 100, 102-103, 109, 111, 118, 121, 132, 135, 137-138
  writing, 84
  summary, 146-147
  teaching techniques, 78-79
    "activities-of-daily living," 78
    functional approach, 78
    one problem at a time, 78
    pupil's needs, 78
    scheduling of children, 78
    various types of activities, 79

Learning centers:
  approach, 70-71
    child's schedule unique, 70
    evaluation, 70
    instructional groups, 71
    interstaff communication, 70
    personal work areas, 70
    self-directed movement, 70
    students involved in planning, 70
    teacher-pupil conferences, 71
  facilities, 74-75
    human element, 75
    open-space building, 74-75
    renovated traditional buildings, 75
  teams, 71-72
    analyzing needs, 71
    evaluating progress, 71
    planning activities, 71
    prescribing activities, 71
    real problems, 72
    self-directing activities, 72
Levels, approach, 292-299 *(see also* Evaluation, continuous)
"Living room" approach:
  children involved, 274-275
    had potential, 275
    lacked motivation, 275
    prior to project, 274
  description, 276-280
    emotional climate, 276
    furnishings, 277
    group direction and policy, 276
    individual differences, meeting, 276
    individual projects, 279
    intellectually stimulating, 276
    not textbook oriented program, 277
    one-to-one relationships, 279
    personal programs, 279
    positive self-concept, 277
    school experiences included, 277
    self-direction, 277
    teaching team, 277
  evaluation, 280-283
    anecdotal records, 280
    child as growing individual, 280
    concepts for everyday living, 280
    guidelines, 282-283

"Living room" approach *(Cont.)*
  reporting to parents, 282
  sociometric diagrams, 280
  standardized achievement tests,
    280
  objectives, 275-276
    general, 275
    specific, 276
  summary, 283
"Living room" corner, 249
Logic and computation, 149, 150

M

Major Concepts for the Social Studies, 212
Maps and globes, 215, 219-220
Master schedule, 68
Materials:
  balance, 36
  Instructional Materials Center,
    244-253 *(see also* Instructional
    Materials Center)
  language arts, 79-82
  mathematics, 151-152
  science learning center, 234-237
  social studies, 215-217
  source lists, 35-36
  two types, 36
  variety, 36
Mathematics:
  activities in center, 152
  goals and objectives, 149-150
    abstraction, 150
    accuracy, 150
    estimation, 149-150
    generalization, 149
    logical reasoning and computa-
      tion, 149, 150
    Mathematics in our society, 149
    practical applications, 149
    problem solving procedures, 149
    universal truths, 149
    validity, 149
    vocabulary, 149
    work habits and attitudes, 149
  guidelines for teaching, 148-149
  materials, 151-152
  skills and evaluations, 152-208
  summary, 208

Mathematics *(Cont.)*
  teaching techniques, 150-151
    activities included, 151
    daily living activities, 150
    functional activities and ex-
      periences, 150
    individualized activities, 151
    life-like experiences, 150
    one problem at time, 150
    organization of activities, 151
    pupils' needs, 150
    scheduling of children, 150-151
    sequential and systematic, 150
    various types activities, 151
Mental needs, 35
Modular schedule, 72
Music, 267-269 *(see also* Special
  Teachers)

N

Nongraded school:
  building, 31
  curriculum, 23-24
  goals and objectives, 31-32
  principal, 26-27
  program, 22-23
  pupil, 27-31
  teacher, 24-26

O

Objectives and goals, 31-32 *(see also*
  Goals and objectives)
On-the-job training, 256
Open-door policy, 303
Oral reporting, informal, 36
Orientation program, 256

P

Peer teachers:
  from other rooms, 271-272
  leadership role, 273
  learn while teaching, 273
  one-to-one basis, 271
  positive self-concept, 273
Permissive atmosphere, 41
Personnel, auxiliary, 254-264 *(see also*
  Auxiliary personnel)

Physical education, 269-270 *(see also* Special teachers)*
Physical needs, 35
Planning, long-range, 35
Planning time, staff, 73-74
Price, Roy A., 212
Program:
  complete understanding of self, 22
  experiences related to environment, 23
  functional value of subjects, 23
  primary function, 23
  problems of everyday living, 23
  society, 23
  successful living, 22
  tools needed for growth, 23
Progress report, 297
Promotion letters, 300
Psychodrama, 277
Pupil:
  his experiences, 27-28
  learns as he lives, 28
  multi-directional living, 28
  part of a group, 28
  rules and regulations, 28
  uniqueness, 28
Puppet shows, 215

R

Reassignment letters, 300
Record keeping, 294
Recreation, 284-289 *(see also* Community School project)
Report card, 300
Research experiences, 36
Responsibility, sense, 35
Role playing, informal, 277

S

Schedules, individualized, 72-73
Science:
  concept development, 225-227
    earth and universe, 226
    living things, 225-226
    materials, energy and change, 227
  Earth and Space Science Laboratory, 238

Earth and Space Science Laboratory *(Cont.)*
  ambulatory, 238
  auxiliary devices, 238
  classroom, 238
  exhibit area, 238
  planetarium, 238
  Spitz AP projector, 238
  two science workrooms, 238
  evaluation, 240-243
  goals of Science program, 224-225
  materials for learning center, 234-237
  Outdoor School, 238-239
    animal life, 239
    astronomy, 239
    classroom learnings more meaningful, 238-239
    correlated with classroom instruction, 238
    mathematics, 239
    plant life, 239
    practical outdoor situations, 238
    rocks and minerals, 239
    weather, 239
  philosophy, 223-224
  problems for study, 227-228
  resource people, 239
  summary, 243
  teaching techniques, 228-234
Scientific thinking, 211
Scrapbooks, 215
Self-direction, 34-58 *(see also* Teaching)
Self-discipline, 34-58 *(see also* Teaching)
Seminar rooms, 249, 251
Sharing experiences, 36
Shelving, 249
Social needs, 35
Social studies:
  activities, 212
    characteristics of program, 212-213
    opportunities provided, 212
  community resources, 217
  concept development, 211-212
  construction and processing materials, 220
  creative experiences, 220-221

Social studies *(Cont.)*
  democratic values, 211
  evaluating materials, 216-217
    appropriateness, 216
    content, 216
    physical qualities, 216
    purpose, 216
    time, effort, expense, 217
    variety, 216
  evaluation, 221-222
  major objectives, 210-211
    creative skills, 211
    good citizenship, 210
    judgement skills, 211
    knowledge and understanding, 210
    social problems, 211
    study skills, 211
  maps and globes, 219-220
  materials for center, 215
    audio-visual, 215
    community resources, 215
    construction, dramatics and creative expression, 215
    reading, 215
  philosophy, 209-210
    human relationships, 209
    major areas of living, 210
    political and social problems, 210
    real life situations, 210
    socialization of children, 210
  sample field trip plan, 217-219
  selecting materials, 215-216
  summary, 222
  teaching techniques, 213-215
    activity selection, 213
    building experiential background, 213
    culminating activities, 214-215
    evaluating activities, 215
    good initiation, 214
    initiating activity, 213-214
    major problems and needs, 214
    stating purposes, 213

Socialization, encouraging, 43-44
  children's problems, 44
  continuous evaluation, 43
  effectively utilize freedom, 43
  group goals, 43
  individual activities, 43

Socialization *(Cont.)*
  larger group activities, 43
  normal children talk, 43
  small group work, 43
  social climate, 44
  teacher is guide, 44
Sociodrama, 277
Sociometric diagrams, 280
Special teachers:
  art, 265-267
    creativity encouraged, 265
    lesson every week, 266
    naturally nongraded, 265
    no time limits, 266
    purposes, art education, 266
    reflects uniqueness, 265
    rich experiences, 266
    role of teacher, 267
    symbols, 266
    variation in every experience, 265
    various art media, 266
  develop creativity, 265
  group activities, 265
  music, 267-269
    at least once weekly, 268
    attitudes, understandings, skills, 268
    creative self-expression, 267
    culminating activities, 268
    instruments, 269
    normal impulse, 267
    role of teacher, 269
    self-direction, 268
    self-expression, 268
    skills developed sequentially, 268
    special interests, 269
    total program, 268
  physical education, 269-270
    homeroom groups scheduled, 270
    individuals and small groups, 270
    major function, 270
    planning program, 270
    purpose of program, 270
    reason for including, 269

Standardized achievement tests, 280
Student government:
  common purposes, 45
  contribution, 45
  needs of group, 45

Student government *(Cont.)*

school paper, 45-57

Study skills, 211

Symbols in art, 266

T

Talking, 43

Teacher:

aides, 254-264 *(see also* Auxiliary personnel)

background of child, 25

close friend of child, 26

each child is unique, 26

"fair shake" for children, 26

faith in children, 25

free reading of child, 24

helping child with problems, 25

helps community, 26

numbers, 24

peer, 271-273 *(see also* Peer teachers)

special teachers, 265-270 *(see also* Special teachers)

Teaching:

encouraging children to socialize, 43-44 *(see also* Socialization, encouraging)

general guidelines, 34-37

balance of materials, 36

classroom environment, 35

discussion experiences, 36

emotional needs, 35

evaluation experiences, 37

group plans, 35

improvements, 37

independent work experiences, 36

informal oral reporting, 36

intellectual environment, 35

interests of children, 35

lagging interest, 37

long-range planning, 35

mental needs, 35

method of self-discipline, 35

physical needs, 35

research experiences, 36

responsibility, sense, 35

sharing experiences, 36

Teaching *(Cont.)*

social needs, 35

source lists for materials, 35-36

two types of materials, 36

group process:

art work, 44

planning activities, 44

putting plans into action, 44

relevant activities and experiences, 44

sharing leadership role, 44

social functions, 44

"style of living," 44

security, providing, 41

self-direction and self-discipline, 34-58

student government and self-direction, 45-57 *(see also* Student government)

summary, 58

teacher is human resource, 41-43

genuine affection, 41-42

member of group, 42

not stereotyped authoritarian role, 42

talk and listen, 43

team teaching, 59-75 *(see also* Team teaching)

variety of experiences, 37-41

adding new meaning, 39

aesthetic values, 39-40

background, 39

correlation between old and new, 39

critical thinking, 40

direct, first-hand, 37

each child unique, 37

multi-directional living, 37

on-going, 39

relevant, 37-39

variety of situations, 40

Team teaching:

characteristics, 61-62

continuous evaluation, 62

interaction increased, 62

no group is static, 62

skill subjects, 61

Social Studies and Science, 61

individualized schedules, 72-73

faith in child, 73

Team teaching *(Cont.)*
   modular schedule, 72
   special projects, 72
   teacher-pupil conferences, 73
  learning centers, 70-72, 74-75 *(see also* Learning centers)
  organizations, 63-66
  planning time, 66-69
   "back-to-back" plan, 68
   continuous evaluation and re-grouping, 68
   flexibility, 67, 68
   graded elementary school, 67
   large group activity, 67
   large time block, 67
   master schedule, 68
   new materials, 66
   principal or vice-principal, 66
   scheduled on school time, 66
   scheduling of specialists, 67
   unscheduled time, 67, 68
  practical approach, 62-63
   children question answers, 62
   close working relationships, 62
   concepts and generalizations, 62
   homerooms, 62
   instructional groups within team, 62
   group and regroup pupils, 62
   Language Arts, 62
   Mathematics, 63
   more productive planning and sharing, 62
   range of achievement, 63
   Science, Social Studies, 63
   students "uncover" subject matter, 62

Team teaching *(Cont.)*
  team, definition, 62
  pros and cons, 59-61
   change of rooms and teachers, 60
   continuous curriculum revisions, 60
   disadvantaged children helped, 60
   individual help, 60
   individualization of instruction, 61
   know pupils better, 60
   lack of modern facilities, 61
   meet needs of children, 60
   more time for teacher, 60
   more time with teacher, 60
   new knowledge in all areas, 60
   offices are lacking, 61
   some teachers don't want, 61
   stimulating, 60
   watching other teachers, 60
  staff planning time, 73-74
  various connotations, 59
Transfer of a child, 298
Typing facilities, 250

V

Validity, mathematical, 149
Viewers, 250
Volunteers, 254-264 *(see also* Auxiliary personnel)

W

Work space, 250
"Written conference," 301

DATE DUE

NOV 16 '72	NOV 15 '72		
APR 4 '73	APR 1 '73		
APR 2 '73	JUN 7 '73		
	JUN 26 '73		
JUN 21 '73	DEC 9 '73		
DEC 11 '73			
OCT 15 '75	OCT 1 '75		
GAYLORD			PRINTED IN U.S.A.